Father's Late Writing

TRACE OF MEMORY

Written by Zheng Chaoqiang

Translated by Zheng Tian zhong

Translated by Zheng Tian zhong

ISBN 978-1-954941-14-4 (softcover)
ISBN 978-1-954941-15-1 (ebook)

Printed in the United States of America.

Book Vine Press
2516 Highland Dr.
Palatine, IL 60067

CONTENTS

PREFACE

Our father Mr. Zheng Chaoqiang Fuzhou, Fujian Province.

In Fuzhou dialect, "husband" was called "Tang Bu (meaning Tang Filler)", while every boy was called "Tang Buer (Tang Filler son)", that was traced back to the prosperous period of the Tang Dynasty, when the Dynasty expanded its territory to Fujian, the army fought against great resistance. At that time, the war was very fierce and a large number of men died, resulting in a serious shortage of men. In order to balance the population and consolidate the rule of the Tang Dynasty in Fujian, a large number of men, known as "Tang Bu", moved to fill Fujian as husbands of Fujianese women.

According to this calculation, the ancestor of Zheng should enter Fujian from Henan in the Tang Dynasty (618~907). After seven or eight hundred years of reproduction, Zheng became one of the big family names in Fujian. Our respected father lived in one of the Zheng Families, that was a large feudal family. Back up our seven and eight generations, there were several Jinshies (The successful candidates in the highest imperial examination) happened in this family. Of course, no successful family was perfect, which might be mixed up with different people from their own life tracks. My father gave a very detailed description of those in this memorial.

My father was just born during the Chinese feudal dynasty was falling apart. The education he received could be both Chinese and Western, with encyclopedic knowledge and sciences. Because he studied hard and always had his own clear life creed, he finished his primary school, middle school and even college in western church schools despite of the influence of feudal family. However, he insisted on studying science and engineering, firmly believed in saving the country by industry. At the same time he did believe neither the feudal superstition nor the western dogmas. Although he lived in a social upheaval time with suffering of several wars, he still kept his life integrity, discipline, willing to teach, eager to help others. He set an excellent example for us.

When we were sorting out our father's heritage, we found this manuscript, and read it carefully. We thought it was very valuable, so we sorted it out and published it. In this way, we could get spiritual comfort for our father. We also hope to give the reader some perceptual knowledge about this book.

Zheng Tianhui
Zheng Tianzhong
July 1, 2020

CHAPTER 1

Infant Name

My Infant Named was Tuan

February 23, 1910 was the 14th day of the first month. It was also the eve of the Lantern Festival. The middle of the night, the moon was round and white and its light fell like water on the front and rear patios of the walled yard in Zheng's mansion. Two white beams of light enter the back room from two skylights in the roof, leaving two rectangular white spots on the ground. By this time, my mother was suffering from abdominal pain and was waiting for her fourth delivery. My grandmother was busy with her eager expectations and made all kinds of preparations. The old-fashioned midwife was also in the room, waiting to show off her skills. At the door to the back hall, The Zheng's Family were busy with another matter as usual, because the Lantern Festival was not over yet, they were still betting on the "12-He". The inner one layer and the outer one layer, surrounded by a long table, connected by two eight Immortals tables, shouted "treasure" and cried "pearl". In spite of the noise, they refused to stop at midnight. The clock in the back room struck eleven, It was on the 15th of the first month, Just after 11 o'clock, before 12 o'clock, I was born. When grandmother and mother knew they had a baby boy, they cried tears of joy. It turned out that my father's first wife had only one daughter, my eldest sister. Later, he remarried my mother and my mother's first child was a girl, my second sister. My mother second child was also a girl, but died before grew up. After that, the third boy was born and died. My mother told me that after the baby was born, he died because he could not defecate, and if that happened today, the baby would not die. So when my mother was pregnant with her fourth child, she was so eager to feed a boy! She was 30 and my father 37, my grandmother embraced the grandchild more. As a 58-year-old woman, she considered herself very old, close to the age of death. She always looks forward to seeing her grandson. My grandmother gave birth to two boys and a girl. But unfortunately, even though my uncle got married, he died at an early age without having any children. She pinned her hopes on my mother's fourth child, long time waiting to get the result, no wonder she cried. To make a supplement for my mother, and handed out snacks and cakes to every Fangs (rooms) of the Zheng's Family for reporting them the good news, my grandmother was busy most of the night. A person's spirit was flourishing when he was happy, and my grandmother's spirit was really flourishing at this time! First of all, she decided that my birthday set as the Lantern Festival of the Gengxu year, that was February 24, 1910, because it was a good day.

My grandmother also wanted to give me a lucky name. When she sew the full moon in the sky, she thought of all the famous people she knew whose names had Tuan. In particular, there was an old man named "Long Tuan" nearby, who was very old and considered a long-lived person, so she decided to name me "Tuan". In this way, when I was a child, the elders called me Tuan Tuan. Until today, all relatives in our family still called me "Tuan", younger brother (Tuan di), elder brother (Tuan xiong), uncle (Tuan shu, Tuan bai) and so on.

I was not superstitious that a person name could determine his life destiny, but I had lived to this day, it could be said to be longevity. Life had its ups and downs, but could be relatively smooth, later life also good. So I had to thank my grandmother, and take pains to bless my life with a sweet prayer.

Super Protected Objects

When I was born, I was regarded as a precious son by my family. Two years later, my mother gave birth to my younger brother, but he was immediately stepped forward to my aunt, and my second sister had already stepped to my aunt. My mother had no more children, so I became the only son under the name of both parents. Of course my parents were precious to me, my grandmother was even more precious to her first grandson. Although my younger brother was born before her death, she was suffering from a serious illness and was mentally weak, that she was unable and unwilling to take care of my younger brother, and soon she died. My grandmother, my parents, my aunt and my elder sister, all of them treated me as their baby, and I was a special focus of protection in my childhood. I also was the first grandson of my maternal grandfather, of course he joined in the ranks of protecting me and I was the special protection of our family. Until one year old, I was almost confined in the back room of 20 square meters, or was carried into the hall. Except to burn incense to god, I never allowed to go outside the eaves. On several occasions my mother took me to my maternal grandfather's house, although it was only a few steps away, we also had to take the sedan chair, and the sedan chair had to be carried to the hall, so that we could get on and off the sedan chair. Without getting much sunlight and breathing enough fresh air, the inevitable result was a weak or sick body. In order to beg for God' blessing, the adults promised me to a witch as her righteous son, I would call her the "three generals righteous mom", because the god she offered was "three generals". There was a statue of Empress Linshui Chen (Fuzhou people call as Lin shui mom) in our home. Every month I had to bow to the statue in order to get her blessing. I also called my third aunt (my mother's cousin) as foster mother, because she already had three sons. As she was a mother with many sons, I could get more sheltered from her. Shortly before I was born, she had just given birth to a baby daughter, and I had suckled her breast milk many times. Every year, at New Year or every festival days, and also on my birthday, I had to eat the food she brought to me. During Chinese New Year and her birthday, I had to kowtow her for thanks. She lived to be nearly 90 years old before died. While she was alive I gave her annual gifts every year. I also used some money when she died. All four of her sons died of illness in middle age, while I was alive over 70 years old. If it was really my foster mother's shelter, she was a great foster mother. Also for superstition, I had to called my father as uncle and my mother as aunt just as the same as my second sister called them. Until the death of my parents, I never changed my name to them.

When I was a kid, I often hung a few charm bags and incense bags on my chest (among them were given by "three generals mom"), and some random things. Around my neck was a silver long life lock, on my wrists and ankles were all equipped with silver bracelets. On my head wear a circle cap (a cap with no top except the brim), and in front of the brim were painted ornaments to ward off evil spirits. A pair of tiger-head shoes were worn on the feet, and there was also a close-fitting one red cloth apron embroidered with a lucky design. Adults in my family just dressed me up in a weird way, these were also for special protection.

On some special days, such as the first month of my life, the fourth month of my life, the first year of my life and also after I became seriously ill, the adults in my family would asked a Taoist priest to help me "get through the barrier." The Taoist priest wore a robe, a crown on his head, horns in his hands, yelled while blowing. The Taoist priest set up a half altar in the middle of the hall, and surrounded by four doors made of bamboo with colored paper. After the Taoist priest had pronounced a few words and prayed for a while, he blowing his horns and led the way and "get through the four barrier". I was carried behind him by the adults, followed by a large group of children in the same Fangs (rooms) and relatives of our family, they also want to follow through these procedures of "get through the barrier". Every time some of them themselves "pass through a barrier", I also followed the same. By the end of the "get through the barrier", the adults burn up all of these four bamboo and colored paper doors. All the while, the children burn incense and kneel down to pray for peace and safety.

All of the above were special protection measures that adults had taken for me, because I was the only super important protection object of the family. It was completely different with my younger brother, he did not seem to take any protective measures. But he and I were still alive to today, both of us were old and in our seventies. This also show that the superstitions of the old society were not only discredited, but also very ridiculous.

CHAPTER 2
Childhood

The most difficult thing for people over 80 to write memoirs was about childhood. The reason was very simple, the time had passed so long. After all, what happened more than 70 years ago was very confusing and unclear in people's minds, not to mention the beginning of childhood confusion. Superficial memories of things would not bear the wear and tear of a long time and would soon be forgotten most. Childhood memories were often piecemeal, incomplete, not their own experience, just witnessed, so it was difficult to recall from the association. A lot of things were learned indirectly through listening to adults rather than through immediate experience at the time. For these reasons, childhood memories must be incomplete, could only write what you remember. What you write must be fragmentary, but it was a dreamlike childhood memory.

Things before the age of three were basically what adults told me later. My grandmother died when I was three years old, but she still had memories in my mind, and the photos she left behind also helped deepen my impression of her. I was the first grandson she had been waiting for a long time, so she cherished me and really loved me. She wouldn't let me eat anything that she thought was "heat" food, such as fried, smoked or baked food, too "cold" or too "heat" fruit, and any food that was too hard or indigestible. One of my young uncles owned a fish shop and often sent her some good fish and aquatic products. Instead of eating them herself, she fed them to me. So when I was a kid, ate a lot of foods containing calcium, so my bones were very strong. However, when she was about to die in bed, she became very greedy and always fought with me for food to eat. Sometimes she even told others that I had eaten up all the good food.

After my grandmother death, because my mother was busy with housework, I followed my widow's aunt for a few years. When I got a little older, my imagination opened up, so I had relatively more memories. Until now I still had an impression of my aunt's sickness and thinness and the sound of wheezing and coughing. I often carried her water smoking pipe, and followed her through the side hall into my aunt's room in the second entrance. She went to play cards with my forth aunt, I sat next to her and watched and sometimes helped her to draw cards. Once, I went with my aunt to my uncle's house in ZhongZhou to see my uncle boat and one of his monkey, all of these I still remembered well. After my aunt died, I began to study in private schools. My eldest sister got married early, but she quite often came back to parents' home and brought me fruit every time. There was a fruit store opposite her house, where she must go through when came back to her parents' home, so she often brings longan (fresh longan), pear, persimmon, loquat and lotus root in summer (Fuzhou people eat lotus root as a fruit) and winter water chestnuts and other fruits. I was very thin as a child, but every year in the fall, I gained weight by eating a lot of longan, which was rich in glucose. Very strange, people in Fuzhou do not treat longan as a "heat" fruit, but treat the dried longan (longan pulp) as a "heat" food. So, although I was forbidden to eat dried longan (longan pulp) by adults, but I was allowed to eat a lot of longan as fruit in summer. At that time, when I wanted to eat fruit, I always looked forward my eldest sister came back home. Sometimes she brought me cakes or toys for me to eat or play. My eldest sister also bought us other fruits such as raw pears and persimmons.

Until now, a few things about my maternal grandfather still remain in my mind. Every year on the first day of the first lunar month, when

I gave him a New Year's greeting, he would like to give me a piece of silver money as the new year's gift. At that time, it was regarded as a big gift. but only for me to keep a few hours, then my mother would confiscate the money, my mother said she would keep it for me. As soon as the Lantern Festival arrives, I hope my maternal grandfather could send me a lamp that I want, such as a pick lotus lamp, a sheep lamp dragged on the ground, and a white horse lamp that could be tied on my body. By the Mid-Autumn Festival in August, I not only could get some cakes with some festival gifts from my maternal grandfather, but also could play with the carp cakes (one kind cake made of flour with carp shape), two carps mouth to mouth, tail to tail connect together, painted with difference colors, for children the carp cake only for playing not for eating. I also like to play with the pagoda game, every year just before Mid-Autumn Festival I would like to clamored my maternal grandfather to buy a mud Buddha for my decoration. Then my maternal grandfather get old and became demented, I was afraid to meet him again.

Every year my oldest maternal uncle gave me one or two lucky money, I remember that very well, because other adults only gave a dime or a few dimes, or two blessed oranges that could not be eaten. When I was a child, the adults of the other relatives in our family did not leave any special impression on me, but a few younger friends impressed me deeply.

The Body Weak

Despite the best protective measures that were as complete as possible, my body was not good as a common child. After born, I always sick and often had a cold, fever, or cough. My grandmother used to thought that I was too "heat", and constantly gave me some refreshing tea, such as Puer tea, rose tea, chrysanthemum tea or reed root soup for dispelling the "heat" inside my body. Among all of these I think the most delicious tea was Puer tea from Yunnan Province. Until now had not drunk Puer tea for more than seventy years, but I could still remember its sweetness today. Probably It was added with some rock sugar, that made it so sweet. I also drank a lot of reed root soup, loofah with winter melon skin soup, rose and white chrysanthemum tea, because elders think all of these kind soups or tea were benefit for dispelling "heat" from my body. I also drank a lot of soy milk, because old people think soy milk was "cold". I was most afraid to drink loofah with winter melon skin soup, it was too astringent. Because of drinking so much "cold" soup and tea throughout my childhood, my appetite became very bad, even lost all my appetite. Later, stomach trouble had haunted me all my life.

After weaning at the age of one, to feed me some food was a very hard job for all women in our family, my grandmother, my mother, my aunt and two of my sisters, even one young maid (country girl). In order to feed me a meal, they had to hold me from the kitchen to the back room, then from front hall to back hall, one person hold me and the other one feed me at the same time. The clay mannequins on the top of the wall, the statues on the wooden door, the swallows on the beam, the sparrows on the roof, the cats and dogs passing through the hall, even the gods images of on the table (in order to deceive me to eat, they had forgotten that was blasphemy against god), all were chose to be accompany or compete with me for to eat. Feeding them a bit, then coax me to open my mouth and cheat me to swallow, went on for years and months, really a very hard job for them.

When I was ill or had a fever, all the women in our house were busier and more restless. My grandmother would only give me some "cold" soup or herbal tea, but my "heat" did not drop and even started to bleed from my nose. That made my grandma believe the internal "heat" inside my body was too strong and still asked me to drink more "cold" soup or herb tea. When I had a nosebleed, the adults had no choice but to roll up a bundle of papyrus, soaked it in water, then stuffed into my nostrils. With regard to my illness, my mother could do nothing but pray for the blessing of Land God and also make a wish to provide small dough or homemade rice dumplings after my illness. Therefore, after I got well, my mother would burn incense with money paper in front of the door, put a plate of rice dumplings and a bowl of clear soup soaked with bamboo shoots, then ask me to bow down for thanks. After thanking the God bless, my mother would spill the soup along with rice dumplings into the streets.

When I had a fever for a few days, my mother would call Dr. Ke to treat me. Dr. Ke clinic was located in a house along Xiangtu Street, not far from our house, which was at the end of a lane. There was a sign boar "Ke Ruo Qiu Medical Clinic" at the gate. Dr. Ke was a doctor of traditional Chinese medicine, and was not very famous in our area, but the prescription he gave me was very effective for my illness. After I took his medicine, I get better. Dr. Ke medicine was hard for me to swallow, after I took the bitter medicine prescribed by Dr. Ke, I still remember the bad taste of the Chinese medicine. Of course, it was much more difficult for adults to feed me Chinese medicine than to give me food. It was a hassle for my grandmother and mother to feed me Chinese medicine. Every time the adults had to pinch my nose and then spoon Chinese medicine into my mouth. They also took rock candy as bait, told me to drink a spoonful of Chinese medicine, and then gave me a piece of rock sugar. It took them a long time to coax me to finish a small bowl of Chinese medicine. Sometimes I spout all the traditional Chinese medicine out, soiling my clothes and bedding, that would keeping my grandmother and mother busy for a while. When I was drinking Chinese medicine, I hated Dr. Ke and cursed him for giving me such a bitter thing. But when I was sick, I also begged the adults to ask Dr. Ke to come and relieve me. In those days, the children or relatives of rich families would call in Dr. koji, one of the Chinese physician, or Dr. Boji, a Japanese doctor of western medicine in the city. They all arrived in a sedan chair carried by three men. Seeing a doctor plus with the money of sedan chair were very expensive. But sometimes they could not cure the disease. It was a mistake to walk so far to get treatment. My family was poor to afford it, but Dr. Ke could cure me well. This was what happens all the time in the world. No extra money was needed to solve the problem, and sometimes spending more money could not solve the problem.

When I was six years old, my fourth uncle (and later my father-in-law) returned home from Malaya, where he was a doctor in Penang. From then on, whenever I was ill, my mother would call him and he would give me some Western medicine. At that time, quinine was very popular. People called it Jinna. I took quinine pills and ate a kind of jinna which was not bitter, like cotton, which was said to be more expensive than gold. When I was sick as a child, the medicine I took was not bitter, but more precious than gold. Sometimes my fourth uncle would give me antiperspirant and Epsom salts. Although it was bitter, but easy to swallow in small amounts. Castor oil was the western medicine which I was most afraid to take, and the sweet cough medicine was my favorite. As time gone on these old drugs were almost completely out of using now.

When I was young because of my lack of appetite, I usually ate very little at every meal, because there was no food to accompany this meal, I did not want to eat. I rarely ate snacks, so I was always very thin, it seemed that there was only a layer of skin outside my chest ribs. Only eating a few food, my body was seriously deficient in vitamin A. As a result, I developed night blindness, which was not noticed by adults until I entered a private school. My fourth uncle found that my body resistance was poor and night blindness, suggested my mother to gave me fish liver oil. So I had been taking cod liver oil since I was six years old for many years. At first I took the very sweet malted cod liver oil, then I changed to almond and clear cod liver oil, both were Norwegian products at that time. Later, I became stronger with less sick.

I don't know why, but when I was a kid, I had a pimple right above the umbilicus of my abdomen. At beginning show small, later gradually grow up. My mother was very worry about that, and used some Chinese medicine to treat it for long time, but did no effect at all, it grew bigger and bigger. Until my fourth uncle came back from Malaya, as a doctor, my uncle switched to use strong iodine several times a day. Probably due to the corrosive effects of high concentrated iodine, the tumor (pimple) gradually shrank and cleared away. As a result, that part of the abdomen was sunken downward, leaving a scar that looked like another umbilicus. Later, whenever I was shirtless, the children and teenage classmates would scream that I had two "umbilicus". More than 70 years passed, my second "umbilicus" was still very obvious in place.

Due to the poor economic conditions of our family, except for three meals a day, my mother hardly bought me any fruit and cake to eat. Kids were usually greedy, and I was no exception, but I did not often had snacks, besides there were many food that adults did not allow me to eat. I never begged for food or asked my mother to buy me snacks, so elders always praised me for not being greedy. In fact, my grandmother and my mother taught me not to accept any food from others without my mother's permission and hand transfer. There were many difference kinds of snacks in Fuzhou, and I was only allowed to eat not "heat", and easy digest food such as dry ZhengDong cake, light cake, milk cake and taro cake, oyster locust cake, shrimp balls and leek crisp stuffing (these had been fried powder shells, relatively "heat"). All of the delicious shell were eaten by adults because they told me that shell of the fried flour was "heat" and dry, not good for my stomach. The freshly baked ZhengDong cakes and pancakes were not allowed to be eaten. These cakes and breads had to put into the pockets of adults to get them not crisp before eating. The cakes, white bread and other snacks were sold by some snack vendors who came along the street and into Zheng's mansion carrying baskets. Zheng's mansion often set up a card table to gamble money, and vendors would bring snacks to the card table for selling. When I was hungry and saw these snacks, I didn't dare to ask the adults for it, and the only way was to avoid it, so I was praised by elders. Because when I was a child, I liked to eat fried snacks, but I didn't eat enough, when I grew up I still did not eat enough, so after leaving my hometown I always want to eat these fried snacks. Every time when I went back to Fuzhou, I always liked to eat these snacks to satisfy my old wishes. In Fuzhou, there was also a soup called "tripod-edge paste", which was made from sea squirrels, clams, or fresh razor shells, diluted in iron pot water and stirred with flour, then scooped into the soup and boiled, followed by a roll of noodles or dumplings with fresh meat. All these snacks that I liked to eat but did not get enough when I was a kid, that became the food I wanted to eat after I left home and munched on when I returned home.

Dress and Play

Most of the clothes I wore as a child were made by my mother out of adult clothes. It was the transition period from the feudal dynasty to the Republic of China. Before I went to private school, my hair was still very long with some braids. Later, when I went to private school, I shaved off my long hair, leaving only bangs on my forehead. As a member of an official family, I was dressed in a long silk robe or long gown, which was covered with a jacket. In the summer, I also wear long shirt. The upper part of the long shirt was resembles a robe, and the lower part was made of cloth from the front and back of a robe. At that time I did not wear short shirts, because only ordinary people wore short shirts when they were working. I often wear a black satin melon cap on my head. Usually the top of the cap was black, but in mourning changed to other color, depending on whose funeral. Of course, when I was a baby, I also wore a fancy hat or hoop hat (a hat with edges but no top) that all babies wore at the time. The brim of the hat was decorated with the head of a tiger in the front or with some other decorations, to ward off evil spirits and pray to God. I used to wear cotton socks and black satin shoes, which I made at home, and I used to wear fancy shoes. My clothes were all made at home, and made out of old clothes, but they fit perfectly, not broken, not beyond repair, which was very difficult for my mother. She always tries to make me look neat and clean and make people respect me, and for that reason, I was quite popular with adults.

My body was weak and unable to move much, and often follows the adult just liked a simmering cat (kitchen cat). So, could say that I was not naughty at all, and never play pranks. I was always praised by adults, they said I was a reasonable and honest boy. Except for occasionally with adults, I hardly go out, or even out of the back room. I was afraid to go to the front gate, because my great-grandfather's housekeeper, RenBo was staying and would kept the children from going out. I was also afraid of "big neck" (the 18th mother), who often sat in the front hall and was very cruel to the children. Except for our own room, I only played in the back hall and backyard, afraid to go the second entrance alone. The only people I played with were my brother, two nephews and two nieces who were close to my age. We just play hide-and-seek and imitating the actions of adults. Because we didn't allow loud noises, our games were mostly quiet. Most of the time, We imitated what the average adult liked to do, such as the Taoist chanting, worshiping god and so on. But my brother and I rarely play with other kids after my brother fell off the table and bleeding from his head injury, my two nieces stopped playing with us because they were afraid of getting into trouble again. My mother also told us not to play with the little nephew who liked to tease us. So our two brothers often only play games in our own room.

But I was sorry to say that there was nothing interesting to play with in our own rooms. Just a little stone Buddha, a hungry little Buddha, some clay figures and three puppets. These clay figures were brought back from Beijing by my father and were made by skillful craftsmen in the capital city. They were of high artistic value. These clay beggars were handmade in different shapes, some standing, some sitting, some lying on their side. These clay beggars about 10 cm high, were all bronzed, presenting the real face of hungry, poor beg and were easily broken due to their small size. When I played with them, some of them broke their hands and feet and wrapped them in cloth. The adults of our family also treated these soil beggars very treasure, seldom took them out to play, and then collected and preserved them immediately. I used to play with three puppets, made of half a log about a foot long. There was a head, with a nose and eyes on one end, and almost nothing on the other end. The whole dress was painted in oil. It turned out that these three puppets were the "double" of my second sister, my younger brother and me. They were called the "lads", and on top of his head was a wooden peg for a man, but not for a woman, whose name was written on the back. These "lads" would stand in a bowl of rice and line up on the altar as offered sacrifices to ancestors and Bodhisattva or asked the Taoist priest to "pass through". When my mother stopped doing this, the three puppets became toys for my younger brother and me. We played with them as dolls, so that the decorative wooden pegs were removed, and the nose on the head was flattened into a marionette with a flat nose. Our childhood was to play with these poor things, but we also had a happy time. Every year during the Chinese Spring Festival, we all had a few days of fun with joy.

Celebrate Spring Festival

Preparation for Spring Festival

Spring Festival, Chinese New Year was my happiest time of the year, I eat a lot and had a good time. Since the beginning of the twelfth lunar month, adults had been busy for celebrating the Spring Festival. First, they began to thoroughly clean all the rooms in and out of our house, sweeping the rooms up and down, scrubbing the floors, doors and walls with shark skin. The People of Fuzhou built their houses of cedar wood. Once the cedar was cleaned, it turns white, so this cleaning method was called "white cleaning". On sunny days, all sheets and mosquito nets would be taken apart and washed. The next step was to wash and polish all the copper and tin utensils in the house, including the candlesticks, pots and pans, and polish the copper sheet on the leather cases. all should be polished to be shiny. The fold ingots of tin foil were hung in strings, ready to be offered to the gods. Then prepare more than a month of pickled and brine products for the New Year, such as fish, chicken, duck, and eggs etc. all put into jars or urns. In addition, there were home-made steamed sweet rice cakes (red and white) and Chufa cakes, and sometimes also taro cakes. Candies the kitchen sugar and kitchen biscuits, dried fruits (longan pulp, black jujube, persimmon cake, persimmon pill, hazelnut, melon seeds and so on), fruits (such as oranges, water chestnuts, etc.) and sugar cane (Fuzhou people known as "section high") should be bought first, incense and firecracker also should be bought early. In this busy time, I would also do some things around the adults, such as polishing copper, folding tin foil ingots, or moving this and that.

The 23rd, Worship to Kitchen God

The 23rd day of the twelfth month was the night to worship the Kitchen God of our family. In front of the Kitchen God tablet filled with a lot of food, especially the kitchen sugar and kitchen biscuits, all set on the tables, then lit candles, burned incense and folded tin foil ingots to Kitchen God of our family. It was said that the Kitchen God was very fond of food, especially sweet food. When the Kitchen God of our family reported to the Jade Emperor in Heaven, he would say more good things for getting bless and removing evil for our family. In fact, it was the children who most like to eat the candies and cake because the Kitchen God was only pretending. As soon as the Kitchen God worship was over, the children were given candies, biscuits and dried fruit to eat slowly, about half a kilo or more for each child. When it was in my hand, I should be my own master and I should eat some every day, as my mother ordered, about a week or so. These crisp candy, twig candy, sesame candy and peanut candy were wrapped in red paper and taste delicious. Every child wanted more of them, but they were very few, and most of these candies were not very delicious. So while the adults were distributing the food, the children clamored for more delicious food, or they divided the food equally among themselves. I tend to eat the bad cakes first and save the good ones for later.

On the evening when we worship the Kitchen God, we would had a big dinner, such as fried sugar cake, fried rice cake (known as white cake in Fuzhou), bean sprout spring rolls, boiled or fried rice noodles and some fish. When it came to eating, there were many adult taboos. The children were not allowed to talk much for fear of saying something unlucky. Adults carry papyrus with them in case a child said something unlucky, and they immediately wipe the child's mouth with papyrus, meaning his mouth was like an ass, and his unlucky words were farts. During the Chinese New Year, there were many oysters in Fuzhou, which were very delicious whether they were fried noodles or fried rice noodles. People of Fuzhou called the oyster as Di (the same pronounced of "younger brother" in Chinese). Whenever I want to eat oysters, say I want to eat "di", immediately a papyrus wipe in my mouth, eat "younger brother" that also had to! To prevent this from happening, the adults devised a trick to get the children to call the oyster as "jasmine". If they want to eat some oyster, just say "I want to eat jasmine" instead of "I want to eat di". There were a lot of taboos! for example, you could not speak of si "death", and wan "die", or words which had the same sound as si or wan. So you could not say anything like that because that was taboo. The adults were happy that the children eat quietly. I was more sensible at eating time and just not to speak, and quite get praise from adults, and only a few times for the adults use papyrus to wipe my mouth.

New Year's Eve Dinner

The 29th night of the twelfth lunar month or the night before New Year's Eve was called Small New Year's Eve, whole family could eat a hearty meal, did not serve for god in advance, but talking in disorder was still taboo. On New Year Eve, the meal was more abundant. Before eating, all the food should be sacrificed to the ancestors, and fold tin foil ingots were burned more. In addition to eating spring rolls and Fried rice noodles, this meal also included hooves, chickens, ducks, and fish and so on. First of all, we should eat fried sugar rice cakes, which means that we were going to rise every year. At last everyone should had some rice, even it was a very little bite of rice. In any case, we should not eat to the bottom of the rice bowl, never let the rice bowl upside down, we should always left some rice. After eating such a big meal with so good food, children were often too full and could not to eat more. If he shout "I am not want to eating more rice", he was breaking a taboo, and the adults immediately rush to get the papyrus and force him to eat, even if it was a little bite of rice, then fill the bowl with more rice for left. This was meaning "there were food to eat, there were food left", and this was a very luck thing.

The First Day in Chines New Year

The first day after New Year's Eve was the first day of the first lunar month, and everyone was one year old. Early in the morning the adults wake me up, then my mother dressed me with the newly reformed outer garment, a silk robe, a black jacket, silk leggings on my legs, new socks and satin shoes on my feet. All of these dressed me like a gentleman. After washed up, we had the first meal of the New Year with our family. The first meal of the New Year must be all vegetarian. First, we must eat celery, in order to show that we should work hard, I don't like to eat celery, but my parents insist that I must eat at least one chopstick. Then we eat a vegetarian rice cake without lard, which means hoping you'll get a higher position or rank. Finally eat dried rice (Fuzhou people usually eat porridge for breakfast, except on the first day of the first lunar month). Side dishes were seven or eight bowls of vegetables and soy products, even soup was vegetarian soup without any meat. I was not like to eat vegetarian food, but I had to make do with it. I dared not say no, and we had to leave some rice in the bowl and not eat it all. When eating this meal, just like the New Year's Eve dinner, no one was allowed to say unlucky words that also to be tabooed.

After the first meal, we began to pay New Year's greetings. The younger generation had to bow to elders. Children had to bow to everyone they meet. After paying New Year's greetings and bow to adults at home, we should also go to other room for paying New Year's Greetings and bow to the elders, relatives and friends. New Year greetings and bows, New Year greetings and bows, almost throughout whole the morning not stop. Then I went to my maternal grandpa's home to pay a New Year greetings to maternal grandfather, uncles and aunts, also the same to bow as well. Some adults gave New Year lucky money wrapped in red paper, some gave two red oranges, some gave nothing at all. When I was a child, I listened to adults, and bowed when they asked me to bow, I bowed. Later, when I grew older, I became disgusted with this feudal custom. After the New Year, the adults who were not busy with housework began to gamble and play dice, and the children played all kinds of games instead of gambling. My body was very weak, unlike the ordinary children hyperactive, just follow the adults, and watching them gambling.

During the first two or three days of the Spring Festival, some boatmen came to Fuzhou. They crossed the streets and entered houses, singing New Year's songs. They would receive some jasmine cakes (including the New Year cake). It was said that even rich boatmen would come out to do such things for good luck.

My two nephews had a set of gongs, a big one, a small one, a drum and a pair of gongs for four children to play with. My younger brother and I joined, happened to be a four-piece percussion group. On the first day of Spring Festival every year, the two nephews would take out all set of the gongs and we would play together. But we only play with one tone, which was the collision of the big gongs, two little gongs colliding, one drum colliding, two little gongs colliding, and then the next big gongs colliding, two gongs colliding, one drum colliding, two gongs colliding. So the four children walked up and down in the room, playing inside Zheng's mansion. When our four children had grown up, we also played on the street, to the nearby Ancestral Hall of Zheng's Family. I mainly play small gongs. At this time, most adults like to let their children play loudly and no longer hate the noise. So we could play for hours without stopping, and played like this until the end of Lantern Festival.

The 10th Day in New Year

The tenth day of the New Year was the first day that the great land king returned to his hometown. At night, people play dragon lanterns in the streets, dance to the accompaniment of drums and gongs. There were also some families who welcome them to perform dragon lanterns with firecrackers and cakes in their yards or halls. Besides, setting off fireworks adds to the fun. At that time, there was a large iron pot in Zheng's mansion yard. A pile of wood had been built on top of the iron pot, and a bonfire had been made, and on the table in the hall there were offerings of all Fangs of Zheng's Family. Light candles, burn incense, and welcome the great land king from the countryside to visit Zheng's mansion. Before the great land king came, men and children were waiting around the fire and the altar. It was a very cold day. It was nice to sit by the fire. When they hear the sound of the dragon lantern dance, the children went out the gate to have a look, and sometimes follow the sound to the neighbor's yard to watch the fireworks. Because there were so many people along the street to welcome the great land king, the great land king usually came to our Zheng's mansion often very late. As soon as the great land king arrived, the men and children of our Zheng's Family were holding incense at the gate of Zheng's mansion to welcome the great land king. After the great land King was carried into the hall and seated. Everyone would burn incense and bow down to him. People in all the Fangs in Zheng's mansion had taken the flag lamps of the great land king to light up every corner in their rooms and kitchen, supposedly to keep everything and everywhere safety and peaceful.

After the tenth day of the New Year, every day there was the great land king traveling in his hometown. All this was busy until the 16th of the New Year.

The 15th day in New Year (Lantern Festival)

The 15th day in New Year (Lantern Festival) was my favorite day, because it was my birthday. In Fuzhou, people eat a bowl of noodles on their birthday. Noodles were thread noodles, commonly known as longevity noodles. Noodle soup could be chicken or broth, topped with chicken or meat pieces, plus two duck eggs, commonly known as longevity (Taipin) noodle. It was said that eating longevity noodles on your birthday would help you live a long and healthy life. So every year on my birthday, I eat a bowl of noodles like this. But I was always asked to eat only one duck egg and had to keep the other one. A few days before the 15th day of the first lunar month, my maternal grandfather would send me lantern to play. Sometimes my oldest sister would also send me lantern. I like to play with these lamps. In the night, I would ask the adult to help me to light the candle inside the lamp. I like to pick up the lantern over my shoulder and played around for a few days.

The 15th day of the first lunar month (The Lantern Festival) was also the day for our family to visit our Ancestral Hall to worship our ancestors. In the morning, I followed the adults to worship ancestors and got meat. In front of the memorial Hall there were several rows of red candles placed on the memorial tablet, all of these red candles were lit up in the Hall. The Ancestral Hall was ablaze with lights and incense smoke. At the beginning of the ceremony, adults and children take turns kneeling. But only men allowed to go, women were not allowed. There were only men and no women inside the Ancestral Hall. After ceremony of offering sacrifices, the administrator of Ancestral Hall would share the meat according to the number of men in each Fang. It was said that each man could get one jin of the meat, but when the Ancestral Hall's public funds were not enough, each man actual income was only half jin or three-quarters jin. There were three men in our family, my father, my younger brother and me, so we could get three shares. At noon, one man in each Fangs of our Family could have a lunch meal at the Ancestral Hall with some dishes and wine. At night, the shrine was still very busy, as many people go there to "accompany" their ancestors. In the Ancestral Hall courtyard, with an iron pot burning a bonfire. Children often go there to play with all kinds of lantern. The children talked and laughed around the campfire late into the night. Because I was young and was taken home early to bed.

The 29th day in New Year (Dark nine porridge)

On the 29th day of the New Year, Fuzhou people would cook sugar porridge for their ancestors. Sugar porridge was made with glutinous rice and brown sugar. It contains peanuts, water chestnuts, black sesame, red dates, longan pulp and other nine ingredients, and deep burn color, so it also was called "dark nine porridge". It was said that because of its ugly color, the devil in hell did not like to eat this kind of porridge, so our ancestors could eat all of them. According to Fuzhou custom, married daughters would send the porridge back to their parents' homes at this time of the year to show filial piety. There was also a custom in Fuzhou, when a person's age number reaches 9, such as 9, 19, 29, 39, 49 and so on, or another kinds of 9 (dark 9), such as 18 years old (Double 9), 27 years old (Triple 9), 36, 45, 54 so on, they should to eat this kind of porridge on the 29th day of the New Year. At the same time, they also should to eat longevity (Taipin) noodle for peace over the "nine". Because this porridge was very sweet, there were many delicious dried fruits and many fragrant sesame seeds, I like sugar porridge very much. But adults forbid me to eat more, they were afraid the property of brown sugar, red jujube, longan pulp were overheating, and would harmful to children.

Qing Ming Festival

Qing Ming Festival nearby, the adults were busy with the tomb sweeping. Because of my age, I was too young to climb the mountain, I could not go with adults. But they allowed me to go when I was older.

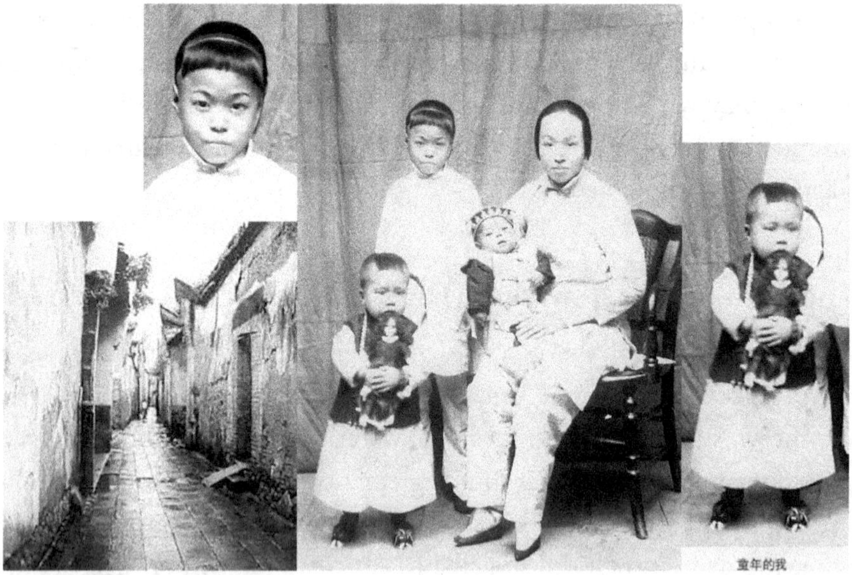

童年的我

Dragon Boat Festival

On the fifth day of the fifth lunar month, I had another happy time. By this time, the weather in Fuzhou was already warm. Children could go shirtless, wearing only one belly pocket and wearing all kinds of sachets on their chest. At this time of year, I wear a red cloth apron with beautiful embroidered patterns, most of which carry auspicious meanings. Adults also bought or made a beautiful perfume pouch to hang on my chest. It was true that hanging sachets was said to drive away evil spirits, because the fragrance could drive away insects such as mosquitoes and ants. During the Dragon Boat Festival, every family makes dumplings, I also eat dumplings, but I could not eat more, because I was still young.

What I was most interested in was watching the dragon boat race. Every year, my parents took me to the Mnjiang River to watch the dragon boat race. One year, my aunt took me to visit my uncle in Zhongzhou. I feel so excited, really happy. At noon on May 5th, we had a big lunch, Before we eat, we should pay tribute to our ancestors.

In Fuzhou, the Dragon Boat Festival was also known as the Health Festival. At this time, calamus were hung on every door and each corner of the room was smoked with a kind of smoke called "yellow smoke". When the smoke was ignited, it only emit yellow smoke, leaving a yellow trail of the smoke for a period of time. It was said that this was to kill insects because the smoke contains sulfur. In addition, realgar (arsenic sulfide) was mixed with yellow rice wine and applied to the child's nostrils, ear holes and other external holes in the body. Adults drink some of this wine to disinfect and ward off disease. In addition to sachets, some children also wear Realgar crystals in various shapes on their chests. And, of course, before the festival, Each family also had a thorough cleaning. During the Dragon Boat Festival, the weather in Fuzhou was quite humid and warm, sometimes very hot. Various insects and ants began to multiply, and the plague also began to spread. At this time, all family should do a good job in environmental hygiene and disinfection, people also pay attention to the health of diet, in order to prevent the gastrointestinal tract infection caused by the mouth. So adults were very careful about what I eaten and drunk.

Children loved to play with insects. I once played with silkworms and dung beetles. Silkworms were mainly raised for me by adults, they beg for a few Silkworms from others and also try to get mulberry leaves. I find it was very interesting to watch silkworms eat mulberry leaves, grow, grow larger and thicker, make cocoons, and then change from pupae to moth. Adults bought this beetle for me to play with in the market. Adults made a little cross out of a bamboo stick, and tied the beetle's legs with thread to the ends of the stick, so that it could fly freely, but not fly away. To feed them, I put a plum on the top of the cross. So I could hold the pole in my hand and spin it around and make it fly with lot of fun.

In Fuzhou, July and August were the summer months, and adults were used to cooling off in the foyer in front of the back well. The foyer was at the top of a lane (Zhengjia Lane) to the east of Zheng's mansion. The wind often blew in from the south along the high wall, and there was no sun in the afternoon, so it was cooler here. The adults liked to go there to sit, sew or talk and children played with them. In summer afternoons, I often went there to cool off and listen to the adults. But there were many things I did not understand, and sometimes when they talked about gods and ghosts, I listen with fear. After that, when I was not with adults at night, I got a little scared.

When persimmons were on the market, my eldest sister often bought them for me. As persimmon had been shown to moisten the lungs and relieve coughing, other children also eat a lot of it. The core of this persimmon was flat, the game that children like to play was "slapping the persimmon core", which was to put the edge of the persimmon core on the table or a stone in the corridor, so that they reach out a little bit of the outer edge, then hit the persimmon nucleus with the palm to see who could hit the persimmon nucleus farthest, I used to like such games. Other children also played the game of throwing copper coins, but forbidden to do so because some people gamble in this way.

Send Out the God of Plague

Around the Hungry Ghost Festival in the seventh month of the lunar calendar, every family presents paper clothes to their ancestors, known as "burning paper clothes". The original paper clothes were only one square foot of paper printed with colorful patterns. Before burning, it had to be rolled, like cloth. I did it for my mother, and found it very interesting. Before burning the paper clothes, ancestors were sacrificed first, and in addition to burning many rolls of paper clothes, also burned many pieces of folded tin foil. This was the season to send out the god of plague. In the street, there were many different gods, were carried forward, in front of the gong, clear the way, welcomed by the people. There were two gods in the world, the God of peace and the God of war. The face of the God of peace was very handsome, not terrible, because wearing a very beautiful pearl crown, wearing a very gorgeous robe, I like to see the God of peace. The God of war such as the impermanence of day and the impermanence of night, one tall, one short, with black fangs, an ugly face, a tall hat, and long robes of terror. I was so scared when I saw them. Some of these gods came from the Temple of Plague (known in Fuzhou as the Temple of the Five Emperors), while others came from families that worship them. Most of these families were wealthy merchants, and their houses had a large hall for keeping them. During the season of expelling the god of plague, they would set up a god's place in their hall, From time to time these gods were carried through the streets.

There was no above Gods in Zheng's mansion, but there was a "old daddy" who wore the official clothes of the Qing Dynasty. The "old daddy" wore a bamboo hat with a red cap, a blue robe and a green jacket, and beads on his chest. "old daddy" was about the size of a real man. Like other gods, head and hands of the "old daddy" were carved out of wood, and his body and arms were made of bamboo. It was empty in the middle and no legs or feet, so it could stand up and walk with the help of a man. The person inside the empty body of the "old daddy" could see out through one of the holes. Zheng's "old daddy" did not take out for decoration every year, and it's never being carried out around the street. But he was allowed to sit in the hall only when epidemics (mainly cholera and bubonic plague) prevailed. It was said that this would suppress the evil spirits against the bubonic plague and would also bless and protect the safety of the whole family. In fact, the "father" did not work well, and some of the Zheng's Family died of the bubonic plague.

Sending the Plague God in Fuzhou was called "Going to sea" and it was carried out in stages. So it was on the last day that the Plague God was actually "Going to sea". Therefore, it took many days before the last day to really send the plague god "Going to the Sea". Earlier, in the Plague Temple, people used bamboo and paper to paste paper boats. In the evening of "Going to Sea", departing from the Temple of Plague, there were many gods queuing to go out and walking on the street, there were also many string bands in the team, playing while walking to welcome the gods. At the end of the procession, there were people carrying paper boats, and there were the so-called plague gods, who were made up of men, and they were dressed purple robes, and their faces were painted with terrible colors, such as green or other colors. Whenever I saw them coming through the door, I was so frightened and I hide my face or walk away from them, afraid to look down. Finally, a god of plague statue was carried in a sedan chair, followed by a row of five lanterns. The entire team walked toward the banks of the Minjiang River, where people burned the paper boats which was regarded as sending the god of plague out to the sea.

Meeting or greeting the god of plague were often held in the countryside of Fuzhou. I remember when I was a child had want to Yixu town to meet the general, to Gaohu town to meet the Tai mountain god, to Xiadu area to meet Tan mountain white horse king and so on. This kind of welcoming meeting was held only once every few years, and always very jollification with a lot of funny. The team was very long, In addition to string orchestras bands in the team, there were many entertainment dance teams, some walking on stilts, some with lotus boat, some with many different acting while walking and dragon dance, lion dance so on. Whenever such a grand welcoming meeting was held, many people from Fuzhou city would went out and lived with relatives in country side for watching the teams and enjoy these entertainments together

Moon Festival and "Tower Show"

The Moon Festival (Mid-Autumn Festival) was also a happy festival for me, because I could play "Tower show" at this time. In the early days, adults helped me grow rice seedlings in small bowls or basins. That was, put some sand in a bowl or basin, add a layer of water, put rice grains on the sand, wait for germination, green rice seedlings were quite beautiful. Shortly before the moon festival on August 15th, I would take out all the small toys and put them in a certain order on the square table in the room. There was a mud tower in the middle, and in front of the high and low were all kinds of clay dolls, which the adults had bought for me.

The stone Maitreya Buddha in the home and some clay beggars were of decorations on the furnishings. In addition, all the small candlesticks, small vase and small porcelains in the home were also brought out and placed, and the seedlings were planted on both sides. So it was kept until a few days after the Mid-Autumn Festival and then pulled down. Children in many families also set up towers in their rooms, and we observed each other, evaluated each other and judged who had done the best job.

At this time, outside Zheng's mansion, some people were playing with large landscape decoration, called "Ao Mountain", for people to see. They were all wealthy families, some alone, some united. I once went to see the nearby "Ao Mountain", with adults, they put on large puppets made up of dramatic characters, such as some characters described in some novels, such as "Journey to the west", "The story of the west chamber" and so on, which I found very nice and interesting.

On the night of the Mid-Autumn Festival, there was a big meal of food and drinks to eat, before eating, we must to offer a sacrifice to our ancestors first. When eating, there were not many taboos like eating New Year's eve dinner. If the weather was fine and there was a full moon in the sky, after dinner we could sit in the yard and watch the moon with the adults. It was said that who ever could see the "yuehua" falling from the sky would have good luck, but I did not know anyone who has seen it. But at this time to listen to the adults tell the story of the "moon beauty Chang e", I think it was very interesting.

During the Mid-Autumn Festival, my grandfather and my eldest sister sent me a lot of moon cakes and seasonal fruits, such as longan pulp, persimmon, pear and so on, which made me gain a lot of weight and made my cheeks grow fat.

In September when adults go to the grave for the tomb-sweeping on Autumn, I was too young to go.

Same Birthday

My maternal grandfather and my eldest uncle were both born on the same day, which was the 13th of the tenth lunar month. Every year they celebrate their birthday and had a big party together. Every ten years, the size of the birthday was larger, in addition to a banquet a few days also invited some troupe to sing and perform. My mother and I used to stay at my grandfather's house for the next day or two until the celebrations were over. At this time of year, my mother dresses me in better clothes and dresses me up as the son of a rich man. My grandfather, uncle's family and other relatives brought their children with them. They were about my age, so everyone had a good time for playing together. The tricks to play were nothing more than hide-and-seek, eagles to catch chicken and so on. Sometimes we do imitation performances, or Taoist recitations. On the night before or the day of birthday of my grandfather and uncle's birthday, everyone wished them a happy birthday, and all the children knelt down and bowed. At this time, the hall was decorated with many colorful paper flowers, birthday cakes and birthday noodles, plate after plate like a tower, the hall was also surrounded by colorful knots, the children seen the red candles on the table was very happy. Children were attracted to the "four real fruits" (fresh pears, apples, bananas and Buddha's hand) on the table. Everyone wants one, especially citron (known as The Buddha's hand in the Fuzhou dialect), which looks beautiful but could not be eaten. Each time, when I get a citron, it could be used to play for many days until it dried and turn dark, then throw it away.

My mother used to take me when someone got married in my maternal grandfather's house. On this special day, people congratulate the parents of the bride and groom and each other. The younger generation kneels to their elders, and the children kneel to almost everyone, which annoys me from a very young age. At this time with other children to play another kind of pattern, that was to imitate the wedding of adults. Maybe because I dressed like a groom, they all wanted me to be the groom, and the bride was dressed by a cousin my age who later really became my wife. We acted out the wedding in exactly the same way adults do, which was still funny in retrospect.

Sixth Aunt's House

I seldom went out when I was a child, and I never went to Fuzhou City. I had not even crossed the Wanshou Bridge. only remember to go to Cang Qian mountain once, that was my 6th aunt took me to her home, until today I still remember the general appearance of her house.

One thing I remember very well was that my 6th aunt told me to stand on the dining table, holding an egg with a small hole in my hand and then told me to make a few drops of my urine into the hole in the egg. I did what she said, but why did she ask me to do it? Of course I didn't understand, but I was confused. It wasn't until I heard from some adults, and realized that boys' urine was thought to contain some "nutrients", and was added to eggs for adults to eat. It was good for adults, but bad for children. That egg must have been eaten by 6th Uncle. I didn't know if it worked or not? But I knew I had nothing to lose. It was superstition, but I did not think this should be done by my 6th aunt.

Shanggan Nephew

The furthest I ever went from home was to my cousin's home in Shanggan township with my second sister. Because of the possibility of war in Fuzhou, my mother asked us to take refuge in the countryside. I remember taking a sedan chair from home to the west end of Nantai Island on the banks of the Minjiang River and crossing the river from there to Shanggan Township. My cousin Lin Peirong was the son of my 4th aunt. He inherited his father's fish wholesale business and owned some land to lease to tenant farmers. In addition, he owned a village bank and later a repair shop too.

My cousin lives in Zaili village, Shanggan Township. I still had some impression of his residence. There were many small streams in the Zaili village, and part of his house was built on a river, so you could pull up a floor and see the water below, and there was a wide river near his house. There were lots of little crabs in the stream, and the children could hook them with a little jellyfish on a rope. I also learned to fish, as long as you open a piece of floor, you could catch some small fish or crabs in the house. But I not dare to catch the crab, because I was afraid of its two claws, it would hurt your fingers when you want to grasp them. I was glad to see the crab bound with a thread, crawling sideways on the ground. Zaili village in Shanggan Township was a rich village in the southern suburbs of Fuzhou, but the villagers there often fight with other villagers for some kind of profit. Therefore, all the strong men in the village had to learn and practice martial arts since childhood, They often gathered at the shrine at night to train and fight with each. My cousin took me to see it once and I still remember that. In Fuzhou people's eyes, the children from Shanggan Township were very barbaric, always ready to beat other people. Some girls of Fuzhou city married shanggan people and brought their sons back to their parents' home. Their sons were regarded as barbarous, so the city people gave these rough children the name of "Shanggan nephew".

My childhood was boring because no one told me stories, taught me how to draw or sing and play musical instruments, and no villain books were given to me (in fact there were no such books at the time), so my childhood probably said there were no artistic or musical skills, it was really mediocre. Adults praised me for being smart, receptive and memorable, but they did not teach me what to learn. Or say I wasted my childhood time. It was a pity to think about that now. If I had learned some useful knowledge or mastered certain skills, I believe that my life would be much richer when I grew up.

CHAPTER 3

Xiadu Zheng's Family

Tengshan Zheng's Family

I was from The Zheng's Family in Fuzhou. Our ancestor's name was Benchu Gong. During the Reign of Emperor Ding of the Yuan Dynasty (1323–1328), Benchu Gong came from the north to be a senior official and settled in Fuzhou with his wife, Mrs. Li. What's his name? I did not know. Maybe I heard it when I was a child, but now I had forget. I remember very well the posthumous title of Benchu Gong that was given by his descendants, not only because I had seen it written on the highest rank of the posthumous title in the Zheng Ancestral Hall, but also on the memorial tablet in the ancestral shrine of our home. Benchu Gong came to Fuzhou as an official, and I did not believe he would live on Tengshan as soon as he came. Most likely that his descendants settled in the land surrounded by fields because of farming. As a result of the proliferation of descendants, formed a large family, known as the Tengshan Zheng's Family.

In order to worship the ancestors, Ancestral Hall was built on the site of Tengshan, named the Tengshan Zheng Ancestral Hall. I did not know when this Ancestral Hall was built or from which generation to start the built. But what I had seen and what I used to go in while I was a child, it was not very old, and seemed to be about the same age as the house of Zheng's mansion in my hometown. I also did not know Whether or not it was rebuilt on the original address. This Tengshan Zheng Ancestral Hall consisted of a large hall facing south, like the main hall of temple, with a front patio but no compartments on both sides, only a narrow corridor connected with the corridor inside the main gate to the south. and there were rain covers on the corridor. Outside the gate was the street formerly known as Xiadu Street, the appearance of the gate was similar to the temple gate. A vertical plaque hanged in the middle of the outside of gate, and the letter "Tengshan Zheng Ancestral Hall" six characters were written on it. There were shrines on the north and both sides of the hall, and there were memorial tablet on several levels. These memorial tablets were called god master tablet by Fuzhou people.

The god master memorial tablet of Benchu Gong was the largest one, placed on the highest level of the middle. Next to and below it were the god master tablets of his descendants according to their generations. The middle shrines were almost filled with god master tablets of early generations, and the god master tablets of later descendants were placed on both sides of the shrines. There may be with some individual prominent figures also placed in the middle shrines. With the exception of the main god master tablet of Benchu Gong, all god master tablets were the same type and the same size. The god master tablets were made of wood, a vertical board was erected on a wooden base. On the middle of the vertical board the name of the man and his generation (that was the generation of the descendants) was written in lacquer. On the top and both sides of the vertical board were carved with pretty patterns, painted with Fujian paint. Only men could be allowed to put up the god master tablet in the Ancestral Hall, which was a manifestation of Patriarchal in old feudal society. It did not have to be after death for his descendants to set up the god master tablet for him, but even those who still alive also could to erect the god master tablet for themselves. As long as he was a descendant of the Tengshan Zheng's Family, whether it was dead or alive, all could be allowed to set up a god master tablet in the Ancestral Hall by paying a certain one-time fee, that was quite a lot of money. The charge for the alive men were much higher than the dead person. All of these god master tablets were customized by the Ancestral Hall, so the size and style were exactly the same. There was a small difference between the signs of the dead men with the alive men. The names of the dead men were written in black paint, while the name of the alive men was written in red, and it would be painted to black after death.

Not at any time could to set up god master tablet in the Ancestral Hal, generally to be launched in the Ancestral Hall, there was also a ceremony, called "entering the lord", I know of only one occasion, at that time, my father participated in the preparations, and many of my kindred entered the god master tablets for their dead ancestors, and others entered their own god master tablet. At this time, the Ancestral Hall received a large amount of money for maintain the worship and repair the Ancestral Hall. At ordinary times, the Ancestral Hall also had the income from the sacrifice field, which was used to employ management and watchmen. The sacrifice field was purchased when the Ancestral Hall was built. There were several houses behind the Ancestral Hall for the management and watchmen to live, and also a kitchen for the banquet at the time of the sacrifice. Every year after the Spring Festival, people from all clans of the same Ancestral Hall offer sacrifices to ancestors on separate days, quite a few days of excitement. On weekdays, the Ancestral Hall were mostly for people of the same tribe or clan to set up schools, or for people who practice medicine.

A large lacquered screen was erected inside the Ancestral Hall, with the full text of Zhu Bailu Family teaching motto on it. There was also a board wrote all the names of total generations from the fist generation (Benchu Gong) to the 40 generation in Fuzhou (for the namc list Fuzhou people called Xing Di), there was a total of 40 words make up ten sentences, as below:

Zi Chong Jing Wen, Shi Ke Ting De, Jun Ren Wei Ren, Zong Gong Sh Zi, Bo Zhong Chao Tian, Shu Ji Guan Guo, Shī Shu li yue, Zhi You Bi De, Yu Shi Qi Yi, Ke Yi Cai Fa.

In the "Xing Di" list of the total generations, the second character in my name was Chao, so I was the Nineteenth grandson of Tengshan Zheng's Family. In our country, the nomenclature given to people could be said to be quite scientific. Most people use three characters to name, the first character was the surname, which represents the family to which you belong; the second character was the family name of the Xing Di, represents which generation you belongs to; the third character was your own name. So whenever two people from the same country had the same first character in their names, it was very likely that they were brothers of the same family and of the same generation. In the same clam, if there was different in the second character of two names, from these two characters, it could be seen that there were several generations apart. Of course, this was the feudal nomenclature, that had now been abandoned by many people, and many people do not use double-word names, but instead use single-word names.

Due to more than a dozen generations of reproduction, the population of Tengshan Zheng's Family had been greatly increased. There were many different professions, farming, business, workmanship, being an official, and so on.

The place of residence had also gradually dispersed, and some still lived in the Tengshan area, and some had moved to other places, but when I was a child, the vast majority of people still lived in Fuzhou, and very few went to other places. With the increase in the number of people and the separation of residence, the family had several clan branch, even those who stay in the Tengshan area. The clan branch that my family belonged to was separated by Shangzhao Gong, because his residence was at the Xiadu area, it was called Xiadu Zheng's Family. Later, my great-grandfather became a Jinshi celebrity and became officials. The local people called our branch of a elegant name with Straw Hal Zheng, but most people still used the name Xiadu Zheng's Family. The date of our visit to Tengshan Zheng Ancestral Hall was arranged on the Lantern Festival, the 15th day of the 1st lunar month. Arranged in this auspicious day for worship our ancestor, It may be that the clansmen gave special care to the Xiadu Zheng's Family, who had made a fortune and had a Jinshi celebrity.

When I was young, that was 60 or 70 years ago, people of our clan basically lived in Zheng's mansion. But now only a few people still live in hometown, most of them had moved to other places, some far away from Fuzhou. I settled in Shanghai 53 years ago, and now there were eleven people in three generations of the family. If family planning was not carried out as in the past, I was afraid there would be at least 20 or 30 people. We could set up another Shanghai branch of Tengshan Zheng's Family. In the next few generations, if they were all in Shanghai, if they still follow the practice of feudalism, this branch may form Shanghai Zheng's Family ancestor with me. This was how the clan of our country formed and developed from the Tengshan Zheng's Family to the Xiadu Zheng's Family and then to the Shanghai Zheng's Family.

Xiadu Zheng's mansion

The north-south Xiadu street under the xiaoling hill had a section of the road turned to the east and west. At Shijing temple, it turns back to the south. There was an old-fashioned residence on the north side of this street. There was an entrance gate hall in the past. It looked a bit like a small government build, that was Xiadu Zheng's mansion, my hometown. Behind the entrance hall was a fire-proof and anti-theft hill wall, which tightly encloses the whole two-and-a-half main house, and the a similar partition hill wall between the first and second entrances, the top of which was higher than the roof.

The entrance gate hall was a row of three wooden houses, the middle was the gate hall, and the two sides rooms for the gatekeepers to live and hide the magnifying lanterns. The entrance gate hall was relatively wide. There were three detachable doors in the front. The middle one was wider. It was only opened when there was the sedan chair in and out. The two next to it were narrow. When the celebration of weddings and funerals was held or the religious Taoist altar was placed in Zheng's mansion, all the doors and thresholds were dismantled to open the entire hall. The ground of the entrance gate hall was slightly higher than the street, and had to walk up two stone steps to enter the entrance gate hall. In the middle of the wall behind the entrance gate hall was a wide door that opened into the house, Inside was a corridor along the hill wall with a rain cover. There was an equally wide plug-in door facing the gate on the gallery, which was normally closed to prevent outsiders from seeing the inside house. This plug-in door was only opened or disassembled when something serious happens. The two-step stone level from behind the plug-in door was the front patio, and the three-step stone level through the front patio before reaching the stone corridor in front of the hall.

On both sides of the front patio were narrow front compartments (referred to by Fuzhou people as front pavilions). The front compartments had doors and windows that open to the front patio, and another door that opens to the hall front stone corridor. In the event of a grand ceremony, the doors and windows, as well as the shutters, were detachable, turn the compartments into a side gallery. Normally, a narrow corridor outside the compartment was connected to the front horizontal corridor for walking on rainy days. Therefore, it was necessary to step up from the front compartments and side gallery to reach the main hall. The front patio and the surrounding corridors were paved with large stones and were extremely flat. The stone corridor in front of the main hall was more than a foot wide, and the two ends were separated by a small room in front of the side room. The Fuzhou people call it Langdou (corridor buckets). The corridor was surrounded by two wooden doors about eight feet high. These could be completely dismantled during the ceremony, so that the front corridor of the main hall extends to the east and west high walls. At the east end of the front corridor, a small door opens to an alley called Zhengjia Lane. The front end of the Zhengjia Lane connects to Xiadu Street. At the west end of the front corridor, there was a small door leads to the lower hall outside the high wall. On both sides, the wooden doors surrounding the gallery were carved with flower hall outside the high wall. On both sides, the wooden doors surrounding the gallery were carved with flowers and birds or figure, and the top of the high wall surrounding the front patio was painted with colorful reliefs of many flowers and birds. Iron beams made of pieces and iron chains hang on the beams near the eaves on the two sides of the front of the hall. When I was young, the carvings on the wooden door had been eroded a lot, and there were only a few pieces of iron horse piece. The sand sculptures on the top of the wall were still clear after 100 years of sun, wind and rain, and the invasion of birds, color was arguable. The surrounding high wall was about two feet thick. It was made of muddy rice with glutinous rice juice. The foot of the wall was made of large stones more than one meter high. There was basically no damage for more than 100 years. These were enough to explain the ancient construction technology with sophisticated materials and sophisticated work.

In· Zheng's mansion the structure of the first entrance was three rooms with seven columns, and four roof trusses were used to carry the roof. Except the front and middle columns of the main hall were square, the remaining twenty-six were all round, and they were quite thick and straight, with a bucket on the top to support the beam. All the beams and columns were made of specialty Fujian fir, which was firm and corrosion-resistant, and the column foundation was made of large granite to raise the pile foot to about one foot away from the floor in the house. Because the floor level in the house was nearly one meter higher than the ground, the roof truss was not affected by the dampness of the ground, and was also protected from termite attacks. The main hall of the first entrance was about two feet wide and three feet deep, and the floor from the second column was paved with Fujian fir. There was a detachable plug-in door in the back of the front hall, and there were doors at right angles to it on both sides into the back hall, with a high threshold. The width of the back hall was the same as that of the front hall, and the depth was only two-thirds of the front hall. There were also three tall doors behind the main hall, and the threshold was also very high. Because it was quite difficult to cross these thresholds, some outsiders even complained about the Zheng Family high threshold and big dog. There was a stone back porch with a width of about four feet outside the door, and a small door at the west end of the back porch leads to the flower hall. Due to the high ground outside the wall, it was necessary to climb the five level stone steps to pass this small door. There were left and right front rooms on both sides of the front hall, and left and right back rooms on both sides of the back hall. They were about one foot and five feet wide and similar in depth. There were connected shallow shelves on the top for storing debris. There was an escalator for going to upstairs. As mentioned above, there was a Langdou (corridor buckets) in front of the front room, which was separated by six tall doors, and the threshold was also high. In addition to the light entering through the Langdou (corridor buckets), the front room also had two small glass skylights. The back room had a door leading to the back hall and back porch, and also had a high threshold, and there was a window above the ground with a dense wooden fence. In addition to the doors and windows, there were also two small glass skylights. There was a door to the side of the front and back rooms near the hall, and the threshold was lower. There was a small Langdou (corridor buckets) outside the door of the back room opening to the back porch, which was actually the two ends of the back porch. There was a door separated from the gallery. The threshold of this door was not high.

Under the corridor of the back hall was the back patio, which was also paved with large stones. There were rear compartments on both sides of the rear patio, called the rear pavilion, with doors and windows opening to the rear patio and another door opening to the small gallery. The rear compartment was also relatively narrow, but slightly wider than the front compartment, and there was also a narrow corridor outside the doors and windows connected to the rear corridor. The ground of the rear patio was one stone level higher than that of the front patio. When It rained, the rainwater slowly flew away from a small semi-circular hole under the back porch, run under the hall floor to the front patio, and then enter a large gutter under the street. If there was heavy rain, the back patio sometimes collects water, but the accumulated water would slowly flow away through the small hole. The strange thing was that this small hole only allows water to pass through, and any floating or settled garbage would not pass through, so the small hole was never blocked, even if you put something into the hole, it would not be washed away by the water.

Behind the rear patio was a horizontal high wall separating front and back, with a gate in the middle, as wide as the gate on the front wall. Because the entire Zheng's mansion was built on a slope, The second entrance was higher than the first entrance. From the back patio to this gate, we had to walk up to the five stone steps. Through this door was the front porch of The second entrance which also had a removable plug-in door. There was a door leading to the small foyer at the east end of the gallery. The small foyer leads to Zhengjia Lane in the front, and there was a small patio at the back with a well for food and drink.

The format of the first entrance and the second entrance was exactly the same, only because of the high floor of the hall, it took four stone steps to walk from the patio, and two stone steps to go from the side corridor. There were also small doors at both ends of the stone corridor in front of the hall. The small door at the east leads to the small foyer and the kitchen behind the well and the small door at the west leads to the flower hall. As same as the back porch in the first entrance, the two entry stone corridors in the second entrance were divided into small Langdou (corridor buckets). The decoration of the second entrance hall was not as sophisticated as that of the first entrance. The floor of the front hall and back hall in the second entrance were not paved with wooden boards, but was made of tabia land surface, because it was convenient for feeding ducks.

Steps up the stone stairs from the back patio were the halls of the third entrance. The halls were very shallow, and there were side rooms on both sides. Because there was no back hall, behind the front hall was the back wall of the whole house, and there was a gate in it, go out the gate to an Yi Garden. Therefore, the third entrance was actually only a half-entry. A hall liked this was called "the three hanging halls" in Fuzhou.

The Yi Garden was located at the highest point of the slope, so it was necessary to go up the level after the gate of the back wall. The garden was originally intended to be the back garden of the Zheng's mansion, but the garden was never created, so it was very empty and desolate, with only a few houses built on it. There were several barn houses on the west side of the garden, which were originally used for storing rice, and later used to house people. There was a small two-story building to the north, which was originally used as a reading building. The large area in the middle and east had never been planted properly. There were only a few trees on it, one of which was a slightly larger litchi tree. It was said that there were ghosts and would make people who walk under the tree to death. My uncle died of plague by sweeping the ground under the tree. In fact, his death was not caused by any ghost, but the plague was prevailing at that time, and many people died who did not go under the tree. Since Fuzhou was a flower tea producing place, many tea merchants (mostly northerners from Beijing and Tianjin) transport tea from Zhejiang, Anhui or other places to Fuzhou to "eat flowers" (smell them with jasmine), and then transport them to north for selling. Xiadu was near the Cangqian Hill area where jasmine was abundant, so there were many tea shops (actually factories for scented tea). The Yi Garden of the Zheng's Family was favored by the tea merchants who wanted to build a factory on it. The Zheng' Family took advantage of this opportunity and gradually leased out plots of land to rent for them to build factories. After signing the agreement, they would only pay a small rent every year for several years (about fifteen years), then the property would also return to the Zheng's Family. In this way, the Zheng's Family increased their income every year, and each Fang of our Family took turns taking charge.

Outside the western wall was a flower hall, and the single-room houses also extend into the back one by one, and also gradually rise with the slope. At the front was an entrance hall, which leaded down to the Xiadu street. There were two rooms deep, and then there was a small courtyard with a corridor by the high wall. There was a small door at one end of the corridor leading to the front hall of the first entrance, and the other end was along a few stone steps, and the upper was the former flower hall. There was a corridor in front of this flower hall, overlooking the courtyard. There were also two rooms deep in the flower hall, followed by a courtyard, with a small door leading to the back hall, a narrow patio along the wall, and a well for washing water at its northern end. Behind this courtyard was the second flower hall, which was narrower than the former flower hall because of the patio next to it. Behind it was a horizontal high wall separated from the first entrance with the second entrance, but there was a small door leading to the second entrance flower hall. The layout of the second entrance flower hall was similar to the first entrance flower hall. There was a firewall in the west of the flower hall, with a small door opened out of the wall. Several kitchens and toilets were built outside along the high wall, and form a row. There were also some courtyards in the middle, then to the west was the dwelling house called Langxuan Li.

When I was a kid, both the patio and the front courtyard of the flower hall were decorated with bonsai and potted flowers, that was very elegant. The corners at both ends of the stone corridor near the south wall often had the old generation life boards (coffin boards bought before death), some two (called the sky floor), and some four (including the sun and moon board), Red paper with the words "Fu" and "Shou" posted on it. Couplets in black lacquered gold were hung on the pillars of the hall. The couplets were very long, and large calligraphy and painting were hung on the walls on both sides. A set of black lacquered Taishi chairs were placed along the two walls. There were eight chairs, four tee tables and four large square stools. The chairs and stools were all made of rattan bases, which was quite simple. Not as luxurious as some people furnish chairs and tables made of mahogany and marble.

Behind the front hall, a large horizontal head table was placed against the plug-in door for the gods like Wenchang Emperor and Kuixing. for bless the idol in the learning. In front of this table was placed a slightly shorter horizontal table for placing incense burners and candlesticks, and in front was a square table named table of eight immortals for offering sacrifices. On the columns on both sides of the plug-in door, there was a couplet on the side writing "Reading the Book of Sages" and on the other side writing "Practice of Benevolence". There was a horizontal plaque on the top of beams, but I had forgotten what wrote on. Ancestral Memorial Tablets (the inhabitant shrine in Fuzhou) was placed on the left behind the front hall, On the right was the door that often walked into the back hall, and the threshold was very high. There was a long escalator for hanging things in the right corner.

There were four large palace lights hanging from the top of the front hall, two on each side, and a large "full house red" light hanging from the center. In the back hall, two in-law niches for ancestors were placed behind plug-in door. The reason for having so many in-law niches was that He-house and Le-house had their own, and some share one. A portrait of Gaozu was hung on the wall of the back hall. A couplet was hung on the west side wall of plug-in door. The names of all generations of Tengshan Zheng descendants from Gaozu were written only for men, not women, except for the name, also written the ranking number.

This side of the back hall was used to park the coffin when someone died, often for seven-seven 49 days. The back room was usually used as dining room. Each Fang in the back room on both sides had a table for eating. When the coffin was parked, the table on the west side would be moved out. On the back patio and back hall corridor was the place for drying clothes, and there were shelves for bamboo poles. The narrow corridor outside the rear pavilion was where the firewood was stacked. In the event of a funeral, in addition to the coffin in the back hall, the plug-in door in the front and back halls must be removed, and the decoration by this door should be removed. And that place should be for the spiritual table for the dead. In addition to a half-size table and a backrest chair, there was also a filial piety curtain, with photos of the deceased hanging behind the filial piety curtain, and paper-made golden bossy in-law niches. Such things often took up to 49 days. In the event of wedding or funerals, the big halls were decorated with red or white colored knots. Sometimes the walls of the galleries and the front of the pavilion were torn down to make a flower hall for guests. Zheng's mansion used to be used to set up the altar, and the hall was to be re-arranged. When the three-entry halls were all furnished, all gates and plug-in door could be opened so that people on the street could always saw the garden behind. Such a big show had never happened since I was born.

In the Feudal era, Xiadu Zheng's Family was once famous, and of course Zheng's mansion was named accordingly. In this residence, three Jinshi had been sent out successively, and it became a Jinshidi. First of all, my great-grandfather was a Jinshi in 1844. People used his name to call this house as the home of Zheng linfu. After that, my uncle Zheng shuzhang was a Jinshi in 1883, people renamed the house as Zheng shuzhang's home. Finally, my brother-in-law Zheng chaochang in the Le-Fang was a scholar (Jinshi), of in 1901, Zheng shuzhang was still alive and he was a Hanlin (within 100 Jinshi) because the Qing dynasty was overthrown soon, so no one called this house as the home of Zheng chaochang. Because these three people had gone through the township examination and the palace examination, and had passed the Juren and Jinshi, several horizontal plaques were hung on the Zheng's mansion's entrance hall and front hall. When you enter through the gate, you could see two hanging on the beams in front of the hall, one on each side of the gallery, and also hanging on the plug-in door. The plaques were inscribed with the characters "Wen Kui" and "Jinshi". A large horizontal board was hung on the entrance hall, which was covered with the official notification and news from the government. The scarlet letters on official papers were white with age.

The house of Zheng's mansion was built in the Jiaqing period (1810–1820) of the Qing Dynasty by Shangzhao Gong, and it had a history of about 170 years. From Shangzhao Gong to the current grandson, total of eight generations had lived, and soon the ninth generation would also be born. Therefore, everyone calls this house an old house. Because it was built earlier, its decoration was less sophisticated than some nearby houses that were built later. But the scale was larger than the others built later, not only more than one entrance, but also more side houses, with a large garden behind. At the same time, because Zheng's mansion was built on the slope, it stepped up from the door, and it looked magnificent. There was a private property on the east side of the Zheng's mansion, and in the west side there were large residential real estates from Langxuanli to Xiaoling Lanet, also the property of Zheng's Family. So at that time, the scope of the Xiadu Zheng's Family industry was quite large. Originally, our ancestor wanted to build a house with a similar scale to Zheng's mansion on these lands, but for some reason it didn't work out.

The condition of Zheng's mansion described above was in my childhood, but it had completely changed today. Many things, such as plaques etc. had been removed long time ago, and even the furniture displayed in the hall was gone, not to mention the paintings and portraits. In a word, all the movable things were gone, only the still strong beams and pillars and the dilapidated floor, and the relatively complete large stone strips. Some of the front and rear pavilions had been widened, the narrow corridors had been squeezed out, and buildings had been added. The buildings above the large houses had also been converted into housing. In order to widen Xiadu Street to become a road, in the 1930s, the entire entrance gate hall was demolished, and the large high wall on the south was exposed on the roadside. It was very likely that the large southwest corner of this wall and the small foyer on the west side would also be removed in the near future in order to widen the road.

When Shangzhao Gong built this house, he originally wanted to live for generations to come. However, the fourth generation changed, and some divisions of Zheng's Family mortgaged the allocated rooms to foreigners (because there was only one deed for the entire main house and side house, which stipulates that it was not allowed to sell to foreigners, so they could only be mortgaged). When I was a child, people from other surnames had moved to live here. Now more of them were actually owned by foreigners, because some divisions of Zheng's Family were extinct, and some had moved to other places. This was the inevitable progress of the times and would not last forever according to the wishes of entrepreneurs.

CHAPTER 4
High Ancestor

My high ancestor, Shangzhao Gong, was the ancestor of our family, and was the 15th grandson of the Tengshan Zheng's Family. His name was Zheng shiyao, also known as Shangzhao, or Guangzhai. All his descendants respected him as Shangzhao Gong. Originally he used to be a farmer, living in a village south of the county, in addition to farming and also raising ducks. Later, he gradually changed to a rice broker, let his wife Lady Sun and his eldest son continued to engage in agriculture. Because he was honestly and responsible, the farmers and the small landlord in the countryside liked to give him the harvested millet to the town for selling. Every time he received the money from the sale, always paid back to the consignor without delay, and they paid him a few commission according to the regulations, which won people's trust. The more millet he resells, the more commissions he got. The family saved money and frugality, plus only two sons, the family was simple, so enabled them to accumulate money over time. With the capital, he further advances the purchase of other millet, hoarding it, and selling it when the grain price was slightly higher, so that the income was more than the commission. He also lends money to other people, and receiving interest was also an income. As a result, he gradually build up money, his savings accelerated, and he made a fortune. He built his house and moved his residence from the countryside to Xiadu Town. Under Xiaoling Hill, not far to the west of Shijing temple, he bought a large area of land and built a house, and also built a side house on the west side as a warehouse and kitchen, forming what people used to call the Xiandu Zheng's mansion, my old home. There was a large vacant lot on the hillside behind the house, called Yi Garden, with a barn built on it, and a two-story building for the second son to study. There were still a lot of land on the west side of Zheng's mansion. There were old houses that had not been demolished and rebuilt, for rented out to people. With such a large fortune, Zheng's Family became one of the four largest families in Xiandu.

Shangzhao Gong's Family business had supported several generations of descendants (currently the 8th generation), and today there were some of his descendants living in the old house that built hundreds years ago. Although his house was sold a lot by some unscrupulous descendants, until the early days of liberation, there were people who depended on his industrial rent to live or subsidize his life. My grandmother and mother used these incomes to support our families, so I also dazzled. The ancestor left their property, and their children and grandchildren depended live on it. It was inevitably produce a number of parasites that did nothing, but rely on family wealth to live a leisurely or luxurious life. The descendants of Shangzhao Gong were no exception. He accumulated so much money to protect his descendants that he was only honored by some children and grandchildren, and he was called a "family treasurer". Long times ago, our ancients had said that governing property for their children would make them "*To be wise and rich was to lose one's will; to be foolish and rich was to gain one's fault.*" These words were quite accurate for the Xiandu Zheng's Family.

Shangzhao Gong had two sons and there seem to be no daughter. I had never heard of a relative like an old aunt. The eldest son's named Zheng zehui, also known as Caiyuan Gong, and he was engaged in farming and raising ducks. After moving to Xiadu new house, he continued to raise ducks. Therefore, Shangzhao Gong gave the first entrance of the Zheng's mansion. to his second son as the official residence, while the second entrance was given to his eldest son. In order to facilitate duck raising, the second entrance hall did not lay the floor, but make tabia land surface. From this matter, we could learn that the filial piety and humility of Caiyuan Gong as a elder brother, the virtue of "only filial piety was your brother". Perhaps for this reason, Shangzhao Gong named two houses of his sons as He-house and Le-house.

Shangzhao Gong eldest son, Caiyuan Gong had three sons, and another may die long ago. I do not know if there was any daughter. Therefore, He-house, had three divisions and lives in second entrance of the Zheng's mansion.

Shangzhao Gong second son was my great ancestor, and his name was Zheng zelian, also known as Caineng Gong. He later became an official, change his name as Peiyun and Linfu. His children and grandchildren called him Peyun Gong, and at that time the people of Fuzhou called him Zheng linfu. He was clever and studious since he was young, and Shangzhao Gong still deliberately trained him to study, not let him manage farming works. After his family moved to Xiandu town, he went to upstairs in the back house in Yi Garden to study, first in the xiucai, then pasted the township test to be Juren, and finally went to Beijing to participate the temple test and getting the Jinshi (1844 the Qing Daoguang years).The selection of the temple test was considered very glorious at the time, and the neighborhood and the people of the Minhou county were all envious. Therefore, the name of Zheng linfu became very famous. Since then, the guests had called Xiadu Zheng's mansion. as the home of Peiyun Gong, Zheng linfu. At this time Shangzhao Gong was extremely pleased, burning all the documents that people borrowed from him and unable to return to him in public, in order to show gratitude and thank God. This matter was quite praiseworthy. Caineng Gong had nine sons and possibly ten, one of whom died early. I only know that the last three were born by Mrs. Yang in Sichuan. For the two Mrs. Chen, I do not know, each gave birth to a few, Caineng Gong may not had any daughter, because I had never heard of an aunt. Of the nine divisions in Le-house, only seven divisions live in the first entrance of Zheng's mansion. and the next flower hall, and the remaining eight divisions and nine divisions lived in the half entrance behind the second entrance (the third entrance had only a shallow anteroom and no backroom) and part of the warehouse in the back garden. Shangzhao Gong had thirteen grandsons, one of whom was not growing up, but still numbered, so the serial number of the three sons born by Mrs. Yang was eleven, twelve and thirteen. But according to Shangzhao Gong, there were only twelve separate, that were He-house three fangs and Le-house nine fangs.

Shangzhao Gong made a fortune in his early years, bought a big property, the second son become an official, and he had so many grandchildren. At that time, he was able to enjoy enough glory, wealth, and prosperity with all of his children and grandchildren. I don't know if it was at his request or out of the admiration of the Tengshan Zheng. Let him to founded the Xiadu Zheng's clan and put the date of the shrine on the best day. However, in terms of political status and wealth, this clan was really admired by local people at that time.

When Shangzhao Gong was sixty years old, it was the most prosperous era of Xiandu Zheng's Family. In order to celebrate his birthday, in addition to held a grand banquet with lanterns and decorations, a number of notables and officials who had worked with my great-grandfather Joint presented a pair of twelve high lacquered screens. On which a great ode was written for praising Shangzhao Gong achievements. When I was a child, every New Year or an older generation celebrated their longevity, this screen was spread out, and surround behind the hall to show glorious and extravagant.

When Shangzhao Gong was still alive, he divided most of his property equally between the two houses, so that each of them had a house to live in and some houses with rental income. In addition, he left land and real estate, such as the garden at the back of the Zheng's mansion's house and the houses above the land, as public property, especially tenant rent, for the worship of tombs during the Spring and Autumn Period and other public expenses. The annual income of this public business was quite rich, stipulating that the two houses should be divided equally, then He--house part again divide equally among three Fangs take turns by each

Fang collection. The Le--house was divided equally with nine Fangs, also takes turns by each Fang collection. In this way, each Fang of He--house shall be charged once every three years, and every Fang in Le--house shall be charged once every nine year. One Fang that collects tenants' rent was responsible for paying public expenses such as sacrifice in the same year, and the balance was used as the additional income of each Fang. Because this additional income was very rich, later a lot of Fangs had relied on this income to maintain the family. Each Fang had its own income from housing and private housing, and after several years, it could also obtain additional income from the public business. If all division in Zheng's Family could live in peace and order, did not waste things, in the family simple, did not meet the circumstances of death and other disasters, life could be basically secure. Everyone respected Shangzhao Gong as the "Family Treasurer" who protected his descendants. But with the exception of a few aspirants, many of their descendants had failed. Some had become parasites that depend on their fortunes, and some had become hooked on gambling addictions and opium smoking habits. To the point of nowhere in life. Later, a part of the public business was sold equally, and the rotation of the rest of the public business income also be changed to divided every year. This of course, was not anticipated by the "Family Treasurer" and also was unwilling to come to mind.

When Shangzhao Gong was alive, he was reputed to be a blessing and a longevity (at that time, people over 60 years even had a longevity). The old man with many sons, of course, had to enjoy mourning when he died. He was buried on the Gaogai Mountain, and the tomb was of course well built, but not as grand as the tomb of his second official son. When I was a child, I had participated in sacrifices for several years, but I did not go because I left Fujian. If his grave still exists? Or has it been destroyed in war or unrest.

CHAPTER 5

He-house and Le-house

Some Things about He-house

The earliest ancestor of He-house was Caiyuan Gong, the eldest son of the high ancestor of Shangzhao Gong in Xiandu Zheng's Family and also the elder brother of my great-grandfather Caineng Gong. Since childhood, he started farming and raising ducks with his father Shangzhao Gong. When their family gradually accumulated wealth and bought real estate, even his younger brother became a jinshi and an official, he still engaged duck farming, eventually his life unchanged. Both two brothers were extremely friendly, although he was the elder brother, voluntarily to live in the second entrance of the Zheng's mansion. and letting the officer's younger brother lived in the first entrance of Zheng's mansion for close the Yi Garden and facilitate duck raising.

In Chinese "He" mean peace, and "Le" mean Happy. So Shangzhao Gong used "He" and "Le" to named the house of his two son's families, as He-house and Le-house that was profound.

When I was a child, I seldom went to the second entrance of the Zheng's mansion, adults seldom talked to me about the second entrance, so I knew little about them. I only knew that Caiyuan Gong had three sons growing up, so He-house was divided into three Fangs. I had not seen these three ancestors, but I had only seen one of their sons, for all of them died young before I could understand.

He-1st Fang, More People More Flourishing

There were more people in He-1st Fang, it was more prosperous, and I had no any idea how many Zhong's generations in the He-1st Fang, but the 8th uncle I had seen was one of them. There was no one decent characters in He-1st Fang. I only heard that there were several opium smokers and gambling lovers among them. The 8th uncle worked as an enlightenment teacher, with a meager income, begged a housemaid to be his wife, and getting married at very old age. The 8th-aunt was a very virtuous woman, spent her all days sewing for others to help the family. She had two sons, both younger than me. The eldest son later became a tailor, and the youngest son did photo work. Not too bad, and they all had children now. The elder brother's family still lived in the warehouse in Zheng's mansion's backyard. The younger brother's family had moved to Fuzhou city. In He-1st Fang, there were two brothers with my same generation, both with strange names, one named Baba 8 Ge and the other Bajiu 9 Ge. It was said that Baba Ge was born one hundred and eight liang, and people called him this name, because of older brother called Baba 8 Ge, his younger brother was called Bajiu 9 Ge.(in Chinese numerical order 8 was followed by 9). Both brothers had been to Gansu, and were working as a little errand under his official brother. Baba 8 Ge married a Gansu girl and took her back to Fuzhou with two daughters. He used to set up a class apprentice in the Ancestral Hall, and he was a mean man just liked Mr. Dong Hong, and also practiced medicine, but was not good one. His life was of course very difficult, and had to rely on his wife to live. Ba Jiu Ge was even worthless, was an opium smoker, never married and I did not see him do any work. But I know there were a second brother and worked on pasting lanterns for living. None of them had any descendants, so now in He-1st Fang only 8th uncle's son and grandson left.

He-2nd Fang, Had a Jinshi

There were very few people in He-2nd Fang, but come out a Jinshi made them glorified. He was my 8th brother of the same generation, named Zheng chaochang, also called as Tingzong. I called him Ba Ge (the 8th brother). Ba Ge was a Jinshi in 1901, a Jinshi in 20 century, also the last Jinshi in Xiadu Zheng's Family. At this time, only 10 years before the fall of Qing Dynasty in 1911. After he passed the Jjinshi examination, he was sent to be an official in Gansu region, the northwestern of China, and I did not know was not he was a county governor or a magistrate. I also didn't remember seeing him or not, because he had always been away. He was greedy for women and prostitute, and died in Gansu in the early years of the Republic of China due to collapse. He left behind two boys and a girl born to his dead wife and concubines in Gansu, they returned to Fuzhou with their mother in great distress. Fuzhou people call concubines as girl, so everyone calls these children's mother as Ba Ge girl or the girl in back hall. When she first arrived in Fuzhou, she didn't speak Fuzhou dialect, she gradually learned it, but always with the northwest accent. She was a nice women, the children of Ba Ge depend on her to raise. Ba Ge still had a widowed sister-in-law, called Sisao, who also lives on Ba Ge girl. Neither of the Ba Ge's sons had ever done anything important, and their bodies were extremely weak, suffering from lung disease, and died shortly after their marriage. Because of father was a Jinshi and the Zheng's Family as a prominent clan, the eldest son of Ba Ge had married a young lady who was the descendant of Lin zexu Family. She was born in a big family, and quite virtuous, but she was poor and her husband died early with many illness, but she still kept the old moral traditions. In the old days it was regarded as a rarity. Ba Ge had no grandchildren, and so the He-2nd Fang died without an heir. The son died early, and the grandson did not show up. This may be due to the fact that Ba Ge was infected with venereal disease by his prostitute, enough to quit for future generations. After her daughter got married, the Ba Ge girl lived with her daughter, and ended up.

He-3rd Fang, with more People

There were many people in He-3rd fang, but I only saw three brothers, my 5th, 6th and 12th brothers. I heard that my 5th brother father had never done one thing in his life. Before his son grew up, he lived by his ancestry, when the son grew up, he lived on his son.

My 5th brother started doing works very young. I did not know what was he to do. Later, he became a real estate agent, buying and selling real estate for others. This kind of person in Fuzhou was called "termite", because he specialized in helping black sheep sell their ancestral or early property for a commission. Therefore, he sometimes earned a lot of money and sometimes got nothing, his life was often difficult to maintain for a long time. My 5th brother's wife, the 5th sister-in-law, Mrs. He, knew a few words and also knew a little about Chinese medicine. She dared to list medicine and practice medicine. There was a "Zheng He's specializing in difficult embolism of men, women and children" put outside. Fortunately, no one asked her to treat disease, otherwise she really hurt people. She had several children. I knew there were four boys and one daughter. But one year measles epidemic in Fuzhou, both of her boys died of measles. Later, the daughter died before married. The eldest son of the 5th brother first worked in the naval hospital, learned some about nursing, and actually he became a doctor. After liberation, he was transferred to the Leprosy Hospital as a doctor. He had two sons, young one nearby 60 year old, had not married, and would probably become a lifelong bachelor, the other one had off spring. The younger son of the 5th brother named Tianshen, a living baby, ridiculous with Stupid, of course poor readers and study, incapable of speech. often see other people in the afternoon and ask do you had breakfast? He hadn't done any work in his whole life, he was a full parasite. But relying on the high threshold of the Zheng's Family, his mother could deceive a girl into marrying such a son, get a girl of equal rank to be her daughter-in-law. This daughter-in-law was also known as a "miss" of the Chen baochen Family in Luozhou. Chen baochen was a teacher of Puyi, prominent figure in Fuzhou. This "Miss" was willing to marry Tianshen, it could to say Tianshen's mother lie to the "Miss", also could to say the "Miss" mother lie to Tianshen. Because the "miss" was a Silly girl. But in addition to beg for a wife, Tianshen also got her dowry to continue his parasite life. After the outbreak the Anti-Japanese War, the Kuomintang troops seized young men everywhere. Tianshen, the living baby who was actually arrested and never returned home, may soon had ended his parasitic life. After Tianshen, disappeared, his foolish wife married once again, but was returned back the next day as a real joke.

The 6th brother and The 12th brother were both cooks. The 6th brother had two sons and one daughter and had offspring, while 12 brother had only one daughter. whether the three brothers in He-3rd fang born to the same father, that was unclear. Strangely after they die, three of their widows lived to be over 80 years old.

At the time, the relatively prosperous He-house had only left a few sparse younger generations. Most of the second entrance and third quarters of Zheng's mansion were occupied by non-Zheng's Family members. So it was nothing more than most of the descendants of the Caiyuan Gong, not only unemployed, relying on the ancestral legacy to be a parasite, but also infected with bad habits such as gambling or opium, and sold out the share of the family business. Many women were also addicted gambling, so the second entrance of Zheng's mansion. once had became a famous gambling nest on Xiadu Street. The women were also join the "catch the flower club", and they were so obsessed even did not care their children. As a result of gambling, his, Life was abandoned and his family ruined. The result of opium smoking was that he could not even find a wife. Many of them died young and at one time as many as six or seven widows in the second entrance. For a living, some widows took their young daughters to the back garden or nearby tea shops to collect tea leaves for a few cents a day. In order to make a living, some widows also at home sewing clothes, Sewing button, rolling shoes, paste tin foil and so on. Under such circumstances, boys were bound to be poor readers, poor learners and far too few achievers. Shangzhao Gong worked hard with elaboration, while Caiyuan Gong worked conscientious with diligently, that was not only for the accumulation of wealth for future generations, but also for the prosperity of future generations. They certainly did not expectation that the 5th generation would fall into such decay. There were an old saying in China, *"Sixty years of luck goes round and round, the losers turn to the winners, the winners turn to the losers"*. That was really a good summary of experience.

Le-house Past Overview

My great-grandfather Peiyun Gong was the ancestor of Le-house. His name was Zheng zelian, also known as Peiyun, Linfu. Peiyun Gong had studied hard from an early age and did not join with his father and brother in farming or any business. He was first to be a Xiucai (scholar), and get advance to be Juren, then get further advance to promoted won the Jinshi. He was the first Jinshi in Xiadu Zheng's Family, and perhaps the first Jinshi in Tengshan Zheng's Clam. He made the Zheng's Family famous in his hometown, so the Zheng's mansion. was called the home of Zheng Linfu. Peiyun Gong had never been an official in Beijing, but he was always in charge of prefectural governments outside his hometown, finally died in office when he was a governor in Sichuan around 1860. Peiyun Gong married two wives, both named Chen, and later in Sichuan he married another wife, Yang. After his first wife Mrs. Chen died, Peiyun Gong remarried his second wife Mrs. Chen. At that time he was already an official and Xiadu Zheng's Family also had become prominent family. His second wife came from a wealthy family, in addition to very rich dowry with a maid, also brought half a hill, called Niu Mian Mountain, at the southern foot of Cangqian Mountain. The entire Niu Mian Mountain was owned by her family, the southern half was for her dowry, and the northern half was for her younger sister's dowry, who married to Cai Family, another prominent family, they got rich by owning a wine shop and wine store in Xiadu.

Our great-grandfather had 9 sons, 6 of them were born to two Mrs. Chen. But I didn't know how many of each, the other 3 sons were born to Mrs. Yang in Sichuan. I didn't know if he had a daughter, but I had never heard of any grandaunt. After the death of great-grandfather in Sichuan, his coffin was taken back to Fuzhou by my grandfather (Gongqing Gong) and buried in Niu Mian Mountain. Come back to Fuzhou together with Mrs. Yang and her three sons, as well as Rebo, the manservant. This just was the time of the Taiping Rebellion, which led to a large-scale anti-Qing war. The journey was extremely difficult.

Peiyun Gong's tomb occupies almost the south-facing half of Niu Mian Mountain. Although the mountain was not high, the front was an open field, so it looked magnificent. The shape of the tomb seemed to be unique to Fujian style, with a resemblance to Maitreya Buddha. The top was relatively small, where several burial chamber located, coffins of Peiyun Gong, three wives, and some sons and daughters-in-law were buried. The number of cavities was single, covered with thick soil, and behind and on both sides were surrounded by low curved earth enclosures, symbolizing a wall. A tombstone was erected in front, and the names and titles of people buried in the tomb were written. There was a tomb table in front of the monument for the memorial service. There were pillars on both sides of the tomb table, symbolize pillars, on which a couplet was engraved on it. In front of the tomb table was a flat area that symbolizes the hall. It was quite large in area, with arc-shaped earth enclosures on both sides, connected with the enclosures above, like the arms of Maitreya Buddha. There was a low wall in front of the door that symbolizes the plug-in door, leaving gaps at both ends for people to enter and exit. In front was a larger vestibule with curved enclosures on both sides, which were connected to the upper enclosure, like the legs of Maitreya Buddha. This vestibule and the "hall" at the back could be used to the descendants to set tables in the cemetery for dinner. Every year during the Spring and Autumn Festival sweep tombs, the people who take part in it could eat there. The food was the chosen offering, dig a temporary oven next to the tomb and cook in a large pot. The Zheng's Family had about six low tables and two dozen low benches, used for eating in a cemetery when offering sacrifices to a tomb. There was no enclosure at the front of the tomb, so it was open. The entire tomb was built with tabia soil. All the tombs, enclosures and "hall" courts were covered with tabia soil which were quite firm and looked like a stone. There were a group of small tombs or graves next to the big tomb. They were all buried by the Zheng's Family. Most of them were minor men and women, these tombs had only small tombstones.

Peiyun Gong had been an official for many years, but I had never heard of his achievements. Although he won the Jinshi, he did not leave any poetry that could be passed down. I had read some of his manuscripts, and now still keeps a "Life Standard", which contained all the words of famous celebrities in the past, and they were listed in categories. I didn't know which quotations were excerpted by him or copied from others' excerpts. But his writing was quite good.

Peiyun Gong grew up with nine sons, so the Le-house was divided into nine Fangs, living in the fist entrance and the flower hall with the back garden barn. Le-1st Fang lived in the east front room and front pavilion, Le-2nd Fang lived in the west front room and front pavilion. I did not know the Ranking number of the uncles in Le-1st Fang and Le-2nd Fang, Because the grands of Shangzhao Gong were sorted together with two houses (he-house and le-house) in the order and so were the grandsons and great-grandsons.

Le-1st Fang of Le-house

The granduncle of Le-1st Fang had only one son and one grandson, his grandson's name was Zheng chaxian, I had seen before, he was a fierce and indifferent person. Very early, he assigned the east front room and the front pavilion of Le-1st Fang changed to Le-3rd Fang, and himself lived in Langxuan Li outside the high wall. His Ranking 14th, and his wife, the 14th Sister-in-law, was a small woman. After the 14th brother death, the 14th Sister-in-law almost cursed Le-3rd Fang every day because Le-3rd Fang occupied their big room. Her house was located on the north side of the kitchen used by Le-3rd Fang.

Every day she faces the kitchen curse. The 14th sister-in-law had two sons and two daughters, and the two daughters were married. The eldest son was died before married and the second son was a compulsive rascal, much like his father, I had never heard of him getting married. After the third generation, no heir of Le-1st Fang.

Le-2nd Fang of Le-house

There no children in Le-2nd Fang, I did not know if his second granduncle had any son or not. long time ago, Le-2nd Fang had been carried on by the Le-6th Fang. later Le-6th Fang had no offspring, and Le-2nd Fang was also had no heir. The west front room and the front pavilions, which were shared by Le-2nd Fang, were also occupied by Le-3rd Fang.

Le-3rd Fang of Le-house

The granduncle in Le-3rd Fang was my 7th granduncle. he was distributed to live in the back room and the back pavilion of the east side. Because he was favored by the official father's favor, and there was a son admitted to academician as an official. He was the most dominant of the nine brothers. Their children and grandchildren inherited his hegemony, bullying and defying the children of other Fangs, as a result, the Le-3rd Fang became the most hated Fang of Le-house. The living room of our Le-4th Fang was in the back room and back pavilion of the west side. So we were opposite to their living room, and dining together in the back hall. Two of my brothers grew up in the same age as the two nephews of the fourth generation of the Le-3rd Fang, so I know a lot about the Le-3rd Fang.

Le-4th Fang of Le-house

Le-4th Fang was my Fang. My grandfather Qing Gong was the fourth son of Peiyun Gong, Ranking 8th. Of course there were quite a few things to talk about.

Le-5th Fang of Le-house

The granduncle in Le-5th Fang was my 9th granduncle, he had two sons, the 32nd Uncle and the 33rd Uncle, both died very early. The 33rd Uncle died before marriage, and the 32nd Aunt was the only old person in the Le-5th Fang I had ever seen. Le-5th Fang was lived in the first two rooms of the flower hall. The 32nd Aunt and her offspring had also been bullied by Le 3rd Fang. My mother got along well with her. We had often given them financial assistance for many years, so I know more about Le-5th Fang.

Le-6th Fang of Le-house

In Le-6th Fang, I had only seen two old person, the 16th Aunts and the 24th Uncles. I saw was them lived outside the second partition outside the separating wall, nearby the room of Le-5th Fang, that was originally a kitchen. They had originally shared the flower room north of Le-5th Fang's living room, but these two rooms were used by Le-7th Fang until I was sensible. It was very likely that they had already sold to Le-7th Fang. Later in the 1930s, the second brother of In Le-6th Fang used the money from renting part of the land in the backyard to demolish the house and rebuild it into a small house to live. Some things of Le-6th Fang were memorized in my memory.

Le-7 8 9th Fangs of Le-house

The granduncle 11th, 12th, and 13th were all born to Mrs. Yang. Peiyun Gong's wife, and were very young when they came to Fuzhou from Sichuan. I had seen the 12th granduncle and the 13th grandaunt, and I still remember it. Originally, Le-7th Fang only lived in the northernmost room of the front flower hall. Later, due to Increase in family size, he bought the rooms of Le-6th Fang. The rooms shared by Le-8th Fang and Le-9th Fang were in the backyard warehouse, but Le-8th Fang later moved out to rent a house, and Le-9th Fang did not had any heirs, and 13th grandaunt also move out with Le-8th Fang. I remember a lot of these things about Le-7 8 9th Fangs.

ReBo, Peiyun Gong's manservant

ReBo was Peiyun Gong's manservant, when he was very young, started followed Peiyun Gong, and later became a home keep. When Peyun Gong's coffin was transported back to Fuzhou for burial, ReBo followed Mrs. Yang to Fuzhou. As the servant and gatekeeper of the Zheng's mansion, ReBo with his family lived in the entrance gate hall and two sides rooms. He had served the Zheng's Family for many decades, and all the juniors in Le-house were in awe of him. His son and daughter-in-law also worked in the Zheng's mansion. for most of their lives. So although they were not the member of Zheng's Family, they were like our own family in the eyes of children. The story of Rebe and his descendants would be described in a section later.

Peiyun Gong had nine sons, and he was regard has the more sons, the more blessings in the old society. But none of his sons had done anything outstanding. When the next generation, a number of Fangs were either heirs or poor. In the case of the population, it had shrunk from one generation to next generation. For a sample, Shangzhao Gong's Family from only two sons jumped to had 13 grandchildren, then to the great-grandfather generation, the Ranking was only 33, to the mysterious grandson generation, that was my generation, ranking only 38. For the next generation was no longer to orchestration, but according to my estimation, the total number of growth was probably no more than 30. This also shows that a feudal family could not be prosperous for a long time, and sooner or later it would fall. The female population was even smaller. I did not hear any great-grandfather had that grandaunt, and which grandfather had an aunt. The sum of the two houses of He-house and Le-house, the father aunt only Ranking 15th, my generation older sister was even less, only 13th, and the younger sister had no one. There were so few girls, and I did not know why. It was likely the result of feudalism that favored men over women. Giving birth to girls did not pay attention to nurturing, and many of them died as minors.

The arrogant Le-3rd Fang

The most domineering 7th granduncle

Among the nine sons of great grandfather Peiyun Gong, my 7th granduncle of Le-3rd Fang was the favorite. The reason was unclear, I could only guess. Probably because the two granduncles of Le-1st Fang and Le-2nd Fang both died early, making 7th granduncle became the eldest of the remaining five brothers. Perhaps he was the first son raised by the second great-grandmother, Mrs. Chen from a rich family, so the first son she raised was more important. Later, Zheng shuzhang, the eldest son of 7th granduncle won the Hanlin. The honor of the son and the father adds to his special status among the brothers. The 7th granduncle was in charge of Le-house's wealth, and all the money Peiyun Gong sent back to be an official income were also under the 7th granduncle control. Considering that there were so many sons in Le-house, the fist entrance and the flower hall of Zheng's mansion. were far from enough for them to live in. So, Peiyun Gong wanted to build a similar house in the west near by the Zheng's mansion. Therefore, he successively sent back a lot of silver to the 7th granduncle to save them for this purpose. The 7th granduncle was a businessman, He used the wealth to do his business. How could a favoured young descendants of the government officials did well in business? The result was that he lost a lot of money and eaten a large portion of family's wealth. Peiyun Gong's plan to build a big house was of course in vain. It stands to reason that the 7th granduncle were so sorry for all of his brothers, they should be treated well. But he was not, by virtue of his being an official father's favorite, and had an official son of Hanlin, the 7th granduncle and his wife did not regard the brothers of the same house as brothers, but as a person inferior to him, arrogant to the extreme. My grandmother had been unreasonably bullied by them. Because my grandmother was the continuation of my grandfather, was born as a maidservant, they took the lead in not recognizing her as a continuation, and forced her to be concubine. For this reason my grandmother was called aunt and old aunt. This incident made all of us in Le-4th Fang feel resentful because all the descendants of Le-4th Fang were born by our grandmother. But our stubborn grandmother also had a chance to give the 7th granduncle and his wife a powerful response. After being a Hanlin, their son Zheng shuzhang worked in the Hanlin Academy and did hard job, and of course payment very little, and also couldn't get any extra money at all. If want to get out as a magistrate, he had to pay bribes, which requires a lot of money. At that time, the 7th granduncle lost money because of his business, and his pockets were almost empty. He had the idea of selling the house, wanted to sell the fist entrance of Zheng's mansion. According to the house rules set by Shangzhao Gong, to sale of the Zheng's Family's real estate must be unanimously agreed by all the Fangs, and each Fang in Zheng's mansion. must be signed and stamped on the sale contract, this was clearly written on the deed. If one Fang refuse to sign and stamp, no one would dare to buy, and the property could not be sold. But the 7th granduncle threatened to sell the Zheng's mansion. and donate for his son to be the high officials. When his son became a high officials, he could make a lot of money to buy a bigger and better house and allocate to everyone..At that time, the Le-3rd Fang already acquired some rooms from Le-1st Fang and Le-2nd Fang. There were only a few rooms in our Le-4th Fang that were out of their control. Because our grandfather had passed away, the 7th granduncle and his wife had to condescend to ask our grandmother to allow them to sell the house. Our grandmother immediately asked them "You want us promise you to sell our house. Do you give us another suitable place to live?" They replied "You'll had to find a place to live ". So our grandmother simply said to them: "In this case, our Le-4th Fang did not agree to sell." In this way, their vicious plans fell through and later they treated us more severely. Both the couple and their grandchildren called us "the son and grandson of concubine", and my mother was very angry with Le-3rd Fang.

The 7th granduncle had three sons and two daughters, more children than other Fang in Le-House. This also increased the strength of the 7th granduncle and his wife disdain for other Fang in Le-House. In the old society, they were indeed a good pair. Their eldest daughter was my 5th Aunt, married a descendant of Lin zexu, and their second daughter was my 8th Aunt, married Chen's Family who were high officials. Both daughters climbed high relatives, which also added luster to the 7th granduncle and his wife. The eldest son of the 7th granduncle was Ranking 17. I called him as the 17th Uncle and he was a Hanlin (academician), He was the second Hanlin of the Zheng's Family. I called the second son of the 7th granduncle as the 18th Uncle. He had won anything, so he was "white Ding". I had no idea what he had done in his life. After I was sensible, I saw him all at home and did nothing. the third son of the 7th granduncle was my 23rd Uncle died very early, and I did not see him. The second generation of Le-3rd Fang could be said to be prosperous, but his third generation was very bad. There was only one grandson in total, and had became a three-Fangs unity. The 18th Uncle had adopted a daughter and The 23rd Uncle had only one daughter. So, the numbers of people in the Le-3rd Fang were greatly reduced from prosperity to decline.

I did not see the 7th granduncle and the 7th grandaunt, both of them died before I was born. It was estimated that neither of them counts as longevity. I did not know what the 7th granduncle looked like when he was alive. I only heard from the adults said that the 7th grandaunt was well fed and over-nourished, so that her body became fat and fat. After death her body were put into a very thick coffin which were painted with multiple paints. But her corpse juice still leaked out and dripped to the ground. Fuzhou people called this situation as "leaky barrel". Her coffin was placed outside the door of our house in the back hall. The leaking of corpse juice kept dripping and smelling for dozens of days. The smell was so bad that people passed by the back hall with their noses covered. Of course, we also suffered terribly. She was really dead and wanted to hurt us.

The second Hanlin "Green Blind Daddy"

The 17th Uncle was the second Jinshi of Xaidu Zheng's Family. It was said that he was diligent in reading when he was young, and he studied in the backyard of the house. The block letters were written well and quite neat. The eight-share article was also very well written, so all exams had been successfully passed, won the Xiucai, Juren and Jinshi. Because he was a Jinshi within 100, he won the title of Hamlin. The original academician was to be selected by the emperor, from the examiner submitted the examination paper to pick out he thought the best one hundred volumes. The emperor mainly looked at the words on the scroll, and the finely written candidates took the advantage. My 17th Uncle with some others won the title of Hamlin by written well. After 17th Uncle won Hanlin, his luck had been bad. First, he had stayed in the Hanlin Academy for a long time, and was neither allowed to be a Beijing official nor a magistrate. It was not easy to sent to be a magistrate as Governor in Anhui, but his father, the 7th granduncle died. According to tradition, in order to show filial piety, he would had to resign because of Ding You. After staying at home for two or three years, he went out to become an official again. Unfortunately, his mother died just at this time, and he had to go home again. When my eldest sister saw him went home, he was creeping from outside to the hall for expressing his intention of bereavement. Later, he also had temporary lived in mourning beside the grave of his parent tomb. It was another two or three years at home.

When he went out again, the Qing dynasty was almost destroyed. As a result, his time as a county magistrate was short, with little salary, not to mention the extra income. After the Revolution of 1911, for a period of time, there was still a long braid on the back of his head, which remained as a vassal of the Qing Dynasty. It wasn't until Zhangxun's restoration failed that his tail was cut off. It's really not a single scourge. At this time, his eyes were almost blind, and he only managed to leave a little vision after undergoing surgery in Shanghai. From this moment on, people jokingly called him a "green blind father" (that was a blind official).

During the period of the Republic of China, the Fujian Provincial Government said that he was a former veteran of the Qing Dynasty, and give him a place in the provincial library and give him some money every month. He was basically at home. If he went out, someone was asking him to be a chapel (that was, a companion to an important guest) for birthday parties or funerals. Because he was a Hanlin, a famous gentleman in the local place, asking him to be a guest with other gentlemen would bring glory to those who did birthday parties or funerals. Every time he went out for such thing, he always wore a robe (shirt) and a gown, and took a sedan chair, followed by a servant. In addition to the sedan chair money and servant rewards paid by the people who invited him, he could get a generous gift. At home, he read ancient books or writes something from morning till night. Because of poor eyesight, he must keep his eyes close to books or papers when reading and writing. I did not know what kind of book he reads or what he wrote, but I know that he has not left any poems that could be passed down. He was completely ignorant of the various new thoughts that filled our country at that time, so he was nothing more than a rotten Confucianist at best.

Most people of the Zheng's Family love gambling, but the 17th Uncle never participates in gambling. The only thing he did with the gambling was to create a poem riddle. He took a sentence from a collection of poems (generally a seven-word poem), copies six word on a piece of paper, left a word blank, and writes it on the paper with four or five words under it, which could be used to fill the vacancy for the person to choose and answer. Such notes were only hung out during the Spring Festival every year. Anyone who want to answer would had to pay a certain amount of money (rarely, only a few copper plates), then to take down the piece of paper, filled in the blank words and gave it back to him. If the words filled in were the same as the words in the original poem, in addition to the returned money, he would had to pay twice as much. If it was not correct, the money would be given to him, but he had to show the source of the original verse. Of course, this kind of gambling—like stuff was only of interest to a very few scholars. Such a thing was called "Shi ba" in Fuzhou. He was very quiet and people rarely hear his voice. In addition to going out occasionally, he always sits at the desk in front of the east front room (formerly the room of Le-1st Fang) reading and writing all day long, and even eating on his desk. So I couldn't see him unless I walked into his room.

I only seen him in his room every year when I pray greeting new years to him. He treated his grandson and nephew equally and did not discriminate. I had very little contact with him, only remember his 70 years birthday, at this time I had moved to Meiwu with my mother, I went to ZhengZai for greeting his birthday. He was so happy to see me, then he tested me and his eldest grandson. As a result, he said his eldest grandson did the right thing, but I forgot how to do it. I didn't know if he ever taught his grandchildren, but I know he never taught any children.

The 17th Uncle's wife died early, I didn't see her. A concubine was bought back to Fuzhou from Anhui, she spook Fuzhou dialect with Anhui accent. In Zheng's mansion people called the Anhui girl as the front hall girl, that was different with the girl in the back hall. She had been serving the 17th Uncle to his death. At the Zheng's Family, there were only three people who accept concubines openly, all of them were won Jingsi or officials. Others were looking for their concubines outside the ZhengZai. but there were very few and none of them were in public. They may not dare to do so in the feudal families. The 17th Uncle passed away in poor just about at the age of 70, and after a few years the front hall girl also died.

The 18th Uncle and "Big Neck"

The 18th Uncle was very serious man, he was usually unsmiling and no more talking. He lived in the west front room of Le-2nd Fang, and often sit in front of the gallery or hall of this front room. The children were a little scared while saw him, and I was no exception. At that time, the children of the Zheng's Family did not dare to play in the hall or the front patio, nor did they dare to make any noise there, otherwise would be scolded by him. The first wife of the 18th Uncle died early, and his second wife was a shrew who was called "Big neck" by us. I did not know what background she had, because I had never seen anyone from her family coming here. But I could be sure that she was an uncultivated woman. Married to the Zheng's Family, and was special an official's Le-3rd Fang. She was very be self-important with self-conscious and more outrageously proud than other Fangs, many people in Zheng's Family were ridiculed by her. Our Le-4th Fang lived just in the back of her room, so my mother suffered most from her unreasonable ridicule. Her sarcastic remarks about us often embarrass my mother, my mother felt the most angry, She all publicly and loudly abused us as "concubine's children". My mother was born in a merchant house, "Big neck" used this to ridicule us and treat people from my mother family with arrogantly. Not only could they not sit in the hall when they came, but even they walked through the hall to be sneered by her cold words. Due to our obstacles, it was impossible for the ambitious Le-3rd Fang to occupy the entire big house alone, and hated us for a long time. Many of them dare not treat us in order to maintain a hypocritical appearance. But this fierce woman did whatever she wants and has no scruples. On several occasions, she was so deceiving, my mother reasoned with her. She actually showed her a hideous ugly face and tried to beat my mother, making my mother extremely angry. She was so explicit, no one in Le-3rd Fang stopped her, which showed that they were concentric with her.

Although Le-5th Fang lived outside the high wall, but was next to "Big neck"'s door, and often walks in front of "Big neck"'s room when entering and leaving. There were only orphans and widows lived in the room and the young son was too naughty. then also become the object of "Big neck"'s bullying, so the 32nd Aunts also suffered by the "Big neck"'s bully. "Big neck" also used some small favors to lure Le-1st Fang's bad grandson Xianxian (14th brother) to do errands for her. "Big neck"'s also lure Zhizhi who was a worthless boy and adopted to Le 2nd Fang to do a lot of chores for her. All day long she had been fed so much that her limbs were immobile causing her body to be bloated with swollen. She often suffered from back pain and arthritis as soon as it was cold. She had to summoned someone to massage and beat her waist, back, shoulders, and limbs. Sometimes Zhizhi were called upon to do this, every time she was lay on the front porch and thrashed by someone. When I saw this, I was very surprised. At this time I was a kid, and I felt in my heart that someone thumped this wicked woman for avenge my mother, that was a pleasure. "Big neck" also suffers from severe thyroid hypertrophy and her neck was very thick, just liked the chicken and duck gizzards just filled with feed, so we all call her "Big neck"s in the her back. "Big neck" shad no children, only adopted a daughter, named Lanlan. "Big neck"s was extremely cruel to Lanlan, often beat and scold, treat the bitter girl as a slave. Sometimes, late at night, Lanlan was asked to knocked her back and thumped her arms until Lanlan was married. Both of 18th Uncle and "Big neck"s lived were not long, and they die before about 60. The death of "Big neck"s was a happy event for my mother. For her, we moved away from Zheng's mansion. and lived with my 4th Uncle and the 6th Aunts for a long time, after "Big neck" died we moved back to Zheng's mansion.

A Filial Dangdang

Dangdang was the only grandson of the 7th granduncle in Le-3rd Fang, Ranking 19, but I always directly called him brother Dang. In Le-hourse. Dangdang was a child of three-Fangs unity, the 17th Uncle, the 18th Uncle and the 23rd Uncle. The 23rd Uncle, the 17th Uncle and the 18th

Aunt all died early. Of course, when they died Dangdang as the filial piety. Later, when the 18th Uncle & Aunt, the 23rd Aunt, and the 17th Aunt died one after another, Dangdang was also as the filial piety. The 17th Uncle's concubine was Dangdang's mother, and it seem that he was also a filial boy when she died. Therefore, as a filial son in his life, he had been worn mourning seven or eight times, he really became a filial man. But I didn't know who gave birth to him, because Dangdang and his wife were afraid of the 18th Uncles and "Big neck". On the surface, they were very filial to this old man. So, I believe Dangdan was born to the fist wife of the 18th Uncle, As the nominally the 23rd Uncle's stepson, after the death of the 23rd Uncle, Dangdang couple should provide for the 23rd Aunts extremely difficult. The 23rd Aunt relied on pasting tin foil and her daughter (the 8th Sister) sew clothes for others to keep their live. The 8th Sister's mother died shortly after she married, then the 8th Sister never returned to the Zheng's Family. In the 1920, during the cholera epidemic in Fuzhou the 8th Sister died of the epidemic. Because everyone was afraid of infection, her coffin must not be rest in the back hall, so be buried after death.

Because of his father, the 17th Uncle, was an formal master, so all elders in Zheng's Family called Dangdang as younger Master Zheng and his wife young Mistress Zheng. Dangdang was a rare son of with three-Fangs unity, When he was young, as his father was an official, he became a dandy, so he basically didn't do anything. Listening to adults, there were many famous ladies in Fuzhou City who had competed to marry him. Whenever there was any event, he was invited to participate, letting him choose among many beautiful girls. Later, the 19 Sister-in-law was really a famous noble girl, with a beautiful appearance. It went without saying that a marriage was ostentatious. But It was pity that Dangdang not being favored by chances, his father's official luck was not good, his career was too bad, wealth and honour was beyond his reach. His family fortunes declined, and the younger Master Dangdang was so frustrated and ruined. At one time, my eldest brother-in-law for Dangdang to got a job in the navy and soon Dangdang would not be able to go to work due to a heart attack. He was sick at home, still receives his monthly salary from my eldest brother-in-law. At that time, people lacked medical knowledge and did not understand the truth that "life is in motion". Dangdang died in his live way, only 40 years old, that seems to be quite short-lived in today.

Dangdang's wife, the 19th Sister-in-law was born in a famous family, and married to Hanlin's son as his wife. In addition, Le-3rd Fang had tradition of contempt for other Fangs in Le-house, so think highly of oneself, feudal ideology was very serious. She regards her husband and two sons as being superior to others. When her husband was alive, although his family was poor, still regarded him as a young master and also wanted others to flatter him like her. After the death of her husband, she was very concerned about his coffin. She wanted the family would be rich someday so she could do some funerals for her husband and build a big tomb for him as a young master. So Dangdang's coffin was not buried, but was placed in the back hall for dozens of days then moved to a Bingshe (known as Dingcuo in Fuzhou), waiting for their luck to turn. But it was been stored around for years, may be 14 or 15 years. During this period, once the windy and rainy season, the 19th Sister-in-law would ask someone to visit Bingshe on her behalf to see if there was any damage or leakage, soaking the "Young Master"'s coffin. She had no money to repair the Bingshe, and only asked others to take care of her "Young Master"'s coffin for free. She was such a woman full thought of Feudal rulers. Later, the young Master's coffin decayed until was about to be scattered, So she had to bury thc coffin in a hurry.

Both of her sons, because they were influenced by her thoughts, also thought they were grandchildren of Hanlin. They were amazing and often bullied other children of the same age in the Le-house. Whenever these two "babies", especially the little "baby", quarrel with other children, the 19th Sister-in-law not only did not teach her son, but always repeats aloud: "My son could not compare with other's sons". In this way she instill ed a sense of superiority into her son. My younger brother and I were about the same age as these two "babies", and were often bullied by the two of them. My mother always pulled my younger brother and me into our room, Ignore them, not talk to them.

The 19th Sister-in-law was a little educated after all, unlike the "Big beck", she didn't do the abusive things, but kept the feudal consciousness too long. She also had a bad habit of casually making others to do this and that for her family. But because her family's situation was not as good as a year, who would like continue to help her. Le-3rd Fang, mainly the 19th-Sister-in-law, had changed the attitude towards our Le-4th Fang, The reason was that as both of our brothers graduated from college, our family was better than them, and we were flourishing. At the same time, we do not remember the past complaints and blame the past. On the contrary, we always help them as much as possible, so that they had to look at us differently. However, they still did not change their contempt for Le-1st Fang, Le-5th Fang etc., who were in poor condition, so they still were ridiculed and hostile. As mentioned before, the 14th Sister-in-law (chaxian's wife) of Le-1st Fang hated Le-3rd Fang for occupying her room, and she kept cursing at them while she were alive. The descendants of Le-5th fang still hate them to this day. The 19th Sister-in-law life was very long. She died at the age of 82. At the time of her death, her little "baby" was far away in the United States, not around the bed, not back to the funeral.

Two Sons of Dangdang

The two sons of Dangdang were deeply poisoned by the traditional feudalism of Le-3rd Fang, and they always considered themselves grandsons of Hanlin. Dangdang elder son had not graduated from high school, so he went to work in the salt department. He had not left Fujian, and he was basically in Fuzhou. After liberation, he worked in a tobacco and alcohol monopoly company until he retired. He had a strong feudal consciousness, so he was ridiculed and hated by most people. The younger son of Dangdang joined church, and church helped him to study at the university. He also went to the United States to study and obtained a doctorate. Later he settled down in the United States and became University professor. With the feudal consciousness, coupled with the foreign doctor title and foreign identity, he even had the idea of "I am the best in the world" in front of the Zheng's Family, even his brother. After liberation, he only returned to China once, except visiting his brother's family in Zheng's mansion, but no one was seen, and the Zheng's Family had an opinion about the two sons of Dangdang.

I was one year younger than Dangdang elder son and three years older than the younger son. We used to play together in childhood, and we had many contacts, both brother's fate were no good. Dangdang elder grandson had some abnormal nerves and not clever. Although barely graduated from college, he was neither talented nor successful. He died of liver disease in his 40, leaving behind his widow and two sons. The second daughter-in-law of Dangdang elder son was killed by stray bullets during the Cultural Revolution. Dangdang elder son and his wife were both over 80 years old. Due to the lack of family economy and the discord of their children, the evening scene was quite depressed. Although Dangdang younger son settled int he Unite States, he was retired at the age of 60, and own foreign-style house with car, and his life was quite good. However, only just a few years, successive disasters had come to him. First of all, his beloved daughter who worked in a chemical research institute was smoked to death by poisonous gas during sleep, then his wife was nervous because of the sentimental loss of her daughter, and was killed by car accident. When his wife died, he was still visiting his son in Hong Kong. He failed to return to the mainland to visit his relatives in Fuzhong, he immediately returned to the United States. Both of these unfortunate incidents made him accidentally receive large pensions and compensation. However, when he returned Fuzhong, he did not give any money to his older brother. He promised to support his second nephew to go to the United States to study for Postgraduate Degree, but asked his brother and nephew who had no financial resources to pay the travel fee for the United States. His oral promise thus became a cake that could not be eaten.

Soon after he returned to the United States, he died suddenly in his house, and no relatives were around. I heard that almost all his legacy after his death was swallowed up by the nanny who he brought from Hong Kong to United States. At present, the only grandson behind Dangdang was working in Hong Kong. I did not know if he had a family?

I did not superstitious, I did not believe in gods or ghosts, and certainly I also did not believe in the practice of burning incense to worship. But there was one thing that puzzled me a little bit. That was the idea of "Good and evil have their deserts", because I had seen too many examples in my life. Le-3rd Fang's prosperity and decline, by domineering and entrap people so that generations after generations of disasters were the most prominent examples. I had heard some retributions could be explained, when a person did bad things, harm people too much, always a little uneasy, because of this uneasiness, it would lead him to get retribution. In addition, the person who did harm would always be cursed by people, people plot or revenge, to deal with him as he did, the result of the fallout on his own. As for itself bad, affect the offspring also bad, in turn harm their own things, could be explained as an example of the results of teaching. But I could not explain the mystery of the evils of the previous generation that would afflict the next.

The Le-4th Fang

My grandfather was Peiyun Gong's fourth son, Ranking 8th, so our own Fang was Le-4th Fang. My grandfather and grandmother had two sons and one daughter, the eldest son was my father, the youngest son was named Yizhuan. I called him the 30th Uncle and the daughter was the 13th Aunt, and died before married.

Things about my grandfather and grandmother, as well as my uncle and aunt, were all described in the chapter "Grandfather and Grandmother".

The Le-5th Fang

There were two brothers the 32nd Uncle and the 33rd Uncle in the Le-5th Fang, but among elders in the Le-5th Fang I only saw the 32nd Aunt. the 33rd Uncle died unmarried. the 32nd Uncle died very early, leaving the 32nd Aunt and three sons, four of them lived mainly on the income from their ancestral estates, therefore had been in poverty for a long time. Except for their elder sons who had received primary education, the other two had only studied in private schools for a few years. They lived in two rooms outside the western wall of Zhangzhai, and they passed in and out their rooms had to through the outer porch of the house where "Big neck" lived. So, the Le-3rd Fang was quite discriminatory against them, especially the evil woman "Big neck", who also regards them as the object of unreasonable abuse and ridicule. The Ranking of the 32nd Aunt lower than my mother (my father Ranking 28), but was older than my mother. The two sisters were bullied together and become more intimate. The 32nd Aunt felt uncomfortable whenever my mother was insulted by "big neck", and expressed sympathy and comfort to my mother. But the 32nd Aunt wasn't as gentle as my mother, when she was insulted by big neck, she would fight back. The 32nd Aunt was the best person of my mother in the Zheng's Family, so we help the Le-5 Fang more than other Fangs in the Le-house. When my mother was alive, she gave them some material help from time to time, and my wife and I also to help them a lot in the following decades. The 32nd Aunt lived to be 82 years old and died just after liberation two or three years. At her death I sent money for a coffin. At this time, her second son and daughter-in-law had all died.

The 32nd Uncle's Eldest Son Zheng chaokai

The 32nd Uncle's eldest son Zheng chaokai, Ranking 28th, I call him Kai Ge. He went to middle school for a few years and was admitted to the postal office before graduation. He became a letter sorter first and then a mail clerk in a few years. At the beginning, he worked at the

Fuzhou Post Office, later was transferred to other places, but always had been in Fujian. In the last few years, he was in Xiamen. After over 60 years old, he retired to Fuzhou due to cancer and died soon. When he was a young student, he suffered from severe disease due to malnutrition. He was older than me and left Fuzhou very early, so I had no contact with him. After going to work, he had not care for his two younger brothers except his mother live. Because of his low salary, and had two boys and two daughters, when the second daughters came down and gave her to someone, a few salary and heavy family burden with limited ability, that was all. Kai Ge's wife was still alive today. Kai Ge's daughter after married, and went to Taiwan. Kai Ge's two sons, both had their own families, the big one in Fuzhou and the small one in Xiamen.

The 32nd Uncle's Second Son Zheng chaojian

The 32nd Uncle second son Zheng chaojian, ranking 32nd and I called him Jian Ge. He was an apprentice in cloth shop since childhood, and later died as a salesman in cloth shop. Due to insufficient nutrition, he was not healthy when he was young, and had always been very thin. He was married and had a son and a daughter. His salary was very low, and his wife was born in a poor family. The 32nd Aunt discriminated against them, so the live of the couple was very hard. Every day he left home early in the morning and returned quite late, working in the cloth shop extremely stifling, fearing unemployment. His wife did all the housework and was busy all day long, fearful and sincere. Every day she gets up earlier than anyone else. It was her who first finds that Zheng chaoji the eldest son of the Le-6th Fang hangs himself outside her door. This incident shocked her greatly. Both the husband and wife worked too long, and the nutrition was far from enough to resist disease. consequence cause tuberculosis. Jian Ge's wife died first during the Anti-Japanese War, and Jian Ge also died on the eve of the victory, both no more than 40 years old.

The 32nd Uncle's Third Son Zheng chaozhi

The 32nd Uncle's third son Zhengchao-zhi, Ranking 33rd only one year older than me. I call him Zhi Ge. When he was a child, he was famously naughty at the Zheng's Family, so he was often scolded by the people of the Le-3rd Fang, especially "Big neck", and my mother would not let my younger brother and me play with him. After growing up, Zhi Ge did not had any fixed occupation. I only knew that he had studied business and worked in a bank. He was married and had one son and three daughters. After the victory of the Anti-Japanese War, he had a period of lavishness. At that time, he and some of his father-in-law's family to do some customs clearance and transportation business, made some money, and also buy many gold ornaments for his wife. At this time, in addition to supporting the elderly mother, the couple also raised the children left by their second brother. Both of them was not stingy with his eldest brother, and could almost get what he wanted and almost did what he wanted. But the good times did not last long, and on the eve of liberation, his business could not continue. After liberation, he had no fixed job, and only helped to write some tax bills as temporary workers at the Finance Bureau of Cangshan District, Fuzhou. Because he was very backward in thought, he could not always figure it out, and he was always dissatisfied with the new society, and gradually became mentally abnormal. Zhi Ge's wife started a small business or some temporary work, of course made very little money. The income was very small, and the old mother and four children had to support, so they had to sell some households to subsidize the family. Soon after, all households were sold out immediately, and the economy became very difficult. It was around 1954 that Zhi Ge's wife found a job and worked as a salesperson at the Dongjiekou department store in the Fuzhou city. Because of her work active and hard, she was promoted to counter chief a few years later. However, it was hard to imagine the difficulty of only relying on her to feed six people and pay for the education of her children. About 1956, angry with her husband, felt unable to survive and wanted to suicide, so she jumped into the Minjiang River Fortunately, she was rescued from death. I inherited my mother's ambition, and from the very beginning I gave financial support to the family of Le-5th Fang. Later, I gave them most of my monthly income in Fuzhou. After the Cultural Revolution, their situation improved with the growth up of their children.

The Le-6th Fang

In the Le-6th Fang the 10th Granduncle had two sons, the 16th Uncle and the 24th Uncle. Because the Le-2nd Fang had no sons, 24th Uncle was succeeded to the Le-2nd Fang become his son, So the Le-6th Fang was carrying on the Le-2nd Fang. The 7th Granduncle Uncle in the Le-3rd Fang had three sons and two daughters, In the ordinary course of events should had been the Le-3rd Fang to carrying on the Le-2nd Fang. But the Le-3rd Fang did not like to do this. I had not heard of the reason, so I could only guess. It may be that the Le-3rd Fang, who had a son as an officials, looks down on the Le-2nd Fang, and not would to give a son to the 2nd Fang. Perhaps the granduncles in these two Fangs were not born from the same mother, and the both brothers were not in harmony. Maybe there was only one grandson in the Le-3rd Fang could not responsibilities of carrying on the Le-2nd Fang. Although the Le-4th Fang and Le-5th Fang each had two sons, but one of them died prematurely. Of course, the only remaining son could not be succeeded. So the responsibilities of carrying on the Le-2nd Fang was fell to the Le-6th Fang.

The 24th Uncle had never been married in his lifetime, and I had no idea what work he had done in their lifetime. I just remember that he seemed to had been at home, and doing nothing. I heard that he wanted to beg a wife very much, maybe without a job he could not get a wife. When someone gets married, he hears the sound of the golden drum (or suona horn) and wants to marry a wife, so he had been derishedly called "golden drum epilepsy".

The 16th Aunt had two sons, Ranking 22 and 23, and a daughter. I called her 6th Sister. Her husband, Chen dagui, was a very strict old-style private school teacher, famous in Xiadu area.

The 22nd Brother, Zheng chaoji

The 22nd brother, Zheng chaoji, was a salesperson of a silk shop, a matchmaker claimed that Zheng's Family owned many houses, tea shops, wine banks and other industries, by cheating to marry a devout schoolgirl. Zheng chaoji's sister also helped the matchmaker, On the wedding day, the 22nd Sister-in-law refused to bow down to heaven and earth and ancestors. She only bowed down to her elders. The false face was of course taken out very quickly, so she was very annoyed by the marriage and had a very bad relationship with ChaoJi. But the both two never yelled aloud, probably because the ChaoJi took care of the "everyone" face, and the schoolgirl kept the character of a cultured person! She only had two daughters and soon she did not want to share the room with her husband. Later, she kept ChaoJi out of the door and refused him to enter the room. ChaoJi often stayed in the store, and whenever he came home, he slept on two square chairs in the hall at night. Around 1935, one day, ChaoJi suddenly hanged himself and died outside his door. This could be said to be a tragedy of the feudal family and an example of deceiving the marriage. The 22nd Sister-in-law died in 1945 because she was depressed and body sick after marriage. Before her death, she was forced into poverty and illness, and she wanted to sell the small building where she lived. However, there was a rule in Zheng's ancestral home that all houses within the confines of Zheng's mansion's residence could not be sold to outsiders (a deadline was permissible). At that time, just after the victory of the War of Resistance against Japan, Zheng's Family was almost in poverty and unable to buy the building for her relief. Not long after my family returned from Shanghai to Fuzhou at that time, my mother thought she was quite pitiful, and if I wanted to bear the building, I had to sell my wife's gold jewelry to buy it. After buying, my mother still let her live until her death. We had never lived in this building ourselves, nor had we benefited from it. On the contrary, it caused trouble that had not been relieved so far.

The 23rd Brother, Zheng chaozhi

The 23 rd Brother, Zheng chaozhi, Everyone in Zheng's Family called him Zhizhi, He was a completely useless person, and had not done anything in all of his life. His mother doted on him, and from very early age he just followed his mother wherever she went, carrying her water pipe, and also carrying a fire cage (a bamboo shell charcoal stove for warming up) in winter when cold until his mother died. When he was young, he was not good at school so he only knew a few words roughly, and he didn't want to be an apprentice and learn some skills. After the death of his mother, someone introduced him to do some work, but only a few days he came back. Either he sneaks back because he was too lazy to do it, or was pushed back by others. Such a person like him was ignorant but conceited, and speaks in a big way, talks as if he knew everything, could do everything, and wished to do big things. Of course he was a bachelor all his life, Which a girl willing to marry him? who dare introduce a girl to marry him? His sister had tried to find a girl for marry him, but after knowing more about her brother Zheng chaozhi's marriage bad consequences, of course she dare not make the same mistake and be laughed at. At the Zheng's Family, he became a villain to educate children. Whenever my child refuses to study or to do things, and just follows his mother, my wife and I would to say that when you grows up, you would become like Zhibo, and you would not have a life. My Younger brother's wife also trained her children. Therefore, in the minds of our children, ZhiBo was a contemptible bad example. He relied on his brother, sister-in-law, and the money taken in turn from the Zheng's Family business to live on. After his brother and sister-in-law died, he still lived a hard life by owning rooms inherited from the Le-2nd Fang and selling broken things. He was wearing a dirty and tattered gown, and worn shoes and socks. he looks exactly like Kongyiji as Described by Luxun. He died of illness just after liberation, ending his life as a parasite.

The 24th Uncle unmarried and had not any children, the 23rd brother Zheng chaozhi was succeeded to him as his son, so he also followed the 24th Uncle, succeeded to the Le-2nd Fang. Later, Chaozhi was also a bachelor, and Chaoji also had no sons, so the Le-2nd Fang and the Le-6th Fang were both heirs. When our family returned to Fuzhou from Shanghai in 1945, Chaozhi himself and some older of the tribe to ask my wife to let our third son take over his career. He thinks that by using the public shares of Le-2nd Fang and Le-6th Fang as bait, we would agree. But we were not greedy for money, and we did not like such feudal family practice, immediately refused.

As I known not one decent person come out in the Le-6th Fang, all of them were almost ignorant people, so in just a few decades, the Le-6th Fang quickly fell into decline and eventually ended.

The Le-7th, Le-8th and Le-9th Fang

The 11th, 12th and 13th Granduncles in the Le-7th, Le-8th and Le-9th Fang were all born in Sichuan by Mrs. Yang. After the death of Peiyun Gong in Sichuan official, the three Granduncles all returned to Fuzhou with their mother. At the time they were all very young.

The 11th Granduncle and 11th Grandaunt

I had seen The 11th Granduncle and 11th Grandaunt, and when I saw them, I was young. the 11th Granduncle worked in the upper reaches of the Minjiang River. I only remember that he often brought food from northern of Fujian for his mother. They lived in the northernmost room of the front flower hall. Because our kitchen was outside the second partition wall, there was a small door just at outside the door of their room. When we go to our kitchen, we had to pass through the small door. Behind their room, there was small door leads to the back flower hall. My aunt often took me went to their room for Gambling. Therefore, the 11th-Grandaunt still had deep impression in my mind, because 11th-Granduncle was mostly not at home and died long ago. Although the 11th-Grandaunt not very old, but perhaps because of illness, most time she stayed in bed. There was a lot of food hidden in her bed, such as dried fruits and biscuits and so on. Fuzhou ants, often patronize her bed food, her eyes dim, could not help but eat ants. If those little ants were also rich in protein like African ants, then the ants who share the bed food with her also become a source of protein in her body. When I was about ten years old, the 11th-Grandaunt died, the 11th Grandaunt had three sons. I had not heard that they had daughters. Two of their sons the 25th Uncle and the 27th Uncle were older than my father. The other one, the 29th Uncle was slightly younger than my father. The 25th Uncle had done some jobs, probably inheriting their father's business. The 27th Uncle and the 29th Uncle not only was unemployed, but both of them were promiscuous and slutty. This was the result of the 11th-Granduncle and his wife's failure to discipline their son.

The 25th Uncle and the 25th Aunt

The 25th Uncle and the 25th Aunt were a couple who resemble the 11th Granduncle and 11th Grandaunt. They had a son named Meng Ge (I called him the 21st Brother), and a daughter named Jiujie (I called her the 9th Sister). The couple also did not educate their sons. I had no idea whether Meng Ge had read a book or whether he has gone to school. I only know that he could write good characters, and it was unclear to what extent he learned ancient Chinese. I had not heard of any errands that he had done, But he once had set up a private school in Zheng's Ancestral Hall, also some addicted to gambling, and his wife the 25th Aunt from time to time quarrel. They had only one child, named Hanhan but died very early. Since he mainly lived on the income derived from his ancestry, he was drinking and whoring outside, Of course, could not make ends meet. When shopping and going to the restaurant, he tended to take credit, fearing both Zheng Former power and his rogue scoundrel behavior, people had to give him credit. Every New Year Eve, an endless stream of debtors came to him, so he run outside to hide his debts, and his mother and wife would handle it. He was nicknamed a "Hao Chen", and when people came to demand debts, shouted the "Hao Chen". Whether he could pay off his debts every year, I did not know because I was young, but after the New Year Eve, he went out to buy credit and eat as usual, and during the next New Year or other festive, the shout of "Hao Chen, Hao Chen!" again. Later, The 25th Uncle with the 25th Aunt and the 21st Sister-in-law died one after another, and I never saw Meng Ge again. I heard that he went to Beijing and lived in the Sanshan Guild Hall, where was a hall set up by Fujianese in other provinces or cities, and Meng Ge died in desperation. Jiujie (9th sister) married to a descendant of Eight banners and left Fuzhou very early.

The 26th Uncle and the 27th Mother

I had not seen the 27th Uncle, because he was die quit early. I heard from elders, he did not work and prefers whoring, and though he was married, he still whoring outside. On one occasion, while visiting a prostitute (probably a boat woman) on a sampan, he was pushed into a river to death at young age because of jealousy. At the time of his death, his wife 27th mother was pregnant with a posthumous child. He was born with the name Dudu, I called him Du Ge (The 15th elder brothers).

The 27th Mother was quite beautiful when she was young, and she had read poetry books and were quite cultural. Young widows was inevitably lonely, let alone coveted? This man did not come from outside, he was inside the Zheng's Family. He was the 26th Uncle, the only son of the 12th Granduncles. When the 27th Uncle died, the 26th Uncle was married, but still young and lustful. Would a lustful young man let go of the beautiful widow nearby. Soon they were hooking up, playing rope games together, make a circle with a piece of string, put it on the fingers of each hand and make a pattern, the other one put a pattern on it with the fingers of his two hands, and then began to play again. The couple of red-blooded young man and woman, of course, did not stop there, and soon had sex. Since then, they had been living together for decades, from semi-public to public, until they decently behave just like husband and wife or husband and concubine. It was not uncommon for such a thing to be done sneakily in a Feudal Families, but rarely to be done so openly and boldly. At that time, mother-in law (the 11th Grandaunt) of the 27th Mother and the farther (the 12th Granduncle) of the 26th Uncle were still alive. There were also a Hanlin (the 17th Uncle) and a Jinshi (Ba Ge) in the Zheng's Family. The Qing Dynasty had not yet fallen, in the traditional family as be known as "family of poetry" and "scholarly family", Such openness was probably unique! The 11th Grandaunt died earlier, and the 12th Granduncle lived for a long time before dying. It was incredible to see that such an "incest" continued in front of him for many years without saying a word. I had not heard any complaints from my the 26th Mother, let alone any quarrels. In the Zheng's Family. I had not heard anyone publicly comment on it (of course there were critics behind it). On the contrary, they were not only surprised but also seem to be supportive.

When the 27th Mother lived in Zheng's house, her room was in the middle of the flower hall (originally shared with the Le-6th Fang, I didn't know when it was owned by the Le-7th Fang), and was separated from our big back room of Le-4th Fang by only one wall. the 27th Mother was very kind to people, love to write poetry, good at lyrics. She also was very good at telling stories of old books and traditional dramas. People were happy to go to her room for a short chat after dinner. Although the interior layout was not valuable, but it was very elegant, and often had hot tea for people to drink, so it was also very attractive to enter, especially the concubines of her peers, including my mother and the 32nd Aunt. Some idle people in the Zheng's Family, such as Zhizhi, and occasionally relatives and friends also often chat in her room. When the 26th Uncle came at night, these people consciously withdrew and let him stay with her. In order to reward everyone "support," the 26th Uncle bought theater tickets once a year, and invites these frequent visitors to watch the Fujian Opera, and then invites them to the restaurant after watching Opera. I remember I followed with my mother went to the room of the 27th Mother two or three times. I also remember when I was about three or four years old, I once went into the room of the 27th Mother early in the morning before she had got up. I went to her bed, opened the curtain, and saw the 26th Uncle in the same bed with her. I run outside and said loudly, "the 26th Uncle and the 27th Mother sleep together." So I accidentally became a little "Hong Ge". The adults did not say anything for hearing this. Probably because I was young, so it was not unusual for them. The reason of the 27th Mother keeps her room open was because her daughter-in-law was going in early in the morning to deliver tea, otherwise how could I got in? Both of them had lived together for decades. The 27th Mother had not had children because of this. I did not know if they had been pregnant. It was likely that she or he has mastered the old methods of contraception or abortion. the 26th Uncle died first. the 27th Mother lived about 20 years longer than the 26th Uncle. When she died, was 82 years old. For her death, I used two times money. First, when she was still 80 years old, her daughter-in-law wrote a letter to Shanghai asking for my help because of illness. I sent 50 yuan for her funeral expenses. As a result, she was not dead, and the money subsidized her living expenses. Later, before really dying, her daughter-in-law sent an urgent letter again, and I remitted 50 yuan for funeral expenses. A few decades ago, the little "Hong Ge" became a coffin giver. I was afraid she could not think of it!

"Broken Things" Dudu

Dudu was a posthumous child, and his mother had indulged him since childhood, and she didn't dare to control when she was older, so that he later became a prodigal wanderer with whore and gambling drink all kinds of bad habits. But he was quite filial to his mother and did not regard her disgrace as a shame at all. For a long period of time, the 27th mother actually moved to the 26th Uncle's family and lived in peace with the 26th mother. She became a wife and concubine of the 26th Uncle, and the Dudu couple also lived with them. Dudu had studied in private schools when he was a child, If there was some knowledge, it was not much. Dudu had never had a career in his life, specialize in doing fraud and harm with cheating people out there. In Fuzhou, people like him were called "broken things", which means rogue or scumbag. I know there was a man who was killed in a foreign county because he had done some bad things in partnership with him. The wife of this man came to his house many times and cried.

In addition to the nickname Dudu, he also used Xihou and Yan Gui as his name. People used to spell his three names as "Du Xigui", which happened to be the name of an admiral at the time. This person was a prominent figure in Fuzhou. Like his cousin Mengmeng, Dudu often did some same things such as compulsory purchases in shops and eating in restaurants without pay. Many people come to collect debts during the holidays, and continue to shout "Xihou". These people had to walk through the small corridor outside our house to his house. On New Year Eve, they walked very diligently, holding a lantern and yelling. Like Meng Meng, Dudu also fled outside to hide his debts and let his mother and his wife to handle. In my young mind, "Haochen!" Xihou! Xihou! Howard!" , And "had no money to eat in our restaurant, and very picky when eating. also had been pushing the table and throwing bowls". These insults seemed to be still in my ears.

During the period when we moved away from Zheng's mansion, the back room was once rented to Dudu, and the monthly rent was only 2 Yuan. In order to claim this little rent, I did not know how many times I had to run. Either he was not at home, or he pushed that there was no money around him, and ask me to go after a few days.

Dudu married a wife and stole a concubine outside, but because he was infected with syphilis, he never had a child. Dudu's wife, the 25th Sister-in-law, was a very honest woman. She not only serves a husband like him, but also pays homage to his mother-in-law. Dudu suffered from stomach disease (probably stomach cancer), and died before about 55 years old. the 25th Sister-in-law died shortly after her mother-in-law's death. I did not know what was like in her family before married. Married to Zheng's Family, act servile humbly without a good day, and at last died of hard work.

The 29th Uncle with his son Yanyan

The 29th Uncle was a full swinger, I did not know what serious affairs he had done. I only know that he was a corrupt element who go round on seek carnal pleasure and messes up the relationship between men and women outside. He married a wife and had a son, named Yanyan, Ranking 30th. His wife died early of grief because of the 29th Uncle life corrupts and pay women to fuck, the 29th Uncle later in Fuzhou could not get along, he took a friend to go far away in Malaya, there he was still kept on behaving as he had been before. The strange thing was that he would live to be in his 80 and become the longest hit in his generation. No one knows when the 29th Uncle die, because he had long been separated from relationship with his son.

As same as his father, Yanyan was also a bad guy who loves to fuck women. Yanyan also married a wife. The 30th Sister-in-law was a diligent woman, having two sons and one daughter. Yanyan could not get along in Fuzhou, He took his wife went to Malaya very early, where Yanyan lived with his wife's sister as his concubine, and later broke away from his wife and children. I heard that he and his concubine (his wife's sister) also had some babies, but I didn't know exactly how many. During the Anti-Japanese War, the 30th Sister-in-law back to Fuzhou with her children, She did everything such as being a hawker and buying and selling old things for others. Their live were very difficulty, It was like a bitter pill to swallow. After the victory, I helped the 30th Sister-in-law with her four children to be repatriated to Malaya by the United Nations Relief Agency as refugees. There they were still separated from Yanyan, who had abandoned his concubine (his wife's sister), and made love to other women one by one. I did not know how the 30th Sister-in-law lived in Nanyang. I only heard that Yanyan's eldest son became a policeman, and her daughter moved to Singapore after marriage. Yanyan's second son returned to China in the early liberation period. He reportedly escaped after stealing his father's car for sale. His father had publicly announced in the local newspaper that he had separated from him and wanted to hunt him down. Yanyan was engaged in fraudulent activities in Malaysia and was mixed with the local Islam. He became the leader of Chinese Christians and had made pilgrimages to Mecca. He defrauded people's money everywhere, and when he got the money, he went to play with the women. He returned to Fuzhou with a very young woman in 1982, when he was in his eighties. I did not know when he would resume his relationship with his second son.

After Yanyan's second son returned to China, he became a truck driver in Fujian and was married. He had a son and a daughter. but I did not know when he succeeded as Dudu's son, he inherited all the houses of the Le-7 Fang. In the late 1920s the house was converted into a building (including the middle and back of the flower hall) when a large rent on the grounds was allocated to each Fang (room) in Le-house. Yanyan second son was also a corrupt person. When he was a driver, he was sentenced to prison twice for messing with the women and corrupt life. After liberation, he was not allowed to run amok on the land of new China. His destiny was, of course, different from his father and grandfather. Strangely, I heard that his son also began to have his father's habits. If it is true, it will become a confluence of four generations.

The 12th Granduncle

The 12th Grandaunt died early, I hadn't seen her. In addition to had their son 26th Uncle, the 12th Granduncle also had a daughter, the 12th aunt. She married to a descendant of Lin zexu. I did not know what work the 12th Granduncle had done. I just remember that when I was sensible, he seemed had stopped doing anythings, and he was at home. the 26th Uncle worked in a government agency and was considered with a professional background. Because of this, he seems to be more decent in the Zheng's Family, the economy was relatively well-off. His family did not live in the barn room assigned to the Le-8th Fang by our ancestors very early. Instead they had moved out into larger houses, and had even moved 27th Aunt to live together. The 26th Mother was a weak woman and had four sons. So the Le 8th Fang was a wealthy Fang at that time, quite envied by some people. But the good times were not long.

Jingjing, the eldest son of the 26th Uncle, Ranking 24. who had read in private schools and handwriting was very good. But his vision was very short, only to focus on the ancestral inheritance. When to share profits and divide gains, fear to lose. I had no idea what he had done. I just think that he was always at home. Jingjing was not go to other places even if there was a job. And his wife, the 24th Sister-in-law always clung to him, and he stayed in idleness for many years. Jingjing had a daughter and two sons. His daughter, after married went to Taiwan with her husband. The eldest son died in a warehouse of the Le-8th Fang in the back garden. The second son after graduation from East China Normal University, stayed in Shanghai as a teacher.

Xikai, the second son of 26th Uncle, Ranking 26. I did not understand why he took this Japanese name. He once worked in the Minbao Newsroom run by the Japanese, but later lost his job for a long time. He was lazy and like eating with many bad habits, As a result, his wife starved to death, a pair of children were sold by him for buy food, and finally he fell to death.

Cencen, the third son of the 26th Uncle, Ranking 29. He also was a "broken thing", actually married the daughter of the 12th Aunts, had a son. During the war of Against Japan, he turned to the Japanese invaders and committed crimes. As a result, he was arrested and sentenced to prison after victory, and died in prison (some people said he was shot). After his wife married to him, it said never had a good day, and then died in poverty. Before liberation, his son had followed his uncle to Nanjing then turned to his uncle's natal family in Anhui. Later, I heard he went to college and joined the revolution, but now I did not know how.

Chichi, the fourth son of the 26th Uncle, Ranking 35. slightly younger than me. was trained in the Central Military Academy to learn artillery skills. He was very brave in the Anti-Japanese War, and was promoted for meritorious service. After the victory, he was sent to the United States Military Academy. After studied at West Point, returned back to work in the Department of Defense. On the eve of the liberation of Shanghai, he told me that he was going to abandon the army and go into business in Fuzhou. At this time, his wife already gone to Taiwan with her brother, and he was also called to Taiwan. His father-in-law was a big landlord in Anhui, and his wife's brothers and most relatives held many important positions in the Kuomintang army, so he could not abandon the army. Soon he was sent through Myanmar and sneak into Yunnan for harassing the mainland. He was immediately captured by the People's Liberation Army and almost to be executed. Later, he was pardoned and served as an artillery instructor for a short period of time before he was imprisoned as a counter-revolutionary. In 1970s, when the Kuomintang military and political personnel were granted amnesty, he was pardoned again and returned to Fuzhou. at this time he was already suffering from severe tracheitis. Because the eldest son of his eldest brother did not provide care or accommodation to him, he lived alone in a corner of the front pavilions owned by the Le-3rd Fang in Zheng's mansion. the situation was rather bad. In order to relieve him, the government assigned him to work in a street factory and receive some monthly salary for living. I did not know when his wife had been transferred from Taiwan to the United States, where she lived as a family nanny and learned the news about he was in Fujian. she once sent money to him, but he soon died of illness. In 1976, when I went back to Fuzhou and I had saw him. It was not long after he was pardoned and returned to his hometown Fuzhou. the situation was deplorable. He was disappointed that on the eve of liberation he had not realized his original intention of abandon the army and entering the business. In mid-1977, I got news of his death.

The 13th Grandaunt

The 13th Granduncle was died early and his wife (the 13th Grandaunt) remained widow for some decades. She was from northern of Fujian and always had an accent from northern Fujian. This shows that the 13th Granduncle may had worked in northern of Fujian. She only gave birth to the 15th Aunt and no son. Chichi once was gave her as a grandson, so she lived with the 26th Uncle family for a long time. Because Chichi had no children, the Le-9th Fang also became a heir.

Both the Le-7th Fang and the Le-8th Fang were wealth and prosperous, and they flourished for a while, but soon declined. The 11 st Granduncle had three sons and the 26th Uncle had four sons. At that time, they were considered lucky people, good fortune and many men. At present, the 11th Granduncle's descendants had only Yanyan was left. I only know that he had two sons, born of Yanyan wife who was marrying. Had Yanyan concubine in Nanyang ever had some son? How many were born? was still his son? I was at a loss, I was afraid no one knows. (I didn't know, and probably nobody knows). At present, the Le-7th Fang had only the second son family of Yanyan in Fuzhou with a grandson. The descendants of the 26th Uncle had only two grandchildren left. Superstitious people believe that the evils created by the Le-7th Fang and the Le-8th Fang were to inflict harm the younger generation. so I also believe this kind of retribution. But I think more deeply that this was the result of not educating the younger generation. Not only did the father not pay attention to educating his son, but his own bad behavior became a very bad example. Of course, he could not control his son, That was why produce "the father is not the father, the son is not the son" corrupt situation. Their biggest mistake lies in for their dissolute and casual sex, and for their frequent visits to prostitutes, resulting in severe venereal disease, resulting in loss of fertility, rapidly shrinking population. Its own not right, could not be taught, its harm was very terrible.

Rebo and Anan, Zheng's Mansion Gatekeepers

Before I was ten years old, there lived an old man about 60 years old in the compartment of entrance hall of Zheng's mansion. His goatee, his face marked with the wrinkles of a lifetime of hard work, and his habitual cough in cold weather, made him look rather old. The upper body was wearing a blue or black cloth gown, the lower body was wearing black cloth trousers, and the black cloth shoes were pedals, which look very dirty. Walking on the road seemed to drag step by step weakly, and crossing the threshold was even more difficult. These impressions were still deeply engraved in my mind. He was the gatekeeper of Zheng's mansion. at the time, but he didn't have the name. The Zheng's Family of my generation, as well as the women of the mother's generation, call him Rebo. I don't know if the words were written like this. No one told me what was his surname. Maybe his surname was Ye. If this was the case, then he should be called Ye Bo, not Rebo, because according to the pronunciation of the Fuzhou people, Ye and Re were homophone. But in my mind at that time, I only knew "hot", so I always thought he was Rebo, let me call him like this now!

Hearing from adult, he came to the Zheng's Family from an early age to serve as the great grandfather Peiyun Gong manservant. Later, he served Peiyun Gong all the time, and Peiyun Gong went to Beijing to take an exam and late as officials. he continued to serve as a housekeeper in Peiyun Gong government office. After Peiyun Gong's death, he accompanied his coffin back to Fuzhou. Since then, he stayed at the Zheng's Family, and because he lived in the entrance gate hall, he became a gatekeeper. In the feudal era, the manservant were generally bought like slave-servants. After they were bought, they changed to the owner surname, and the owner gave him another name, mostly in auspicious words. If so, his name might be Yi. The pronunciation of Fuzhou in this word was very similar to that of Re and Ye.

I did not see Re mother, and I did not hear anyone say there was a Re mother, so I was not sure if he ever married a wife. But he had a son named Anan, whether he was born or adopted, I did not know. Anan was married and everyone called his wife Anansao. Rebo and his daughter-in-law both cook their own meals instead of relying on which Fang of Zheng's house, but I did not know where his kitchen was. Their family's life was probably supported by a certain amount of public funds from Le-house. It was not sufficient, so Anan often did odd jobs, and Anansao often helped others with housework and earns some subsidies.

Because Rebo had been following Peiyun Gong for many years, the juniors all respected him, and the children were even more in awe of him. He also contributed to the Zheng's Family and sometimes dared to criticize the behavior of the juniors. In the entrance hall he was very authoritative and could prevent outsiders from walking in casually, and could also stop the children in the house from slipping out. He was very dissatisfied with some women of the Zheng's Family standing at the door and looking at the street, especially with younger grandma and girls. Although the feudal dynasty had been overthrown at that time, the sense of feudalism was still very strong. The elderly still think that women should be less exposed outside, and it was not appropriate to go out. However, some women were unwilling to be lonely. When there was space, they want to stand at the door to see the liveliness of the street. Rebo would criticize without politeness or reprimanded the girl for doing so. He whispered to the young grandmother who he dared not criticize in person: "What's so good on the street, let people see how good you were?" This kind of murmur sometimes makes them embarrassed to retreat into their room. At that time, the women of the Zheng's Family went out and took the sedan chair. The sedan chair was lifted to the patio or hall. After the people sat down, the curtain of the sedan chair was put down, and then it was carried out. Every time the sedan chair entered and exited he took the task of opening and closing the door. In the evening, closing the door and the side door was also his responsibility. After closing the door, if someone comes back to knock on the door, he would inevitably get up and open the door. If there was any wedding or funeral event in a certain Fang of the Zheng's Family, it was certainly his business to participate in helping. On this day and during the Chinese New Year, every room of the Zheng's Family would gave him food and some money. In addition to managing the foyer, he often bought food for this Fang or other Fang. People often told him to buy some things at night. He could buy it from a shoulder vendor who walks through the door, or he could go to a nearby vegetable stall to buy them. He was honest enough not to skimp, and always tried his best to buy cost-effective dishes. Whenever a certain Fang asked him to buy too many dishes that were too good or too expensive on weekdays, he would make criticism: "It's very inappropriate to eat such expensive things! Why buy so much and spend so much money?" Because had seen the prosperity and development of the Zheng's Family in the Peiyun Gong era, and he also had seen the decay of some descendants, and always feel uncomfortable in his heart. As a servant, he did not dare to control, and could only offer advice or mutter in the back. He snapped at the child, for people respected him and dared not refute his chatter.

After Rebo death, the Anan family still lived in a compartment of the entrance hall. Anan could not act as a deterrent for his father, so the Zheng's mansion entrance gate was opened. Anyone who picks up hawkers, collects old things, picks up trash, or any other people, as well as wild dogs, could enter and leave the gate casually. The shouts of selling vegetables, fruits, pastries and buying old furniture, scraps, tin foil ash etc. inside the house could be heard from time to time. They not only enter the hall but also enter the room. The women watched the street and the children slipped out of the gates. However, the Anan couple continued to do things like purchasing side dishes, opening and closing doors, helping with chores, etc. Whether the Zheng's Family still uses some public funds to send them, I did not know. but it was possible that they did not send them anymore. But the festival and some Fangs had worship day, still gave them food with a few money.

Anan was a man with a small head and a simple brain. He was so honest that he could not to talk about some thing and stutters. Sometimes people talk to him, he could not even hear clearly, so he could not do much. Rebo wanted to train him to be a servant of the Zheng's Family. However, because the Zheng's Family did not had any people who needed to be on duty at the time, and because he was not very flexible, he could not be trained. Only when Zheng Shuzhang (the Hanlin) was invited to attend birthday party or funeral, he was sent to take a temporary messenger. A unlucky "green blind father" and a stupid messenger really make a pair of treasures. Every time he went out in this way, he was rewarded with a piece of money. Apart from this, which was a soft job for him, sometimes he worked as a laborer to earn some money for the families who held wedding or funerals, he also carried water and chopped firewood for some of the Zheng's Family. When he went out to work, he wore a long, faded blue and white shirt, as he usually did in a short waistcoat. Anansao spends most of her time as a domestic worker. She once worked as a domestic worker in Le-3rd Fang for a long time. When no one hired her, she also carried water and did some temporary work. The tea shop required the woman worker to pick up the stalks of tea leaves, and at one time she did so, and was paid every day according to the weight picked up. She was slow and did not pick much, so she got less than others. This couple had some children, how many of them I forget. In order to maintain the life of the family, their poverty was imaginable.

In the early 1930s, Xiadu Street was widened and replaced by a road. The entrance hall of Zheng's mansion. was completely demolished. The family of Anan had to move to a broken room in Langang li. At that time Anan died some time ago. What would happen to Anansao and her children? I did not know, since I was not in Fuzhou. When I returned back in 1945, without seeing.

CHAPTER 6

Grandparents

My Grandfather

My grandfather was Peiyungong fourth son, ranking 8th. So, we was the Le-4th Fang in Le-Horse, we lived in the back room and the back porch on the west side of the First entrance in Zheng's mansion. Between the back room and the back porch was a gallery, But this gallery was not for private use, because it was the passage to the flower hall and the of kitchen of the Le-3rd Fang. Our kitchen was outside the second partition, the most norther one, far away from our room, which was very inconvenient, so we often eat in the kitchen. On the west side of the back hall there was a door leading to the back room, where our dining tables were placed, but this place was often occupied by parking coffins from time to time, so that the dining tables had to be moved and the meals were eaten in the room or kitchen. It was for this and some other reasons that the western back room of the Chinese-style south-facing house was the worst in the whole house. When setting up the house, the master carpenter would take the axe up to build the beam, and then throw the axe to the floor of this back room after setting up, also because this room was the worst. But I heard from an adult that the six sons of the two great-grandmothers were all raised in this room. It could be seen that they had all lived in this room. For this reason, this room was quite good.

About my grandfather name, I had forgotten what his name was and I could not to ask. Now I only knew that he was called Shaoqing Gong. He died very early, even my mother did not see him, so I knew very little about my grandfather. When my grandmother died, I was still young, so she didn't talk to me more about my grandfather. My father only told me a few things of him. In addition, I also heard some from adult conversations. Now I could only wrote down about the grandfather's two or three things from some traces of the past that left in my memory. My grandfather was a bit lame, but he was not a disabled person.

Carry Father Coffin Back

My grandfather once did something that was considered a great filial piety and virtue in his life. When his farther Peiyun Gong died of illness in Sichuan Province, he rushed from Fuzhou to Sichuan to carry his father coffin back. As the fourth son, why did he go instead of one of the three elder brothers? I could not say clearly, I only could guess. His first and second brothers may had already died prematurely, or they may not be able to go or be sent away for other reasons. His third brothers controlled all the property of the Le-horse with great power and could not or would not go. The two younger brothers were too young to take on this important task, so the arduous hard task fell to my grandfather. The journey from Fujian to Sichuan with the return of the coffin, that was rather difficult to travel thousands of miles between the mountains and rivers. At this time, just during the Taiping Heavenly Kingdom war, many difficulties were added. During every battle on the way, my grandfather would bury the coffin into the soil temporarily. When the fighting was over and the road was quiet, the coffin was exhumed out and continue to move to next place. It was said that happened several times, each time had to be delayed for a period of dates, so the return journey took more than a year. Peiyun Gong's coffin was made of the best timber from Sichuan Province, and It was very large and heavy. There were a lot of hardships in the long-distance transportation, such as climbing mountains, crossing ridges and wading through rivers. The most difficult thing was that my grandfather had to take care Peiyun Gong's wife Mrs. Yang and three brothers along the way, helping him on the journey only Rebo, Peiyun Gong servant. Mrs. Yang originally from Sichuan, she was unwilling to come to Fuzhou, after much advice from my grandfather, she was willing to go along. Through all the hardships of the journey, she was full of complaints. My grandfather was really painstaking about his second mother and three younger brothers. The journey was so long, and was so difficult to walk. Stopping and waiting till the battle was over, then he had to look for a suitable shelter, all kinds of problems must be determined by him. The intentions could be seen, the road cost was huge, could also be seen. It was a pity that my grandfather did not write down this matter in his diary. If someone could experience the situation, it would all be described in detail, coupled with the literary rendering, that would be able to write a thrilling novel, famous all over the world.

Before or after carrying father's coffin back, my grandfather worked in a pawnshop. There were still expired and unredeemed collateral, my grandfather bought back. There were two camphor boxes, two large suitcases and ancient bottles. The things were quite good.

Official Service in Jinhua

Later, my grandfather worked in the government office in Jinhua, Zhejiang Province. The Master of that station was the husband uncle of the "*three gu eight aunts*". Speaking of this Magistrate, I once heard one thing from my father. The man had a twin brother, who was also a governor. The two brothers were not in the same place, but whenever one was ill, the other was ill with the same disease. They had the same fate from childhood. They both won the imperial examinations and were exactly the same in official affairs. Later, whether they died at the same time, my father did not say, I did not know. From this instance and others I had heard throughout my life, I had been puzzled and half doubted by the story of fate. The twin brothers were born at exactly the same time, were their fates really the same? I really couldn't explain it.

My grandfather died while working in Jinhua. My father took his coffin back to Fuzhou and buried him in Qian Mountain. This was the second generation of my family, after my grandfather died, my father carried his coffin home. The second means of transport was of course easier than the first, because the journey was shorter and there was no war. But at that time, the traffic between Fujian and Zhejiang was not developed, all the places passed by were like mountainous areas, so there were still a lot of difficulties. When my father told me about it, he said I could take his coffin home, too, and be the third generation to take his father's coffin home. There was a saying in Fuzhou: "If there were two times, there would be three times". But in his words, I became the son carrying father's coffin home, which would happen later.

The 4th Aunt and Her Husband

Mrs. Feng was the first wife of my grandfather, She died early, leaved only a daughter, I called her the 4th Aunt. she was married to Lin family in Shanggan Township, the 4th aunt's husband was a businessman, in addition to own some farm property in the countryside, also with his cousin owned a small bank, and set up a Hengyuan fish shop in Fuzhou Zhongting Street, wholesale and separate sale fresh and salty aquatic products. Although the 4th Aunt was not born to my grandmother, she was very filial to my grandmother and cared for our family. She often asked her husband to bring good fish and shrimp with food produced in the village to my grandmother. Although the 4th aunt and her birth mother died prematurely, my grandfather passed away early. After the death of the 4th aunt, the family of 4th aunt's husband still often communicates with our family. The 4th aunt husband still continue to sent some good aquatic products, such as the yellow Croaker and Green crab etc. to our home.

After the death of the first wife of my grandfather, he remarried again. I didn't know what the reason was, but it was probably because the family declined after Peiyun Gong died, and also because my grandfather had foot problems, remarried grandmother was a maid from a large family. For these reasons, my grandmother was treated as a concubine by the Zheng's Family, especially the 7th granduncle and his wife. People in Zheng's Family only called my grandmother as aunt. But she was my beloved grandmother.

My Grandmother

My grandmother died when I was three. I hadn't been with her very long, just over two years. In that chaotic year, my knowledge was not open, so she had little direct impression in my mind. But I had kept a full six and a half inch picture of her, from which I could recall some indirect impression of her in my mind. This was early photography, of course the technique wasn't very good, but I didn't know when this picture was taken. I just didn't think this was a picture of her at 60, because it looks like she's still healthy and not sick, but thin and with deep wrinkles around the corners of her mouth. She looks nervous and serious, probably because of photography. At that time, there were still a lot of people who were superstitious about photography and thought that people souls would be taken away, so they were very cautious. My grandmother left this photo, showed that she was a brave old lady, just a little nervous in the photo.

My Deal Grandmother

When I was young, my parents and my older sister would sometimes told me about my grandmother. The most common topic was how she loved me and how I was loved by her in every possible way. Of course, she didn't know the proper way to feed a baby. The methods she used were old fashioned from her own experience, which were very unscientific. Because she loved me, she kept me in a "greenhouse" liked keeping delicate flowers. I was born in a cold January, and I spent almost a few months wrapped in a cotton-padded jacket in her and my mother's arms. In the first month after my mother gave birth, my grandmother wouldn't let me go out. Later, she wouldn't let me go out in the morning or in the evening, also in rainy days. Even if I leaved home, I would not allowed went to the eave, patio, let alone outside the door. Even my mother occasionally tried to carry me back to her mother's house, just a few feet away, and also asked her to go in a sedan chair. The empty sedan chair must be carried into the hall. After my mother and I get into the sedan chair, my grandmother had to hang up the curtain and seal it tightly by hand before she let it out. Sitting in the sedan chair, I was warm from head to foot and could not afford any negligence. These measures were designed to protect me from the wind and evil. The wind was the weather, and sheltering from the wind was to protect me from cold attacks. Evil refers to the ghosts, and sheltering from evil was to protect me from ghosts. In the past, there was a superstition that the life of a precious son was most easily robbed by ghosts. So, although there were many evil spirits around me, the adults were still anxious to keep me as quiet as possible and not to let me go out. My grandmother kept very Strictly control my diet. She didn't allow me eat a lot of food, not only too "cold" but also too "cold". Because it was said that "heat" food could harm the liver, while "cold". food could hinder the stomach and cause diarrhea. Foods like crab and shrimp were considered poisonous because they may cause allergies, except one type, that Fuzhou people called blue crab. Sugar was what children like to eat, I could only eat some rock sugar and winter melon sugar. I could not eat smoked and fried snacks. I could only eat cake, fragrant cake and cloud flakes. Even the Zhengdong cakes and shortcakes commonly eaten by Fuzhou people at that time could only be eaten by hiding them in rice jars or adult aprons, then let me eat. In terms of fruit, only let me eat a lot of longan (fresh longan), because Fuzhou people think it was the best supplement for children.

Autumn was my happiest season and also my fattest season, a large amount of longan provides provided me with rich glucose, and it also makes my appetite open and I could eat more. However, dried longan never allowed me to eat because it was considered too "heat". Oranges were also considered too "heat" by grandmother and were rarely eaten. Peaches, plums and bananas were not allowed, let alone watermelons. Under the guidance of my grandmother, my mother later controlled my diet for a long time.

Poor Grandmother

My grandmother's life was miserable. She was a handmaid, so when she married the Zheng's Family, she was forced to be a concubine by some feudal barbarians. Although she was my grandfather's remarried wife, but the Zheng's Family only called her Aunt, and when she got old changed her name to old Auntie, that often left her musing and depressed, but as I had already mentioned above, she had also made justifiable counterattacks and revenges. After coming to ZhengZai, she suffered many things, she had two sons and a daughter. The second son (my uncle) died of illness before he could finish his studies, and the daughter died before a teenager, my grandfather died in Jinhua before he was old. After my grandfather's death, all the burden of our family was on my grandmother. Before I was born, there were six people in our family, besides my parents, my young widowed aunt and two of my sisters. My father had no fixed occupation, was often at leisure, and was addicted to gambling, which was of little help to the burden at home. My grandmother lived on the rent from our ancestral estate that distributed to Le-4th Fang and sold some household items to maintain family life. I didn't know if my grandmother ever worked with my mother and aunt to earn some money to support the family, but I believe that it would not be much. The reason why our family could survive was mainly due to her frugality and diligence. I had heard a lot about her frugality from older people. She was really reluctant to eat, reluctant to wear, tighten belt and live frugally. it could said that she had no one good days in her life, except her Sixtieth birthday. When my grandmother was 60, my father earned a salary in Beijing by copying Lin Shu's translations of foreign novels, that was a wage income. So our family feted guests on her birthday, and my father asked for a painting of cranes and pines that Lin Shu had painted. (The painting had disappeared during the Cultural Revolution). The 4th aunts and her husband who lived in Shanggan Township often send fish and shrimp and some good food to my grandmother. But my grandmother reluctant to eat, as far as possible to feed me. It was only when she was dying that she wanted to eat more, and complained that I compete with her for food, the family saw this as bad ominous sign, Later, whenever I heard adults talking about it, I felt a little ashamed that I was too young and ignorant at that time, if I had known early, I should not compete with my sick grandmother like that. In the old days, every serious illness that happened to a person in 60, was considered to be an incurable old disease, and could only lie in bed and die without any cure. In fact, my grandmother was suffering from lung disease, wouldn't had died so early. How I wish she could live for more than twenty years, till she was over 80, which was not so rare now, till I had graduated from university, and could support her more, so that she could live a happy life! My grandmother virtue of thrift had become a good family style in our home. My mother had been very diligent all her life, and she kept claimed that her virtue was taught by my grandmother. After liberation, my family had been rated as one of the "Five good families" in Shanghai for several years in a row, and in 1984 was also rated as one of the "Five good families" in our country of 10,000. The foremost was diligent and frugal family, only diligent and frugal could educate the children, and make the family harmonious, no matter how hard the economy was, we could ride it out safely. After reviewing the past, I had to admit that this advice and teachings left by my grandmother.

Teaching Method of My Grandmother

Grandmother was illiterate, but she had been brought up in a family of propriety, and had learned how to instruct children in the little matters of life. She taught me how to sit and stand, also how to eat in right style. When I started eating by myself, she taught me how to properly hold chopsticks, not too high (that was too far from the tip) and not too low. At that time, People were used to beg a wife to coax the boys, said chopsticks if hold too high, the future would go to far away to beg a wife; also used the same words of to coax girls, said chopsticks if hold too high, the future would marry far away. When had a meal, should took chopsticks in your right hand and hold the rice bowl in your left hand. It was said that if you did not hold the rice bowl firmly, you would not hold the job firmly in the future, because in the old society doing work was often said to hold the rice bowl. When you eat, should sit up straight and upright and did not rest your feet on the chair (because you were sitting in an adult chair, the children's feet could not touch the ground, and so they often raise their feet to the chair because of discomfort), otherwise, when you grew up, you would to do the job of lifting sedan chair. Grains of rice should not be spread on the table or on the ground, also not be left at the bottom of the bowl without eating all. My grandmother did not know how to recite some ancient poems such as "each grain of rice in your bowl was a fruit of arduous labor", also she did not know how to say "we should cherish every grain of rice that was our farmers' uncle had worked so hard to grow". She still used the begging wife to trick her children, and saying that the rice was scattered all over the table, the wife you beg in the future must be pockmarked, the face of your wife was pockmarked, how ugly! As for eating dishes, it was more sophisticated. First of all, you should not eat too much, but you should save them, this was because she was poor at home. She could not to let children eat to much, don't eat your favorite dishes alone. She taught me that should eat a mouthful of rice and a mouthful of vegetables, instead of connecting eat them with each other. That was to say you could not clip several dishes to eat, more not allowed this dish clip one, other dish clip one to eat. Fish or meat bones and dregs must be spit in a pile in front of you own, not casually spit a large piece. After eating, put your chopsticks neatly placed on the empty bowl to show respect to those who eat with you. After my grandmother's instructive teaching, I gradually developed habits, so far when I eat, I could still maintain these habits, but I was not so economical when eating food. It seemed that my chopsticks were hold better than others and clip food from the dishes also better than others. The impact of these lessons from my grandmother had convinced me the importance of education starting from young children, and the *"five good and four beautiful"* civilization education should also start from a young age.

My uncle and aunt

My grandfather and grandmother had two sons and one daughter. The eldest son was my father. The second son was my uncle, named Yi zhuan. I called him the 30th Uncle and the daughter was the 13th Aunt, die young before marriage.

Early Cadet of Chinese Navy

My uncle Zheng yizhuan entered Mawei Naval Academy in his early years and studied hard. I had seen his copied a lot of mathematics notes with practice problems in more than ten thick textbooks, the calligraphy was very neat and the geometric drawings also very fine, but it was a pity that he studied French, of course I could not read them when I was a child. Unfortunately, he died from plague just before graduated, leaving behind my aunt who had just married into our family and had no children. When he died, my mother had not came to our home, so even my mother had not seen my uncle. My uncle was an early cadet in China Navy and his classmates later became senior Naval officer. If he had not died young, he would certainly become a high official and our family would had been very different. But, by that time he was still at the Naval Academy, opium smoking was fashionable in the Navy. My uncle told his family that he would also smoke opium after graduated, which if true, would had some bad effects on our family. My uncle died of epidemic disease, I was told, because he got up early and disrespected the tree god by sweeping the ground under lychee tree in the back garden, of course this was superstition. Long time ago, Zheng's Family had already set up a forbidden zone under the tree, and there was a shrine to the tree god. Perhaps my uncle had read foreign books and did not believe in the superstition that could not sweep the ground under lychee tree. Unfortunately, when the plague came, my uncle died without noticing that he was infected, and that added to people's superstitious thinking, which was very wrong. After my uncle died, my young aunt remained widowed and eventually died of lung disease at the age of 40. Since my aunt had no children, and my parents followed my grandmother's will, my second sister (my mother's first child) and younger brother were adopted to her. However, my aunt liked me better and left deep impression on me.

Widowed Young Aunt

My 30th Aunt died before I was ten, but to this day, I still had an impression of her. My 30th aunt's surname was Song, but I didn't know her name, because my uncle ranks 30th and the Zheng's Family calls her the 30th Mother or 30th Aunt. When she married into our family, my uncle was still studied at Mawei Naval Academy. Before graduating, my uncle died of plague. It could be seen how young my aunt was when she was widowed, maybe about 20 years old? I reckon that she may only spend two or three years or less with my uncle. To be widowed and bereaved at such a young age, the situation was very sad, even not to mention childless. At that time, families like Zheng's Family had such profound feudal ideology that no one dared to think about the remarriage of young widow. Just like her, the 23rd Aunt was a young widow, living in the West rear wing in Zheng's mansion. The other lived in the east rear wing, too, but the 23rd Aunt had a daughter, which was somewhat of a comfort.

By the time my mother married the Zheng's Family, my 30th uncle and my grandfather had already died. So, we had two widows (grandmother and aunt) in our the Le-4th Fang. As soon as my mother arrived at Zheng's Family, my grandmother told her in advance that if she gave birth to a daughter, she would give the daughter to aunt as the 30th Aunt's daughter. If she could raise two boys, she would give the second one to the 30th Aunt as auntie's son.

Later, my mother raised my second sister first, just as she agreed to give her to the 30th Aunt, and called her mother and called my mother as aunt. Later, my mother raised a daughter and a boy, but neither grew up, and then my mother raised my younger brother and me. As soon as my younger brother was born and was adopted to my aunt. Strangely, my aunt did not like my second sister and my younger brother, but favored me, who was not called her mother.

When I was two years old, my grandmother died. My mother was busy with housework and feeding my brother. I was mainly cared by my aunt and followed her until she was too ill to rise. That was probably why she likes me and why she always impressed me. My aunt was ill and her body was thin and weak. In winter, she would carries a charcoal cage to warm her body. My aunt smoked hookah and went there casually at home, and the copper hookah would be carried there. When I was a little boy, I helped her to carry the copper hookah, followed her there, and carried the copper hookah there.

My aunt often went the back west flower hall to play cards with the 4th sister-in-low, a pale young widow also childless. When my aunt went to back hall, she did not through the back patio, instead, she walked through a room of the 11th-grandaunt in the back flower hall on the west side. In the room of the 11th-grandaunt there was a small door led into the back hall. My aunt went there to play cards, and I followed. While they were playing cards, I sat beside her and watched quietly. People praise me for being good boy. In fact, I was very weak in my childhood, could not like the general health children as active fun, or even naughty. I was quiet and followed my aunt like a puppy, so my aunt liked me. Watching her play cards for a long time, I knew a lot about Mahjong and PaiJiu, but I never had a hobby of gambling.

In addition to following my aunt stayed in Zheng's mansion, sometimes she went out and took me to visit her relatives. One of my aunt's sisters married a merchantman lived on a small island called Zhongzhou in the Minjiang River which lies between Nantai Island and the northern shore of jiangbei. From the north bank of Nantai Island to jiangbei, there were two stone bridges, the shorter one connected to Zhongzhou, named Jiangnan Bridge, and the longer one connected Zhongzhou to the north bank, named Wanshou Bridge. In the past, they were main passage from Nantai Island to the north shore and even the Fuzhou city. As a result, both the north and south ends of the bridge and Zhongzhou had become bustling, with many shops. I call the businessman as uncle, I did not know what business he did, I only know that he was very wealthy. The house he lived in was near the river, the scenery was quite good, and could overlook the downstream. He was probably in his 50, and his wife maybe had died prematurely, I did not see. He had several daughters, all of them were married. I only remember these women named 6th sister, 7th sister, and 10th sister. The husband of 6th sister died early and also was a young widow, but I did not remember the husbands of 7th sister and 10th sister. My aunt was there to visit these nieces and play with them. Sometimes they play cards, sometimes they talk. I remember one or two times when they talked, they would not let a boy to listen, and asked me to go outdoors to play, it was really fun. The uncle's house was a two-story parallel wooden house. There were three or four rooms in a row, and there were promenades outside the wooden house. The room downstairs was probably used for business. People lived upstairs. I liked to play on the corridor, because at the end of the corridor you could see boat on the river. I could stand on the railing and watch long time. Especially interesting was that they had a male monkey in their house who was restrained by an iron chain in the opposite corridor near the empty corridor. I stood on the corridor to see the monkey over there, watching the monkey jump and scratch it and peel peanuts to eat. I was very impressed. Although more than 70 years had passed, I could still remember it.

My 4th aunt had lung disease at a very young age. I still remember a tin spitting jar on her bed. Every morning, she would dump the sputum and replace it with a piece of straw paper. At that time, there were many people with tuberculosis, and many of them were young. My 4th aunt probably had this disease for a long time. Later, she got bloating disease and her belly swelled greatly. Because there was no specific medicine for lung disease at that time, my 4th uncle was powerless to treat the disease. He had once treated her ascites with needles, but it swelled soon. In the end probably had a heart problem and her face was so swollen that she couldn't even open her eyes so that she couldn't get up in bed. At this time, my second sister and younger brother were not afraid to see her, but I was very afraid. I would not dare to see her again, and my aunt died soon. I had followed her for several years. I had been with her almost all day except not sleeping with her at night. I had not contracted tuberculosis, which was a bit strange. Because I suffered from night blindness when I was young, I took cod liver oil for a long time according to the instructions of my 4th uncle since young age, and I also took the some sheep liver and Guzhencao according to the prescription of Chinese medicine. Cod liver oil was rich in vitamins A and D, and the Chinese medicine may be also rich in these two vitamins, which was beneficial to enhance my bodies resistance. That was probably the case, and I had not contracted with lung disease. When I was 20 years old, the first time a doctor performed a lung X-ray for me, I was told that there were some calcified spots in my lungs. Therefore, it was also possible that I had tuberculosis when I was young and then I grew up and the tuberculosis healed itself. I was a bit shudder at the thought of this.

CHAPTER 7

Maternal Grandparents

My maternal grandfather's family name was Chen, and also a large family. Because their ancestors did not have a big house like Zheng's mansion, so they were scattered in several places. In Xiadu there was another Chen's family, known as Qingyuan Chen. Their ancestral hall was near Zheng's mansion, next to Shijing ancestral hall. But my maternal grandfather was not related to this family, so this ancestral hall had no relationship with him. And I never heard whether his family also had an ancestral hall.

There was another difference between the maternal grandfather's family and the Zheng's Family. None of the Chen had ever held an official post, and a few of them had ever educated. They were basically business people, traders, shopkeepers, clerks, In feudal society, such a family was called a common family or people's family or the private family. Although not all people of the Zheng's Family had been educated or had been in contact with officials, some people of the Zheng's Family had done business and worked as shop assistants and brokers. But some of them had passed the imperial examinations and served as officials, so they were called officials and scholarly family. With this difference, the two clan had formed a different feudal hierarchy, and even the dates of praying the Kitchen God were different. The Zheng's Family was the official family, and the Kitchen God was prayed on the 23rd of the twelfth lunar month.

But in the Chen's Family, the Stove God was prayed one day later, that was, on the 24th of the twelfth lunar month. Whether the Stove God was also hierarchical, I did not know. In the past, children most enjoyed to pay their respects to the cooking stove, because on this day, they could share a lot of sugar cakes, and I could get two days of sugar cakes, so I still remember this feudal custom.

Although the feudal monarchy had been overthrown for a long time, the Zheng's Family still retained the tradition of the 23rd day of the stove festival, and the Chen's family still adhered to the rules of the 24th day. Were there any other differences between the official family and the private family? I did not know the details.

What did the Chen's ancestors do? I had not heard any.

Descendant of Granduncle's Brothers

My maternal grandfather had six brothers and he was the second boy.

The Eldest Maternal Granduncle

The eldest maternal granduncle died early. When I was a child, I only saw my eldest maternal grandaunt. So far I still remember her. At that time, she was only sixty years old, because she was short with dry skin, was looked pretty old. Everyone called her old grandaunt, someone called her short-grandaunt. In those days, a woman over age 40 was a long live. There were very few women in age 60s. She was the only old woman in the Chen's Family, so she became a typical old woman. People often mentioned her in their conversations, "It would be better to live the old grandaunt", "Someone was older than the old grandaunt" and so on. My old grandaunt had no son, but only one daughter whom, I called the 3rd aunt.

It was said by my mother that the eldest maternal granduncle did not do any work but lived on the renting of the property left by his ancestors.

There was a piece of real estate on the hill behind Zheng's mansion, very close to the back garden of Zheng's mansion. This land had been purchased by the Fujian Provincial Negotiations Agency (the diplomatic organization based in Fuzhou at that time) in very high price. My mother often said to me: "The eldest maternal granduncle and his wife sold their ancestors then got a basket of silver and hired men to carry it home. The couple did nothing but eating and drinking, in a few years they had spent the whole basket of silver, no penny left at all. And later their life became hard" My mother liked to quote this example to educate me and other teenagers in our relatives, "Don't be fond of enjoyment and averse to work!"

Not long after the 3rd aunt got married, her husband died. They had a son named Yi-Chuo. Later, the old grandaunt lived with the 3rd aunt in a hard life and died before her age 70. Yi-Chuo was about my age, so when I had the opportunity to meet him, we played with other similar age children. Due to his family poverty, Yi-Chuo did not get education, but his hand was very clever, and he could use colored paper paste to make all kinds of things. I did not know if he had been an apprentice later. But I heard that he lived by making things out of colored paper for funeral. Since the early 1920, I had not seen him again.

The 2nd Maternal Granduncle

The 2nd maternal granduncle was my grandfather.

The 3rd Maternal Granduncle

The 3rd uncle

I never heard what kind of work the 3rd uncle did, but my mother often said that the life of his family was very good. However, she often said that when the 3rd maternal granduncle and his wife died, the 3rd uncle lied that there was no money for the funeral, and asked my maternal grandfather to support him. My mother said with contempt for both 3rd uncle and aunt. I didn't have impression about him, because the 3rd uncle died when I was very young. Before I was born and when I was a baby, during that time my 3rd uncle family lived in the east front room and front pavilions, near Zheng's mansion back door. Those rooms were mortgaged to him by the He-1st fang in he-house. So our family was very close to his family.

The 3rd aunt was my host mother

The 3rd aunt had four boys and two daughters, so she was a lucky women with many boys. The second daughter was born at about the same time as me, only slightly older than me. Because this girl was aunt's fifth child, and there were already three boys and a girl. The 3rd uncle originally wanted to give her to other family as an adopted daughter, but considered she was so beautiful when she was born, that he was reluctant to give up, On the other hand, his family had the conditions to raise her, then kept her at family and gave her a name Stay-Sister. When I was born, I was a late son and a rare son. My grandmother and my mother were very precious to me. They wanted to find a mother with more boys to be my host mother, So that I had more dependence. The nearby 3rd aunt was chosen, and respected as my host mother. She just give birth to Stay-Sister, and had plenty of milk. I also had sucked her milk! From that time on, we would give her annual festival and birthday gifts. She brought me food in the New Year and my birthday. It was said that I could live forever by eating her food like this. Later, I sent money to her every year, but the rest of her life was unfortunate. After the 3rd uncle died, her life became difficult.

The second son of the 3rd aunt named Qi-Qi, when he grew up and was a clerk, became crazy for wanting a wife (Fuzhou people said it was peach blossom epilepsy). He went to beat people, Then he was chained to his house, and soon died.

The third son, named Shuofu due to life difficulties, the 3rd aunt sent him to the 5th uncle as his stepson.

The youngest son of the 33rd aunt went to Nanyang before reached adulthood and after he left home no further news, probably already died.

The eldest daughter of my 3rd aunt died prematurely of illness.

The younger daughter (stay-sister) was sent to the 9th aunt as her stepdaughter.(the 9th aunt was the daughter of the 6th granduncle).

At last, the 3rd aunts only had one elder son Qian-Fu stayed with her. Qian-Fu had studied in a foreign school. Before graduation, he was admitted to the branch of the British Dadong Telegraph Bureau in Fuzhou as a telegraph operator. Qian-Fu had two sons and one daughter in his family. Qian-Fu was mediocre and very satisfied to had a stable job working in this foreign merchant. He had no ambitions and was afraid to leave Fuzhou. Once the Dadong Telegraph Bureau planned to send him to work at the Shanghai General Administration. He refused to go, and in the end the other people who went to Shanghai got benefits. He stayed and waited until the Anti-Japanese War occurred, Fuzhou fell, and the Dadong Telegraph Bureau was closed. He had to go to the inner land of Fujian to work for the China Telegraph Bureau. Soon the couple died of illness, they left their mother and children behind. The grandma and grandchildren depended on each other in living. It could be imagined how hard their life was. Later, the eldest grandson went to work as an apprentice. Later he was promoted as a shop assistant, the granddaughter got marriage in Shanggan County. After the victory of the Anti-Japanese War, I introduced the 2nd grandson into an orphanage. After liberation, he was trained by the people's government and became a meteorologist. The 3rd son Shuofu adopted by the 5th uncle as stepson also died of illness during the Anti-Japanese War. The 3rd aunt lived a long life and died in the mid-1960s. She was almost ninety years old. At this time, the six children she gave birth had only stay-sister alive. When talking about the later desolate situation of the 3rd uncle's family, my mother said that this was the deserved retribution of his un-filial parents. My mother often used this example to warn her children and other juniors to be filial to their parents.

The 3rd Aunt' Mother Lincuo aunt

The 3rd aunt had a mother who was widowed at her early age, and everyone called her Lincuo aunt because the 3rd aunt came from the Lin family. Why did I call her aunt? Because the 3rd aunt was my host mother, so I called her mother as maternal grandmother. She had only the 3rd aunt, because her husband died early, she followed the 3rd aunt live together, rely on the 3rd aunts support, of course also increased the difficulties of the 3rd aunt. Lincuo aunt was an interesting character that was deep in my mind. She was a well-known greedy. When she walked to some one's houses, she always wanted to eat something from others. It did not matter, even they laugh at her face to face. More interesting was that she was very sensitive to food, as long as she walked under the food basket (Fuzhou people often put the burned and leftover food in the basket in order to prevent rats from stealing, and hang the basket on the roof beam with a long rope), she could smell something delicious on it. She liked children very much and would tease children jokingly, so the children also like her. Of course she likes me more because I called her grandmother. Sometimes she would Sometimes she would take a pancake or a Zongdong cake (all made of flour) from her bosom. The former was a bit more salty and baked more brittle, while the latter was a little more sugar, slightly cooked and not brittle at all. It was said that these two kinds of cakes were specially made by Qijiguang for feeding the hunger soldiers during the war. There were small holes in the cakes for hanging from a rope on the body. Recalling that these cakes were hidden in her unclean arms for few days, and It could be contaminated, I still feel sick. Lin Cuo aunt died when I was a teenager.

The 5th Uncle

The 5th uncle worked as a sales person in a silk shop with very little salary. He could not afford a proper wife. He only found a prostitute as a wife, and of course had no children. The 3rd aunt gave a boy (the third son Shuofu,) to him as his stepson, and my 4th uncle gave a girl to him as his stepdaughter. The 5th uncle was suffering from lung disease and was very thin. The cheekbones on both sides of his face were prominent. He was full of sullen language when he spoke, that was very harsh when hearing it. The 5th uncle died of lung disease before he was 50. Owing to her background, the 5th aunt was not very decent. After the 5th uncle died, she lived on Shuofu, who had been married, also died of malnutrition and malaria at a young age, leaving two sons. Before liberation, the eldest son served as a sailor in the Kuomintang navy and sailed for Taiwan, his life and death were still unknown.

The second son was a teacher at Fuzhou Normal University. the adopted daughter Yiyu (the 4th uncle's girl) was my wife Pinying's younger sister and now lived in Kuala Lumpur, Malaysia.

The 4th Granduncle

The 4th granduncle was a man who had never married. He had been helping to do business in an oil store run by his brother, the 7th granduncle. He was extremely honest and solitary, His eyes were squint and he was silent all day, working silently in the shop. He got up at dawn every day, then open the store door, sell oil and collect money, did not leave the store one step, had been busy until the night closes the door to fall asleep, he sleep in a small room beside the store hall. I didn't remember that he once said a word to me, and I hadn't heard him talk a lot to the relative. In my mind, he seemed to be very old. In fact, he ended his silent life before he was 50.

The 5th Grandduncle

The 5th granduncle I had not seen, nor had seen or heard of his descendants. I only seemed to had heard my mother and her younger sister 6th aunt, talked about he had went to Nanyan, never to return, without any news.

The 6th Granduncle

The 6th granduncle, I did not remember if I had ever seen him. Maybe he died before I knew any better. The aunt was very thin and has two daughters and one son.

The 9th Aunt

The 9th aunt was the eldest daughter of the 6th granduncle, and married to Xiadu Weng Family, soon widowed, and no children, so she took Stay sister, the 3rd aunt's daughter as stepdaughter. The mother and daughter lived in poverty for a long time, and it was very difficult. Later, Stay sister married her husband who worked in southern Fujian, and soon the 9th aunt also went to accompany her daughter and son-in-law in Southern Fujian. Unfortunately, the son-in-law fell ill and died soon after, and Stay sister also widowed very early. She gave birth to only one daughter, HaoHao, a strange nickname. Three generations, three women, suffer from very hard life together, and lived such a places in Southern Fujian, without any close relatives to take care of them, After HaoHao married, the 9th aunt feel old, do not want to die in Southern Fujian, and want return to Fuzhou, still lived in her old house. Stay sister lived with her daughter (HaoHao) and son-in-law in Zhangzhou, southern Fujian province, just like her mother used to do. In Fuzhou, the 9th aunt had no other source of income, except by Stay sister to send some money for her live. In the early 1950s, my mother asked me to send her some money every month from the rent income in Fuzhou, and sometime remitted money from Shanghai to help her pass the day until she died in the mid-1960s. Of course, the 9th aunt life was extremely hard.

The 10th Aunt

The 10th aunt was the second daughter of the 6th granduncle, Her life was also very hard. when she grow up, married a husband who had leprosy. she was afraid every day because If her husband was found out by the neighbors, would be put in a leprosy hospital. She had one son and several daughters, but only one of them grew up, and her daughters die one by one, and none lived to be a year old. His only son, Ekin, follows his ancestors as they cut bamboo. He lived in Warehouse district, in front of a shop, back home, there were several bamboo shops in the area, all of them were backed by the Minjiang River. The moso bamboos, from the upstream drifted to Fuzhou, after the shore bamboo shop cut bamboo blocks and processed into bamboo.

The 15th Uncle

The 15th uncle was the only son of the 6th granduncle, Working in a silk shop, from apprentice to clerk, for a very low salary. His sister the 9th aunt was poisoned by feudal tradition. In order to prevent her family from heir, the 9th aunt hope younger brother gets married. Unexpectedly the matchmaker found a girl with a more serious mental illness. As a result, there was a problem in the bridal chamber night. Soon the 15th uncle left home and went to Nanyang with anger. Since then, there had been no news, and he had probably died in a different place.

The 7th Granduncle

The 7th granduncle and grandaunt, I had seen them long enough to know them best. The 7th granduncle was in business. What was his name, I did not remember. Their level of education was very low, he may have only studied in private school for a few years as a child, read a few words, but he could calculate with an abacus. Strangely, he wrote in large letters so well that many shopkeepers near Xiadu asked him to write signs. At that time, one of the four major xiadu families, the Wang family, there was a man named "Ailu" whose write, like Zheng Xiaoxu's, were very famous. He wrote signs for shops in and out of town, all signed his name, of course he received a high pay. The 7th granduncle was not famous. The signboards he wrote was unsigned. I don't know if he get paid or not, probably he was a volunteer to write. In my young eyes, I think the signboards he wrote was not inferior.

The 7th granduncle opened an oil shop along Xiadu Street near by Zheng's mansion. The shop front was originally the foyer of a private residence, it was as wide as two ordinary shops, but not deep enough. The 7th granduncle's family lived in the back of the shop. The whole house was probably within the scope of Shang Zhaogong's property, as it was surrounded by Zheng's Family property. The shop name was Tongcheng, and the sign of "Tongcheng Oil Shop" was hanging outside the door, probably my 7th granduncle wrote it himself. The oil shop was divided into two sides, against the wall were buckets, tanks and boxes containing various oils. There were two types of oil stored in shops vegetable oils and petroleum. Vegetable oils include colza oil, tea oil, peanut oil, and soybean oil. At that time there was only one kind of kerosene for lighting, there were original one, each five gallons, and also bucket oil for retail. To separate, each oil occupies one side of the shop, with kerosene on the left and vegetable oil on the right. Kerosene was sold on behalf of Mobil Oil Company, so there was a black lacquered gold marketing character issued by Mobil Company, with the kerosene trademark distributed on it, with the words "Mobil Oil Mobil Oil Company Agency". At that time, electric lights in Fuzhou were not yet common. Most people used kerosene lamps, and some poor people were still using vegetable oil lamps. Every time when had a wedding or funeral, people rent gas lamps, which use kerosene, so they were called Mobil lamps. The sales of kerosene on behalf of Tongcheng Oil Co. Many villagers on Nantai Island came to his shop to buy kerosene. Most people usually bring bottles to buy retail sales, but sometimes, large households buy the original one. The torch was also sold in the shop for use in the country's evening reception. This torch was soaked with kerosene on the day of the reception. The business in the shop was mainly managed by the 7th granduncle himself. The goods coming in from outside, as well as bookkeeping and disbursement were all taken by him. Sometimes he also receives and serves for customers. In addition to the 4th granduncles, his eldest son and later his third son also helped him worked in the oil shop. Therefore, the oil shop was a family shop and worked with family members, no outsiders or apprentices were hired. Because the cost of the shop was very low, kerosene was sold for Mobil, and a commission could be charged according to the quantity. The price was completely set by Mobil, and had no risk. At that time, the oil price was basically stable, he was able to make money at the wholesale and retail prices. So at the end of each year he always knew the settlement amount, he would make a net profit of about two thousand yuan, which was quite large for a small shop. The 7th grandaunt was an old fashioned housewife. She was busy with housework all day long. Although the house was behind the shop, she did not care about any things in the shop. I had not seen her in the shop, never heard her talk to anyone. The couple gave birth to six sons and unknown how many daughters, because except for one daughter, the rest were given away at birth. You could imagine the hardships of a woman who was constantly raising children and doing most of the housework. The burden on a man to support such a large family was also conceivable. The two of them endure so much hard work that it was not easy to accumulate several hundred yuan a year. I didn't know how many years later, they bought a piece of land in the alley across from the shop, and built a small house, then moved their family there.

The Eldest Son of the 7th Granduncle

The eldest son of the 7th Granduncle, the nickname was GanGan. After growing up, worked for his father in the oil business. Ranking 17, so I called him 17th uncle. He was very taciturnity, I only saw him selling oil in the shop and to collect money, nothing else saw what he did. the 7th granduncle find a pretty beautiful girl to married him as his wife, they had not yet any children. The 17th uncle died of the epidemic disease, and the 17th aunt became a young widow. Forced by feudal ethics, she could no remarry and only remain widowing. Later, she suffered from mental illness and became a mad woman. She looked extremely pitiful, and a few years later, she died of famine and cold during the Anti-Japanese War. She was the first crazy woman I ever met in my maternal grandfather's family.

The Second Son of the 7th Granduncle

The second son of the 7th Granduncle, the nickname was GanDi. Ranking 19. Of course this name was continuation of his brother's nickname. I called him 19th uncle. He was lucky, had studied in Foreign Language School several years and was admitted to the post office without graduation. The 7th Granduncle also begged a good-looking wife for him. The couple gave birth to several children, as I knew was all were daughters. The 19th uncle and his wife were on regular incomes and could eat well. As a result of obesity they had died of vascular disease, and their lived were not long.

The Third Son of the 7th Granduncle

The third son of the 7th Granduncle, the nickname was very strange, called the Chicken Horn (rooster). I don't know if he worked in the shop, because he couldn't study at school. He died early due to lung disease.

The Forth Son of the 7th Granduncle

The forth son of the 7th Granduncle, the nickname was even stranger, called LuoLuo. Probably it could be a strange-shaped bump on his head at birth. He studied at the Foreign Language School for several years and later worked at the post office until retire. The 7th Granduncle also chose a beautiful girl to be his wife, and had several children. I only know that two of his sons became doctors.

The Fifth Son of the 7th Granduncle

The fifth son of the 7th Granduncle, the nickname was PangPang, because he was very fat when he was born. The 7th Granduncle loved him very much. Whenever he got chance, he stuffed him with food, even to the point where made him unable to swallow. After the death of the 7th Granduncle, he was captured by army during the War of Resistance Against Japan, and then no any news. Of course, he died young. Everyone laughed, the Kuomintang army caught these fools to be their soldiers, in the Zheng's Family was Tiansheng, and the Chen's Family was Pangpang, was it a coincidence?

The Sixth Son of the 7th Granduncle

The sixth son of the 7th Granduncle, Ranking 23. Now, I heard that he was in Hong Kong, he used to be a Western cub.

The only Daughter of the 7th Granduncle

The only daughter left by the 7th Granduncle was the youngest girl of the Chen's Family, most people called her 11th aunt, but I often call her XiXi aunt.

From the difference between the ranking of men and women, we could find out how favored boys over girls in the old days. The uncle of the Chen's Family Ranking to 23, and the Ranking of the youngest son (sixth son) of the 7th Granduncle was only 23rd. But for the aunt of the Chen's Family Ranking only 11, less than half. Not only because there were too many males, but also some of the females were given away to other family. The other part was badly fed and died early. The Zheng's Family was also more male than female. The main reason, I was afraid, also was contempt for girls, not paying attention to feeding them after born. But at the Zheng's Family, I had never heard of giving away baby girls.

The 11th aunt was illiterate, when she was a child she had to help her mother take care of her younger brother and did the housework. After grew up, she married Lin zexiao as his wife. Lin zexiao had studied at the Foreign School and had only worked in the post office all his life. Therefore, in the 7th Granduncle's family there were three people working in the post office, one son-in-law and two sons. The nickname of Lin zhexiao father was very strange and indecent, that was Toilet. I was not sure why he got the nickname, but it was probably because his head looked like a toilet. Fuzhou people often comment on people's appearance, besides toilet heads, there were taro and leopard heads. Lin zexiao liked playing Mahjong, he came to my 7th Granduncle's house to play Mahjong almost every day after work. He was so skilled that he won money most of the time. Besides playing Mahjong, he also had dinner at Chen's house, because he was a greedy person, people often made fun of him, but he did not mind. The 11th aunt gave birth to three sons and several daughters, leaving only one daughter. The 11th aunt died at the age of 40 due to overwork. Later, Lin zhexiao remarried again and gave birth to several children.

The 7th Grandaunt

The 7th Grandaunt had too many children with heavy housework. I think she was very tired and weak. She died shortly after raising her youngest son. The man of the Chen's Family seemed had a remarry character. After the death of the 7th grandaunt, the 7th Granduncles wanted to remarry again. Although he already had a large number of children, he wanted to find a good-looking girl as his wife, but he was already in his 50. At that time, he was an old man, where could he find a decent woman? When the 7th Grandaunt raised her last son, her family had hire a helper called Nanny, the Nanny turned up her eyes and was grotesquely ugly. After the death of the 7th Grandaunt, Nanny wanted to be the continuation of the 7th Granduncle, The 7th Granduncle could not find a suitable woman, so at period he also wanted to marry Nanny, and late he gave up because he was laughed at, that was an excuse to mock him. He died a few years later, at the age of 60. Since no one continued to operate the oil shop after his death, Tongcheng Oil Shop closed.

Above was about my maternal grandfather's six contemporaries and their descendants, that reflected was the typical life of ordinary citizens at that time. There seemed to be only life and death. Some members of the Zheng's Family took advantage of feudal evil to deceive others, but not the Chen family. They tended to grin and bear it, distanced themselves from worldly success and live a mediocre life. In fact, there was nothing up or down in the daily live between the two families. The only difference was the class consciousness.

Descendant of My Maternal Grandfather

My maternal grandmother died before I was born, so I know nothing about her.

My Maternal Grandfather

My maternal grandfather, Chen lianchen, was a merchant. Before retired, he sold dried longan, bamboo shoots and other Fujian native products to Shanghai. All I know was that he sold in one direction, that was, he shipped the products from Fujian to Shanghai for sale, but did not ship the products from Shanghai back to Fujian for sale. Of course, he often told his mother about the new things he saw in Shanghai. Every year after coming back from Shanghai, he would rest at home. At that time, his job was very difficult, because he had to guarantee the cargo and cross the sea. and, Fuzhou external traffic mainly relied on wooden ships, which were less than 100 tons deadweight. Later, although there were ships, they could not carry more than 1,000 tons. Affected by the traffic difficulties, Fuzhou was very crowded. most people were afraid to go too far, thinking it was too risky. Therefore, a lot of money could be made by shipping the products from Fujian to Shanghai for sale. My maternal grandfather took risks, so he made more money than his peers, and his life was much better than theirs. Because of the risk and difficulty, my maternal grandfather retired before the age of 60, and he had accumulated a sum of money. He did not buy a house, the house was probably rented or might be pawn he had bought some landed property, but not much.

In his days, Fuzhou people were content with some property and did not want to be aggressive, so it was difficult to find a rich man in Fuzhou. This was not the case in coastal cities such as Xiamen, Ningbo, Shantou, and Guangzhou, where there were many entrepreneurs who were willing to venture to make a fortune. Fuzhou people went as far as Nanyang, only when they could not make a living at home. After making a fortune, they returned home to spend their old age in peace and did not go out again.

My grandfather had this idea, so he retired early and did nothing. Meanwhile, due to the early death of my grandmother, he soon found a maid to be his concubine and wanted to enjoy the blessings of his old age. The concubine's name was "Wentao", I didn't know if that's her name. My mother and aunts used to call her that, but I never asked them what it meant. "Wentao" was about the same age as my mother. My maternal grandfather loved her very much, and soon they had a boy named Yanyan, Yanyan became my maternal grandfather's favorite son. Since "Wentao" could not get along well in this big family, after my grandfather married "Wentao", he separated from his sons and lived with her and Yanyan. All this happened before I was born. I was my grandfather's first grandchild, and he should have been happy for me, but since Yanyan was about my age, he had to distance himself from the love of his grandson and save it for his youngest son. He seldom came to see me, and my mother rarely took me to see them at his house. I only remember that my grandfather would give me lucky money every New Year when I paid him a New Year greetings. The Lantern Festival was my birthday, every year before the Lantern Festival, he would give me a paper lamp as usual, it makes me very happy, I never forget.

My Maternal Grandfather's Birthday

My maternal grandfather liked birthday very much, the eldest uncle's birthday happened to be the same day with his birthday, that was October 13 (lunar calendar), so father and son were celebrating their birthday together every year, particularly lively. At this time of the year, relatives and children of the Chen's family, were very happy to have the opportunity to play together and attend several parties. At the main banquet there was a lot of fruit to share, sometimes you could get funny citron with special good smelling, Although could not eat, but could be played for a long time, and it was very fragrant even gets dry and dark. There were many birthday peaches and birthday noodle sent by relatives placed on the table in the hall, decorated with paper flowers and some gadgets that made all children happy. After the birthday, when these decorated gadgets were removed, you could take some to home for playing, the peaches or cakes could be taken back to eat.

Encounter my grandfather or eldest uncle meetten birthday, did the scale of birthday celebration was particularly grand. Not only were guests invited to the birthday party, with ten tables set up in the hall, but guests were invited to warm the birthday one day before. A few days earlier, the birthday hall and the shrines, the patios, the corridors, and the doorways were all decorated with lights, and the sky curtains were hung above the patios, making the whole environment magnificent. In addition to holding a grand banquet, but also after the banquet to increase entertainment. On ordinary birthdays, only the Kabuki team was invited to sing opera dramas with band accompaniment, the opera dramas would be ordered by the guest or host. The singers were mostly younger girls who were not immune to teasing. they were asked to perform, they could also sing in costume, which was called "hanging clothes" and, of course, costs more than a cappella. In the event of a big birthday, you must set up a stage in the patio and invite the Fujian opera team to perform. It was a cultural entertainment program arranged on the birthday day, which was performed consecutively day and night. They only performed one or two folds, not the entire book. I could understand some dramas, but some did not understand all of them. I just think that some arias were very nice, and I had learned to hum once or twice. On the birthday, the troupe of Fujian opera was brought by my maternal grandfather and eldest uncle. In addition to this, sometimes some relatives paid money for a choir or "hanging clothes" to sing one or two days as their gift for birthday.

Before the birthday also held religious superstition activities, invited the Taoists to chant sutras, pray for longevity. Most people only invite a Taoist priest to "Tian Tai Sui" on their birthday, and put a small table in front of the hall with several offerings, including a small dumpling (a bun without filling). The Taoist priest took the rattle and wobbled while chanting words. Of course I could not understand what he was saying. Before he prayed, had to tell him about the birthday person's horoscope. After about a quarter of an hour, the priest threw the small bun on the patio, which was regarded as alms to the devil. Afterwards, he burned a spell he brought, even if the ceremony was over. In prayer, the juniors bow down to the sky and burn the paper foil. My maternal grandfather and eldest uncle's birthday held religious events on a much larger scale than others, and it took at least half a day. First, an altar was to be set up in the hall. A lot of Eight Immortals tables and Six Immortals tables (half of the Eight Immortals tables) were stacked. One of the altars was three tables high, while the two sides were two tables high. My maternal grandfather and eldest uncle's birthday held religious events on a much larger scale than others, and it took at least half a day. First, an altar was to be set up in the hall. A lot of Eight Immortals tables and Six Immortals tables (half of the Eight Immortals tables) were stacked. One of the altars was three tables high, while the two sides were two tables high. In addition to general musical instruments, the Taoists also used a horn as an implement. The family, especially the juniors, need to cooperate from time to time, kneeling with bow down and burn paper foil. On the altar there were also offerings including small dumplings. At the end of the ceremony, the Taoists threw the buns from a height, saying that it was alms to the imp, but in fact they were all snatched and eaten by the children. Taoist charms were also burnt during the ceremony. What interests me the most was that the Taoists who came here was a man named "Monk". He was a contractor and a leader. The other four people were employed by him. The Taoists took the silver and kept most of it, the rest was distributed with four people as employment fees. I had seen this Taoist named "Monk" many times, because he often makes a dojo for the mourning family.

My eldest aunt's birthday was also must to do every year. Except for each tenth birthday, the scale was relatively small, much less extravagant than the birthdays of my maternal grandfather and eldest uncle. Another feature of their birthday was most relatives and friends come very early. After worshiping with birthday greeting, they sit down and pay Mahjong, often several tables at the same time. Therefore, the crackling cards and loud vocals all day long added a lot of excitement. They not only participated in the grand dinner, but also participated in a simpler luncheon (known as breakfast in Fuzhou) at noon.

When I was a kid, I participated in the birthday celebrations of many adults. Most of them just had a birthday greeting and had a dinner. Like my maternal grandfather's family, I had never seen in other one's home, in Zheng's Family no one such longevity. It took a lot of money to celebrate one's birthday, and my maternal grandfather and eldest uncle had money for this extravagance because they had made a fortune in business. Although they could receive gifts from others, but there was no cash at that time. Most people send only the birthday noodles and peaches placed on the table in the hall, or the birthday shaft hanging on the wall, with red or gold paper couplets. There were also some people invite the singing team to sing for joy, only few people who send money, but not much money, so most of the expenses had to be paid by themselves. My maternal grandfather's family spend so much money to celebrated their birthday just for meaning that they were rich, on other hand, it also meaning blessing, which arouses people envy. My mother was very envious, soshe also liked birthday very much.

Is My Maternal Grandfather Really Blessed?

Was my maternal grandfather really blessed? This is not necessarily the case. In order to beg a young concubine with the youngest son, instead of living with all of his elder sons, the three of them lived in another house. Although he spoiled on concubine and youngest son, they give him no pleasure, on the contrary, a lot of distressing stimulation. In addition, some unfortunate events also made him feel deeply, such as the early death of the grandson and the death of two great-grandchildren etc. Later, he was traumatized due to mental psyche, so that he developed mental illness. He was just insane, incoherent, and did some strange things, such as riding in a rickshaw instead of sitting in a seat, but sitting on a pedal, saying he was in a third-class car. Probably because he took the third-class train in Shanghai instead of the first-class train. When he was delirium, he also graded the rickshaws and thought the seats were first class, so he did not sit. When he became mentally ill, he did not scold or fight, but did some strange things that made people laugh, but did not fear him. At that time, mental illness seemed to be incurable, so the family left him alone. He died a few years later, aged 69, with just one year left to reach his 70 years old.

The funeral after the death of my maternal grandfather was very grand, more lavish than birthday. Held the en coffin ceremony was on the day of his death, exactly in accordance with the ceremony in Fuzhou at that time. The coffin used the shouban that had purchased in his early years and invited the craftsman to make the coffins and put his body in within a day. The coffin was placed in the back hall for a total of 60 days. there were also be spiritual seats in the back of the hall for 60 days. On the day of encoffin ceremony, the Taoist priest was invited to hold a religious ceremony, It was also the Taoist priest with the name "monk". After that, religious services were held every seven days. The Ashram of first-seven and second-seven was to invite nuns (Fuzhou people call Cai Po) to chant sutras. The third-seven, fourth-seven, and sixth-seven asked the Taoist priest to do the same as the "top seat". The fifth-seven was the day of the egg opening day. Advance announcements were made for relatives and friends to pay their respects. It was almost as if it were a birthday, and the halls, patios, corridors, and gates were all decorated with lanterns, but all the lanterns were plain or white. or blue, no red. Because there were many people who send cloth (or plain silk) shafts or elegiac couplet, it was not enough to hang all the walls of the halls and corridors. The side aisles and places where they could be hung were all hung with bamboo frames. This day was a day for the living to show off for the dead. In addition to informing all his friends and relatives, they also specially spent money to invite the gentry to accompany the guests. The Former Qing dynasties and Officials of the Republic of China were invited to sit in a hall decorated with a cedar. There were many banquets on that day, just like birthday, but there was no entertainment program. The Ashram of the third-seven and fourth-seven were sponsored and organized by the close relatives and friends, the Ashram of sixth-seven was paid by daughter (my mother and my 6th aunt) as usual. The burial was held 60 days after death because the tomb was outside the west gate, near the Hongshan Bridge, far away from home, so the coffin had to be transported by boat. The funeral procession went only from the house to the dock, most of the people went back. Only family members and close relatives took the casket with them to the grave. As soon as the boat arrived at Hongshan Bridge pier, villagers from the cemetery carried the coffin up the hill for burial. That was the end of the funeral, and it was a good deal of money.

Soon after my grandfather's funeral, Wen Tao and YanYan ran away. It was said that a man ran away with them. The Chen's Family did not pursue it at all, so later no one knew how the mother and son were.

My maternal grandfather got married very early, and he had several children with my maternal grandmother. I did not know clearly, but I headed they had three sons with two daughters.

The eldest maternal uncle

The eldest maternal uncle's business

As same as my maternal grandfather, my eldest maternal uncle, Chen shengzhang, also was a merchant. Instead of going north to Shanghai, he went south to Guangzhou, He shipped out Fujian native produce, then brought back fragrant silk and summer cloth to Fuzhou for sell. He had been an apprentice in a cloth shop and knew how to do the cloth business. Because he was a trader later than his father, Fujian-Guangzhou, transportation was much more convenient than his father's time. There was a regular British merchant ship between Fuzhou and Guangzhou, calling at Hong Kong every time, and possibly xiamen and Shantou as well. Another point was that unlike his father, he was not a single-handed business, but had set a Guangzhuang shop in Guangzhou. In addition to his second and third son help him doing business, he also hired some others, some of whom were relatives brought from Fuzhou. So he did pretty big business. A large part of the goods sold in Fuzhou, such as fragrant yarn silk and summer cloth, were supplied by him. So, he made a lot of money, not only "grass", but "top ten grass". Many businessmen in Fuzhou were jealous of this, and his business was a bit mean, which made some people hateful. He made a fortune and spent a lot of money to buy real estate, including a Chinese-style big house in Xiadu Xiaoling, with a garden and rather large tea factory (tea and baked jasmine factory) in front.

At the end of the 1920, my eldest maternal uncle opened a new cloth shop in the lively Taijiang area. In order to attract people to buy, he gave the shop a lucky name called "TianSun". I never thought that the name of this auspicious shop was too unlucky for him. Soon after the shop was opened, all the shop were burned out by a fire, which caused him to owe a lot of money. At that time, people ridiculed at him, and said the name of the store "TianSun" meant that it might suffer misfortune, which just satirizes him for the result of his mean and stingy. He defaulted on the money lost by the fire, people went to the court to sue him, and he lost the case. Because still refuse to pay back the money. As a result, the big house in Xiaolingding was closed by the court. Fortunately, my cousin, Liu boyu, who was an official at the time, argued for him to the court, The seal was not posted outside the gate, but inside the gate, outside passers-by could not see, and there was also still a side door enter and leave. The upstairs rooms were still occupied by his four sons. In return for his help, he gave her several downstairs rooms to live in for a while. The seal attached to the inside gate was always covered with a large bamboo grate. Later, how to remove the seal was unknown because I was not in Fuzhou.

The house bought by my eldest uncle was named Qinglu by him. But he had never lived there except prepare to die there. At beginning he divided the four rooms in upstairs to his four sons. But he rented a house and lived with his concubine. Just like his father, he also begged a maidservant to be his concubine and also had a little son with her. But when he accepted his concubine, his wife was still alive. After he separated from his sons, My eldest maternal aunt lived with their four sons in Qinglu. Everyone calls that concubine as girl. This was what Fuzhou people usually call a concubine. When he was still in business, the girl followed him to Guangzhou. My eldest maternal uncle retired before the age of 60, and the business in Guangzhuang let his two sons to continue. As same as his father, my eldest maternal uncle also rejoices to had a birthday, which was smaller than when his father and him were doing it together. After bought Qinglu, my eldest maternal uncle to do his birthday there, but had never to invite the troupe to play.

The eldest maternal uncle and the eldest aunt had five sons and two daughters, but the fifth son had not grown up. So the eldest maternal uncle and the concubine had a little son named Yiliu. All of other four sons had married and had their children.

The Eldest Maternal Uncle's Family

The Eldest Son of the Eldest Maternal Uncle

The eldest son of the eldest maternal uncle, Zhongfu died of the epidemic very early, leaving behind widowed wife with two son and one daughter. His fist baby was a boy who was named Shunguan by my maternal grandfather, but died soon after birth. The second baby was also a boy was named Jieguan, as soon as Jieguan grew up, the eldest maternal uncle ask him to get married first, but less than two years later Jieguan fell ill and died, leaving behind his young pregnant wife. So there were two generations of widows in the eldest maternal uncle's home, one mother-in-law and one daughter-in-law, very pitiful. Late The daughter-in-law gave birth of a girl, the eldest maternal uncle Immediately hugged a baby boy and pretended to be a twin sister and brother. We called the Jieguan's widowed wife as young mistress, Being a widowed for decades could be quite lonely. After her daughter graduated from University and got married, then she lived with her daughter together. Late she became mentally ill due to her eccentric temperament, and often quarreled with her daughter and daughter-in-law. The adopted son, named Xiaojie, failed to study, when grew up, and I introduced him to an orphanage on my behalf. Later, I heard when he grew up, get a good job, I didn't know anything more. Jieguan's sister, the eldest maternal uncle's eldest granddaughter, was arguably the most outstanding of the eldest uncle's descendants. She once went to college to specialize in physics, and became the first bachelor in the Chen's Family after graduation. Before liberation, she followed her husband to Taiwan and worked as a professor of physics in Taiwan University. Now she had retired and lived in the United States.

The Second Son of the Eldest Maternal Uncle

The second son of the eldest maternal uncle Shanfu was indulge in wine, life was extremely corrupt, and his life was not long. He died shortly after the death of the eldest maternal uncle, leaving two daughters and one son. The eldest daughter was a little silly and betrothed to a merchant's son but died unmarried. Although her second daughter finished high school, she did not do any important work and after married became a housewife. The son was not talented, and after the victory of the Anti-Japanese War, he went to Taiwan and never returned, no any news and probably died early. Shanfu's wife lived with her second daughter and soon became demented. It took many years to die with extremely miserable.

The third Son of the Eldest Maternal Uncle

The third son of the eldest maternal uncle Xiaofu, first inherited his father's business in Guangzhou. After his father's death, he set up Shenzhuang in Shanghai, to do cotton business, and shipped cotton back to Fujian for batch sale, quite developed. During and after the Anti-Japanese War, a lot of National Hardship Money and Victory Money were made. In addition to set up Shenzhuang in Shanghai, he also set up Rongzhuang in Fuzhou. He was quite mean and stingy, even more than his father. After the liberation, he suffered a lot during the five-anti-movement. Shenzhuang and Rongzhuang closed down one after another. He was forced to work as a salesperson in a cloth shop, and the property accumulated in the past almost disappeared. In the anti-right movement, he was classified as a rightist then was expelled home. Later, both he and his wife died of illness, at the age about 70. He had several children. I only know that his eldest daughter was a physician, his second daughter was an accountant in Tianjin and the third daughter was an engineer in the railway system.

The fourth Son of the Eldest Maternal Uncle

The fourth son of the eldest maternal uncle Junfu, When he was born, he was called "eighty-one" because his parents' age adds up to was eighty-one. He was born almost at the same time as the eldest grandson of his father, that was spread as a story. When he grew up, he did business with his third brother and mainly stayed in Fuzhou Rongzhuang as preside. He was cunning too, but not so cunning as the others. He married a wife, but died early, leaving behind two daughters and a son, and then he married again and gave birth to several children. I had no idea about the situation of his children. His first wife was the only daughter of my 6th uncle's first wife who had graduated from high school but never had worked. After getting married, the husband and wife were in love with each other. After his first wife's death, he set up a tombstone for her and wrote "The tomb of my dearest wife ". At that time, Fuzhou people had not yet opened up to accept such writing, some people thought it was quite annoying, some thought it was a good story, then it was spread as a joke. But shortly after his wife's death, He had remarried without sadness, and also had a concubine. After Rongzhuang closed, he was assigned to be a manager of a small cotton cloth shop, and died of illness before 60.

The Eldest Daughter of the Eldest Maternal Uncle

The eldest daughter of the eldest maternal uncle, the nickname was Xiximei, No culture, a little bit silly. But was married to a college graduate who was rare at the time. This college student believes in Christianity, for this reason the Chen's Family called him "Jesus". Such a couple was certainly not close together, so they did not live together after they had a daughter. This religious Jesus actually lived with his cousin who had same religious with him, and later "Jesus" worked under Lei xingbang, a bandit head in northern Fujian. All of these only God knows.

The Second Daughter of the Eldest Maternal Uncle

The second daughter of the eldest maternal uncle had entered the church girls' middle school, but failed to study, and later married with a businessman, with much dowry. But as a businessman, the son-in-law, gambling, alcoholism and all other bad habits were complete, the family property were all ruined away, the wife's dowry also were ruined away. Late she was also infected with syphilis, causing her to become blind and finally die of a stroke. Her husband had to make a living as a small clerk working in Hang Sengzhuang until died at the end of the war. Due to the severe syphilis, they had no children but I heard that he had adopted a son.

The Eldest Maternal Uncle's House-Qinglu

The eldest maternal uncle did not buy any land, only purchased Qinglu in his heyday. This western style building was built by Guangdong businessman Lu zhanquan. Downstairs there were three rooms in front and three in back, among which were the front and back halls, two living rooms beside the front hall, and spacious rooms on both sides of the back hall. There were wide corridors in front of the anteroom and living room, and under the corridor was the garden. The entire floor below was covered with colored tiles, doors and windows were well-made, and in the halls and living rooms, the uncle used high quality mahogany furniture bought from Guangdong, and the mahogany frames and inlays were hung on the walls, exquisite Cantonese embroidery was even more magnificent. But for the sake of his concubine, he did not live in this house, only when his disease (possibly stomach cancer) was critical, just moved here to breathe his last, then die. Of course, every year he celebrates his birthday in this house, they were all very lively. The whole house was not big enough to be extravagant, and even the tea shop in front of it was set up for a banquet. The funeral after his death was also handled in this house, because I was not in Fuzhou at the time, and I did not know its details without seeing the scene. He was only 69 years old, just like his father. Father and son had almost the same fate experience on the same birthday, which was indeed surprising. I did not know if the both two people were exactly the same. If they were so, then it seemed that the destiny was doomed by the "eight characters".

Were it credible?

The eldest maternal aunt died two or three years earlier than the eldest uncle. The eldest maternal aunt was a virtuous wife and mother in feudal times. she did not care about any major issues. I had almost no impression of her.

The house of Qinglu seemed to be very unlucky. The Lu zhanquan family built it and lived inside only a shout time and sold it, because of business failure. Soon after the eldest maternal uncle bought it, he lost his lawsuit because the "Tian Sun" was burned and even closed the door. His second son died after moving in a very short period, his grandson married in the house, and died of illness less than two years, and then died the fourth son "wife" who had married in the house. After the eldest maternal aunt died, the eldest maternal uncle died. Five people died in about ten years, which was really bad luck. There was an open space next to Qinglu, which was originally the ruins of a temple. The red wall of the temple along the road had remained for a long time. There was also a stove for burning waste paper at one end of the wall. When I was a child, I often saw a lunatic dressed like Kuixing, with long hair on his head, bare chest drawing a gossip Tai Chi picture, and his face was pained red, red with green, green which was terrible. He walked along the red wall and from time to time he reached into the hearth to retrieve the word paper. He still read words in his mouth. This way he added a lot of mystery to the ruins inside the red wall. Someone said, The house in Qinglu was built on the open space beside the temple. I wonder if this was the case? I heard that after the eldest maternal uncle's sons moved into the house, there was a haunt in the house. Some people saw ghosts at night, and some heard ghosts? These superstitious words were connected with a series of misfortunes of my eldest maternal uncle's family, which was really difficult to explain. After the death of the eldest maternal uncle, his eldest and second sons obtained the property, no longer taking part in business, it was not long before difficulties arose. On the contrary, the third and the forth sons continue to do the business together and gather more money, especially third son. If all of his sons were in harmony, the third and fourth sons should help the eldest and second son family, but they were not. After the eldest son wife died, only a young widowed niece and young children left, they were very pitiful. the third and the fourth sons swallowed the rooms with the furniture in the public areas and halls downstairs that were belonged to the eldest and second son family. The mahogany furniture, which had been promised by my eldest maternal uncle in his will to his the eldest grandson and daughter-in-law, but all of these had been bought by the third son at a very low price without any mercy. The third and the forth sons made a big fortune during the war of resistance against Japan. They bought many industries, including houses for their own residence, and sold Qinglu, as well as the tea house that the their father reserved for the sacrifice. It was said that there were almost no contact in each families. After the death of the eldest maternal uncle, the girl who not like Wen Tao, just go with others, but she rented another house and took Yiliu to live alone. Because she did not know how to be thrifty, she soon ate up all the money left by the eldest maternal uncle, and it was very difficult afterwards. The mother and son were regarded as passers by the Chen's family and cut off all contact. Yiliu married a woman who delivered milk, had a son and finally lived on her. A few years later Yiliu and then his mother die. Yi liu's son once came to Shanghai to borrow money from me, Since then,

I had never heard any news from him again. That my eldest maternal uncle, so prosperous in life, should decline so rapidly after his death, was it really out of reach, was it retribution for being mean? was it just paying attention to preparing material conditions for our children and ignoring the results of their education? I was afraid each had its own reasons.

The Second Maternal Uncle

My second maternal uncle died very early. I didn't see him. I only heard that he was extremely honest and worked as a shop assistant while he was young. The second maternal aunt was very weak. She had a small square black plaster on her forehead attached to her forehead almost all the year round. She lived until she was over 60 years old and died. She gave birth to two boys and a girl.

The Eldest Son of Second Maternal Uncle

The eldest son of the second maternal uncle **Chenqiu** had studied at Yinghua College for several years, then had been admitted by the Post Office. He was not only extremely satisfied with this work, but also proud of it. He believed that he was the most reliable golden rice bowl. After married, he had a son who was the eldest granduncles' first grandson, and named Yao guan by his great-grandfather. Later, another daughter was born. Unfortunately, both Yaoguan and his uncle's grandson, Shun Guan, both were died young of the measles. The maternal granduncle loved Yaoguan very much, just as he loved his younger son Yanyan, so the death of Yaoguan made the grandfather extremely sad. Later, it was the same with the death of Shunguan. Some said he should not named his great-grandson after the sage Yao and Shun and they thought it was presumptuous of him to do so, so that they all had to die. My second maternal uncle was death only at the age of 65, when he saw his fourth generation, that shows that he and his grandchildren got married quite early. Chenqiu's first wife died after giving birth to a daughter. Chenqiu could not wait and get remarried again, giving birth to several children. His second wife believed in Christianity and extremely unfilial to her mother-in-law, and also not kind to the former wife's daughter. But both of her son and daughter were quit good, The eldest son later became a University professor but her eldest daughter was not filial as her mother-in-law. Due to political ignorance, Chenqiu broke his "golden rice bowl" himself at the beginning of liberation and was expelled from the post office to return home. He could not even get retirement benefits, making life very difficult. Eventually he died of a stroke, and his second wife hanged herself a few days later. The children were numerous, and they had all grown up. Was such a suicide a form of revenge?

The Second Son of Second Maternal Uncle

The second son of the second maternal uncle was Physiologically impaired, eyes squinted, stuttering in speech, no culture, often unemployed due to lack of work. He was also married and gave birth to two boys and two daughters. Of course life was often difficult, but his brother did not help him at all. Before liberation, I introduced him a job, but was soon dismissed. He used to be a helper at Rongzhuang, but he didn't do much. Fortunately, he found a job as a clerk in a small stationery store on the eve of the liberation. After the liberation, the store was changed from private-owned to state-owned. He could to continue working, and he would enjoy labor insurance treatment for nearly 20 years after retirement. However, he had a wife and five children, and also had to support an old maternal uncle. The hardship of life could be imagined. Before the "Cultural Revolution", I often remitted money to him, and also sent tuition fees to his second girl when she was study in the middle school. The strange thing was although he was poor all his life, he didn't die until he was 76 years old. He was the man with the longest life span of the Chen Family.

The Daughter of Second Maternal Uncle

The daughter of the second maternal uncle after grew up, her marriage had its ups and downs, broken off by a college student to whom she was engaged. Later married to a husband working in post office as second wife. They had a few children all were excellent. Unfortunately, she did not live long, dying of a stroke at the age of 60, her husband died before her.

The Fourth Maternal Uncle

The 4th maternal uncle was the third son of the maternal grandfather, named Chen liangdong. When he was young, studied at Yinghua College in Fuzhou. At that time, students had pigtails at the back of their heads in class. The men in the Chen's Family got married early, when he at school and already married. His fist wife braid him in the morning.

Fanzai Uncle Come Back from Nanyang

Yinghua College in Fuzhou was an American church-run school, all students must read foreign books (called Fanza in Fuzhou). So. he was called Fanza or Uncle Fan by the Chen's Family. His fist wife unborn any child and died prematurely, so he remarried again. Before graduating from high school, he went to Nanyang (known as Fanbian in Fuzhou) to work in Tropical Infectious Hospital in Penang, Malaya and later was promoted to doctor. The 4th aunt had four daughters and two boys, most of whom were raised in Malaya. The 4th uncle later suffered from lung disease with poor health. He retired early and returned to his country to enjoy retirement treatment. He received a monthly pension from the British Consulate in Fuzhou. At that time, during the First World War, the price of gold plummeted, and the exchange rate of British pounds to silver dollars was greatly reduced. He did not receive enough silver dollars every month. Unfortunately, the 4th aunt died prematurely at this time. She suffered from gastrointestinal disease, because the medical technique was still very backward at that time, otherwise she would not die before she was 40 years old. After her death, the 4th uncle soon remarried another maidservant under the age of 20. She was a girl of Lu danquan Family. She was from Guangdong and could speak Cantonese and Fuzhou. In just a few years, she gave birth to three girls and one boy, leaving one boy and one girl. The other two girls were given to others as soon as they were born. One was given to a neighbor and later was found, and the other disappeared.

Western Pharmacy Doctor

The 4th uncle originally planned to open a western pharmacy, and oneself hold a doctor concurrently. The cabinets of the pharmacy had already bought, and the medicines also enters in batches, even the sign of "Jianren Pharmacy" also did well first, only need to pay taxes to start the business. It was said that the 4th uncle opposed the payment of taxes, refused to pay tax money, so there was no Official Medical Practice Certificate, the signboards were not hung out, could not start the business. But the 4th uncle often gave people medical treatment for free, even the medicine also free, Apart from relatives and friends, I occasionally see boat people with schistosomiasis who come to him to have their ascites removed. The 4th uncle could be said to treat all kind illness and disease. In addition to medical diseases, he also often tread some surgical diseases, such as treatment of boils, swollen boils, rotten feet and so on. There were only a few varieties of western medicine at that time, I only saw him using quinine to treat malaria, fever tablets (as if it was APC or aspirin) to treat fever, Cough pill or cough syrup for bronchitis, sesame oil or Epsom salt (magnesium sulfate) for indigestion disease, and for treating skin diseases. He used iodine and his own white, yellow, and black ointments, and he also often prepares medicine powder for patient. Cholera and dysentery were prevalent almost every year in Fuzhou, he gave people Brandy or "Gorocho" potions.

Every summer, the 4th uncle advises everyone to be cautious about eating and drinking, not to eat aquatic products, and should eat eggs every day because he thinks eggs were the most hygienic. At that time, there were very few west doctors in Fuzhou, and good doctors were rare, the 4th uncle knowing west medical skills. Once he went to a hot spring bath with my eldest uncle, on his way home found a man hanging himself, he saved him by artificial respiration, because this he was a novelty in Fuzhou at that time, so he was regarded by passers-by Living Fairy. The 4th uncle was not listed to practice medicine, it was a great loss. If he practise medicine well, he was likely to make a fortune.

The 4th Maternal Uncle's Friends

The 4th uncle did not do serious things, but indulged in gambling. Almost every night his friends come to his house to play Mahjong or Poker and it started to disperse at midnight. It was strange to say that all the people he made were small townsmen, such as a butcher who opened a butcher's shop in Guanyinjing, a boss who opened a stationery shop in Meiwukou, a stall owner of a vegetable stall and a fishery stall. All of these people called him "Western Medicine fourth ". Gambling money every night was both laborious and damaging to the body hearth. Coupled with his bad temper, he was furious when he lost his money, and he cursed people badly, often scolding his children for no reason. Treating the ex-wife's daughter could be said to had failed to fulfill the father's duties. When his children went to school and had to pay tuition and fees, he was very reluctant to hand over the money. He often scolded them bitterly, and when he gave the money, he was so rude as to throw the money on the ground for child to pickup.

The 4th Maternal Uncle's House

When The 4th uncle came back from Nanyang, he brought a sum of money and received a monthly pension at home. He also had some savings. So soon he purchased an old-fashioned house located at Meiwukou near

Guanyinwell with jointly his younger sister, my 6th aunts. In the old house, there was a back room downstairs that was transformed into a silver warehouse with thick walls and a heavy iron door to prevent fire and anti-theft. He and the 6th aunts lived together in this house for about two or three years. At that time, because my father was basically far away in the northeast, my mother also moved to live with them. Later, there was a money shop that want to bought the house at a high price. The 4th uncles and the 6th aunts sold it, and all three families moved to Chen yikai's new two-story house near Tianan Temple to share the building. At the same time, the 4th uncle and the 6th aunt bought a piece of land opposite Meiwu Dingmingan Temple (Bengshen Temple) by using the money from the sale of the banker house. Pay money to the poor inhabitants there to move out and hired hands to build two two-story houses on top of them, two three-story rooms on the back side of them, and a two-story shop house on the front road. After the building of the top of the Meiwu, he and six aunt each share a building, behind the three-storey side house to him, in front of the shop house to six aunt. In order to supervise the construction of this house, The 4th uncle worked very hard. He had lung problems, which led him to retire early from Malaya. Unfortunately, the 4th uncle was too not self-love, in addition to not paying attention to body maintenance with the health care. After moving to his new house in Meiwuding in 1926, His lung disease was more serious. Later he was bedridden and died of illness. He was 49 at the time, not 50 as he thought he would have been.

The 4th Maternal Uncle's Family

The 4th uncles and his wife gave birth to four daughters and two sons. When the 4th uncle died, his eldest daughter was married, and the second daughter was about to graduate from high school. The eldest son was already 15 years old, had not yet graduated from junior high school, but he was admitted to the Dadong Telegraph Bureau as a telegraph operator. The forth daughter had been succeeded to the 5th uncle before her mother's death. The most pitiful thing was that both the third daughter and her second son were still young, and they were still studying in junior high school. The stepmother was only in her twenties when she was widowed, and it was also pitiful to raise a fairly young girl and a boy. Shortly after the death of the 4th uncle, his second son was forced to drop out of school and go to Nanyang, and the second daughter married, leaving only the third daughter Pinying lonely, almost helpless, and graduating from junior high school, she had to drop out of school, work as a teacher in kindergarten, lived in the Baoshengtang (formerly Yuyingtang), with some orphans. This poor girl was none other than my wife Pinying.

Since the 4th uncle and the 6th aunts jointly purchased the Qianzhuang house in Meiwu, my mother took me with my second sister and my younger brother left Zheng's mansion. move to live with them. Until more than a year after the death of my 4th uncle and then moved back to Zheng's mansion. My 4th uncle probably thought that Pinying was very pitiful, and at the same time he also fell in take a fancy to me, his nephew. So when he would die, he asked my mother to sit in front of his bed and shed tears and told to my mother "After I die, please take the ball (Nickname of Pinying), she was very poor, I want to betrothal her to Tuantuan, Could you agree?" My mother replied immediately "If Tuantuan was grown up and become a useful person, I could accept her as my daughter-in-low". So the two adults reached an oral agreement. We two children were kept in the dark about it. But such things were hard to keep secret, and it didn't take long for them to come to light. I quickly guessed from the letter come from my father. It turned out that my mother informed my father about the 4th uncle's will and asked for his opinion. After receiving the letter from the Northeast, my father immediately wrote back to my mother and told her that she was the master of the matter. He had no opinion. This letter consists of three sheets of writing paper, and the matter was written on the first one, and the next two tell other things. My mother would not let me see the first one, and only showed me the next two, said that my father probably forgot to put the first one in the envelope. I knew from a young age that my father had always done things very carefully, never neglect sending a piece of writing paper short, so I guessed the mystery. Of course, I heard people talking about it from ear to ear, and my mother decided that we should move back to Zheng's mansion for avoid suspicion for my marriage.

The Eldest Son of the 4th Maternal Uncle

Named Chen **Bingfu,** was my wife Pinying's eldest brother. He married within 100 days of my 4th uncle's death. After marriage, he gave birth to three sons and one daughter. Except for the early death of one son, they had all grown up and were in good condition. After working in the Fuzhou Dadong Telegraph Bureau for a few years, he was transferred to the Shanghai Bureau. When the Pacific War began, the Shanghai Bureau was occupied by Japanese invaders, and he returned to Fujian with his family. He went to Nanping to work as a telegraph operator at the China Telegraph Bureau, and his family remained in Fuzhou. After the victory of the Anti-Japanese War, he went to work at the Hong Kong Dadong Telegraph Bureau. Unfortunately, he died of hypertension and stroke shortly after retirement, was in his 50 years old. Fortunately, the eldest son around him had already worked in Dadong, and later transferred to the Hong Kong Observatory's newspaper office until he retired. He was still settled in Hong Kong, and had many children, all had been growing.

Bingfu's wife, also my wife Pinying's sister-in-law. She had been a senior student who graduated from Fujian Normal University, and once named the school flower. The combination of her and Bingfu was completely dominated by her parents. After the death of the 4th uncle, they hurriedly married. she was very dissatisfied and suffered from schizophrenia and depression within a few years of marriage. After returning to Fuzhou from Shanghai, Bingfu's stepmother refused to take care of her, and also had been refused shelter by her mother, the 5th aunt took care of her. she was so ill-treated that died as mad woman. That was the only misfortune of the descendants of the 4th uncle, and the rest of his descendants were very prosperous and still the same today.

The Younger Son of the 4th Maternal Uncle

Named Taiying My wife Pinying's younger brother. After being forced to go to Malaya, received the help of my 4th uncle's old friend, where he graduated from high school, and then worked as a teacher and principal in the elementary school run by overseas Chinese until his retirement. He died in 1987, at the age of 77, he had two sons, both had a family.

The Eldest Daughter of the 4th maternal uncle

Named **Guiying**, was my wife Pinying's eldest sister. She gave birth to three son and two daughters, and moved to Taiwan and the United States. The situation was pretty good.

The Second Daughter of the 4th maternal uncle

Named **Lanying**, was my wife Pinying's second sister. After married, she gave birth to 3 sons. The eldest son died early. Later, she and her husband and sons went to Malaya. During the Pacific War, Malaya was occupied by Japanese invaders. She had the misfortune die there. Now she had 16 grandsons and granddaughters living in Malaya, and all had formed family.

The Third Daughter of the 4th maternal uncle

Named **Pinying,** was my wife. About my wife, I would statement later.

The Forth Daughter of the 4th maternal uncle

Named **Yuying**, was my wife Pinying's younger sister, after being a daughter of the 5th uncle, now lived in Malaya and had many children and grandchildren.

The Widow of the 4th maternal uncle

The widow of the 4th maternal uncle lived to 80 years old, and a pair of her children were married and each has several children. After the death of the 4th uncle, she lived in a period of hardship. but soon came to rely on Bingfu, the eldest son of the 4th uncle who worked at the Hong Kong Dadong Telegraph Bureau, to maintain a stable life. Later, Bingfu's eldest son continued to remit money from Hong Kong to support her life to death.

The 4th maternal uncle was different from the eldest maternal uncle, he wad loyal and treats people with no harshness. He often made friends with people even killed pigs and sold meat in the market, set up stalls to sell vegetables, and opened small shops. He was compassionate, would to treat people and save people, without charge. But to the rich people the 4th uncle instead disdains no more interaction. The 2nd maternal aunt had a hard time when the son was not growing up, the 4th uncle gave her all the rent money of the land that 4th uncle got from his grandfather, for his nephew to go to school. It was credible that the offspring of the 4th uncle would prosper and they would be able to establish a career at home and abroad. The 4th uncles were not without any shortcomings, his language was extremely rude, liked my eldest maternal uncle and the 5th maternal uncle, While he was speaking, was full of curses, especially when he swear, terrible to hear. So I was afraid of him when I was young. one was afraid of his scolding and the other was afraid of he would giving me bitter medicines such as castor oil and quinine. But once my mother got sick, and my 4th uncles brought her back to life. The 4th uncles had cured of tumor on my abdominal wall and my night blindness. One summer I was suffering from a cholera-like illness that was also cured by my 4th uncle that made me remember him for the rest of my life. I could say that I could live to the 80 years old today, that I believe had something to do with my 4th uncles also my father-in-law.

The Eldest Daughter of My Grandfather

My mother was the eldest daughter of my maternal grandfather. because her brother (the 4th maternal uncles) was called Fanzai, So, my mother was called Fanzaimei by her family.

About my mother, I will write another chapter.

The Second Daughter of My Grandfather

The sixth maternal aunt

The 6th maternal aunt was the second daughter of the maternal grandfather. Her parents engaged her early to a man, but the men died before married. At that time, many people in the Chen's family had strong feudal ideas and Some even advocated keeping her chastity. Fortunately, my 4th uncle (Uncle Fanzai) had advanced ideas, strongly opposed and advocated her go to church girls' school. Later, she went to school, but she dropped out of school and married to Uncle Zheng quan, a member of the Tengshan Zheng's Family, participated in the revolution at his early years and followed Mr. Sun yatsen. His first wife died early, left a daughter, and Zheng quan wanted to remarry for Inherit the family. The 6th maternal aunts married him and gave birth to an only boy. In addition to participating in the revolution, Uncle Zhengquan, once taught geometry at Shanghai Public School, and also translated a geometry textbook written by American Winder worth into Chinese. After the success of the 1911 Revolution, he ceased to be a teacher and changed to government work. I heard that he served for a short time as governor of Zhenjiang during the anti-Qing uprising. Later, he worked for some time in the Revolutionary government of Guangzhou, and suddenly, he went to Beijing as secretary of the Council of Pigs, the sixth aunt followed him. After that, he lived in Fuzhou for a time and worked as a tax collector in a small place, and was panicking over a question. After the establishment of the Nanjing government, he went to work in Nanjing with the help of Ding Chaowu and became a member of the Kuomintang Historical Editorial Committee. He later told me that after years of editing, the first sentence of party history could not be written because of divisions between the parties. When the War of Resistance against Japanese broke out, his family moved to Chongqing. Unfortunately, the 6th aunt died midway by a stroke. A few years later, during the Japanese bombing of Chongqing, uncle died of hypertension. The 6th aunt died less than 60 years old, the 6th uncle also about 60 years old, before death, the 6th uncle's eyes had been almost blind. They had only one son, had married and had a boy. At present, the father was in Taiwan, the son was a professor in the United States, has become Naturalized American. had three sons, each of whom was successful with achievements.

My maternal grandfather died around 1920, and his grandson and greet-grandson now had multiplied extends into the sixth generation, the total number was very large. My great-grandfather died around 1850, and the children and grandchildren had reached the eighth generation so far. However, if we compare the Zheng Families with Chen Families, the Zheng's Family would reproduce more slowly and the total number would be smaller. Investigate the reason, I could say that all the men of the Chen Family get married early, and early marriage would inevitably lead to early childbirth, so they would multiply quickly. The men of the Zheng's Family married late, and some did not get married at all, so there was little increase in later generations.

At the same time, the Zheng's Family had more corruption, and opium smoking and prostitutes seriously affected fertility, and some even later became no heir. The great-grandfather had nine sons, and now four Fangs had been no heir. The number of people in the two houses (He-house and Le-house) had dropped sharply, which was the result of life corruption. There were several widowed wives left in the Chen Family due to early marriage and early death, but the Zheng's Family was rarely the case. Judging from the population reproduction situation of these two Families, without control, China's population expansion would be unbearable. In the past, in addition to being restrained by natural and man-made disasters, the population did not grow indefinitely. Diseases and corruption also played a big role. In today's era of scientific progress, the impact of natural disasters had been greatly reduced, and the forces of peace had gradually overcome the scourge of war. If mankind do not implement family planning, excessive population expansion would become the biggest scourge. Therefore, not only should family planning be promoted, but it must be strictly implemented.

CHAPTER 8

Parents

My Father Zheng Yiju

My father name was Zheng Yiju, Fengxiang. He was born on March 26, 1874. Originally, in our Zheng's Family my father belong "Zhong"'s generation, unfortunately some named of "Zhong"'s persons easy died early. So later abandoned the use of "Zhong", instead of other word. Both my father and my uncle were using "Yi" replaced with "zhong" as their first name, but my uncle still died prematurely.

My father was born to my step-grandmother, and was the eldest son of my grandfather. At the time of his birth, my grandfather was quit old, so my father was considered as a rare son and much loved by my grandmother, especially after my uncle's death. When my father was young, he went to school, but not study for a long time, and failed in the imperial examinations, he never learned to had any skills, so there was no fixed career, spent most of his time unemployed at home. Zheng's mansion. was famous for gambling, which made him also infected with gambling addiction, and my step-grandmother, Mrs. Feng's nature also liked gambling, which further promoted my father's hobby. But in his young age, he had done a good deed, which was worthy of commemoration for his children and grandchildren. My grandfather worked in Zhejiang Province Jinhua as City official in old age and died there due to illness. My grandfather's coffin was brought back by my father, just like my grandfather went to Sichuan to bring back our great grandfather's coffin. Jinhua was much closer Fuzhou than Sichuan, and at that time, the chaos of the Taiping Heavenly Kingdom was flat, the road was calmer. My father's work was less harder than that of my grandfather. It took about three years for my grandfather to transport my great-grandfather's coffin back, but my father only took a few months to transport my grandfather's coffin back.

Travel North and South

After grandfather's death, the family lived on grandmother's hard work, thrift and ancestral income. My grandmother, had only one daughter, but died soon. I heard that after my grandmother death, all her boxes were empty, most of the clothes were sold by the couple for gambling, and another part was generous to help others. After my father remarried my mother, they had given birth to two daughters and three sons, one of the boys was not alive, one daughter died before 15 years old. As the family grew up, my father had to take on the responsibility of supporting the family. Some relatives and friends told me that my father originally worked in Beijing capital Wucheng School. The principal of the school was Yan Fu. So, we had four calligraphy written by Yan at home, but the signed one was lost during the Cultural Revolution. Later, my father had copied Lin Shu's translated novels for him, so there were some of Lin Shu's manuscripts in our home. Lin Shu gave my grandmother a painting of pine trees and cranes for her birthday and a couplet to my father. In the couplet wrote sentence was *"Thirsty bee peeping at Yanshui, swiftly swallowing and hooking"* It was a pity that all these things were lost, as they were nowhere to be found today, most likely it was all lost during Cultural Revolution.

Later, as a messenger, my father and Chen Lu visited the Kulun in outer Mongolia. Everyone rode camels across the desert. My father also told me that the death row prisoners in outer Mongolia were confined in coffins, there was a small hole in the top of the coffin for eating, and other small hole in the bottom of the coffin for the prisoners to relieve themselves. I could still remember this strange thing until today. Yan Fu, Lin Shu and Chen Lu were all from Minhou County in Fujian province, So our relatives recommended my father to work under them, but they were all "Five day Beijing officials ", not long time. Once in the same year when my father went to Coulum he had made a trip to Malaya, where my 4th uncle was working there as a doctor, my father tried to find work there, but could not, and soon returned back. Once time my father told me that he had ridden a camel across the desert wearing a leather jacket and a large cloak on the summer day, and that in winter he had to ride his horse shirtless in the water to keep the heat out. This was a story he told me that was strange to me when I was a kid.

Because my father had written for Lin Shu for a while, Lin Shu later asked him to help his son Lin boheng. Lin boheng had always been a small county magistrate or police chief in the Northeast. And mostly in the frontier, I only remember the two place names of Heihe and Wuzhuhe. My father was a financial officer in the government office. He once told me that working in the Northern of Heilongjiang the most painful work was sending money to Province Government Office. Because the places he had to walk through were desolate, sparsely populated with wolves, the roads were dangerous. In the winter, when it was freezing, the winds were bone-chilling and especially harsh. At that time, bandits were extremely rampant in the Northeast. If you met them on the road, not only money would be robbed, but lives would be at stake and difficult to protect. During this period, my father often did not return home for several years, the longest was 5 years in Heihe. Heihe was located on the border between China and Russia. I did not understand why it was used Russian currency. At the end of the First World War and the early days of the Soviet Union, the Russian currency had depreciated so much that my father hardly had any money to send home. I remember that I only went to the post office to get his remittance of more than 100 yuan at that time. He also sent back or brought back from the Northeast ginseng beard, rana, alexandre (colored stone) and Xiachan (the xiachan cloth produced in the Northeast) in small quantities. At that time, most of his salary was invested in joint ventures to set up a machine-milled flour mill (called the Northeast Fire Mill), but I had never heard my father receive any dividends from this company. It was likely that this company had eaten up all capital, or all his capital was swallowed.

Lin boheng was a young man who was extremely corrupt and had one wife with two concubines. Whenever he go to any new official place, usually taken along with them. He was arrogant and extravagant in his office, also he loves gambling. He did not know how to handle official business, so repeatedly transferred. He was able to owed his official position, entirely on the help of his father's old friends in the Beiyang Government. After his father died, he immediately lost his backer and could no longer find any official position again. My father worked under him and would inevitably accompany him to play Mahjong with him or his concubines. So my father gambling habits remained unchanged. When Lin boheng failed to become an official, my father stopped leaving Fujian. He also realized how difficult it was for my mother to support the family during these years he was away. So he decided to quit gambling, since then my father had not gambling again.

In Fuzhou, my father got a job worked in the Chamber of Commerce, but he quit soon because of the low pay. At that time, my father cousin Liu boyu was in Fujian, relied on Zheng zaiyu as a chief of the civil affairs department, Liu boyu got a official position to be the county magistrate in Zhangbu County. My father worked with Liu boyu as a financial officer in the county government, later worked with him at the Jiaoling Police Station. Because Liu boyu was very corrupt and soon lost his official position and stay at home. Since then, my father also stay at home and would no longer leave home, my mother would not let him go out. My father set up private schools to teach some enlightenment students. And once in Qing Lu taught the 4th uncle's son and several grandchildren.

Run the Family Business

By the time I graduated from college in 1932, my father had been 50 years old and out of work for several years at home. Since he was the oldest living person in the Zheng's Family, he had became the "biological parent", and the Zheng's Family left some public property under his control. The garden behind Zheng's mansion. was the place where Fuzhou tea merchants gather. In the early years, the land was rented to tea merchants to build tea workshop. After a few years, the Zheng's Family would own the workshop. A house was built by Zheng's Family, then rented out for getting rent used to sacrifice the ancestral tomb. There was also a vacant lot that hadn't been used for years. Someone want to rent for building a factory and agree first pay the Zheng's Family a sum of money. 15 years later, the factory house was returned as the Zheng's Family property for collecting rent. My father presided over the matter, which made everyone very happy, because the amount of money was not small, and it was distributed to each Fang (room) for alleviate their financially difficult. The L-5th Fang, L-6th Fang, and L-7th Fang used this money to repair or rebuild their houses. Our the L-4th Fang used the money to build a new kitchen in a small space outside the second wall on the west side to make kitchen closer to our room.

In addition, My father also held a joint ceremony with his clansmen to enter the Zheng Ancestral Hall (a ceremony of putting the god master tablets of ancestor and some living men into a shrine) that would increase the revenue of Ancestral Hall, and enriched the fund for the annual memorial service. During the years in Fuzhou, my father spent his time doing several good deeds, which well received by Zheng's Family and people in the clan.

My father spent much of his life in the officialdom and public service, all worked in finance, but he was innocent, without any corruption, so he did not have much money to support our family, the life in our family had been quite difficult. My childhood was very painful, even suffered from malnutrition. Looking back on those days, I had no complaints against my father, On the contrary, I was proud of his integrity.

"The chicken is a kilo and the son is ten"

Because my father had never had a permanent job all his life, It was spent a lot of time to get a job but lost quickly, so soon had to running from south to north for looking a new job, that made my father quite tired. So he often urged me to work as soon as I grew up to relieve some burden of our family. I remember when I was just ten years old, my father came back from the Northeast, when he was waiting for a new job at home, feel so depressed. He used to said to my mother several times in front of me about a Fuzhou proverb *"The chicken is a kilo and the son is ten"*. This mean a chicken weighing half a kilogram could be sold in market for money and the child over ten years old should go out to work to earn money, help support family, or do not just stay at home and being raised by family. At that time, children in poor families reached the age of ten, and most went out to become apprentices. Zheng's Family and other relatives had several such boys. I had the possibility of being suspended from school to become an apprentice at any time. Fortunately, my mother and father had different ideas, she saw the misery and hardship of my father had not a work regularly. She also saw that some of our relatives of the Chen Family held "iron rice bowls" in the post office or telegraph office. She hope I could hold such a "iron rice bowl" so she insists on letting me go to church school for a few years in middle school, and then fond an opportunity to enter the post office, telegraph office or customs to work. So I was able to continue my studies, first thank to my mother assertion and ideas that let me could graduate from college.

I started working as soon as I graduated, and my father stopped teaching private school, and all the family burden was on me. At the beginning, my father and my mother lived in Fuzhou. I remit money from Shanghai every month to support them. Later, they sometimes came to Shanghai and live with us, sometimes back to Fuzhou. Before the Anti-Japanese War, they spent more long time in Shanghai. My father had seen our raised first boy and a daughter, and he was very fond of his grandchildren. During his early days in Shanghai, he was in good health and looked not like a person over 60 years old. He almost went to the park for a walk every day, but he had to carry a walking stick when he went out. At first I lived in Shanghai West Wanhangdu Road. He went to Zhaofeng Park (now Zhongshan Park). After I moved to Fuxing Middle Road, he went to Fuxing Park (now French Park). One day in 1938, he was holding his grandson, the grandson suddenly clutched the thermos on top of the cupboard. Boiling water poured over his head and scalded his forehead, but not eyes. After being sent to the hospital, he was cured by medical treatment, leaving only a scar on his forehead. But my father was taken aback and blamed himself for hurting his grandson. Since then, he had been very unhappy, and as a result, his quality of life had gradually deteriorated. My mother disapproved of sending him to the hospital for treatment, she had always believed that he was suffering from what she called "old age" and that there was no way to cure him. At the time of the War of Resistance Against Japan, the family's economy was very difficult. We can't get a good doctor to treat him, so he didn't even know what's wrong with him. It could be tuberculosis of the gut, it could be gastrointestinal cancer, he vomited a lot, afterwards, vomited blood with unpleasant smelly things in it, and the pain was terrible. After more than a year, my father finally died in early 1941, on the 25th day of the 12th lunar month, at the age of 65. At the end of his life, except for the second sister in Fuzhou, my eldest sister and my younger brother were all by his side. We had a big funeral for my father at the Funeral parlor and used a large coffin to hold my father body. The coffin was placed at the Paradise Funeral Home, and the rent was high. It was not until after the War of Resistance against Japanese Aggression that I arranged for my father coffin to be brought back to Fuzhou and buried in our ancestral grave. After my father death my mother flew back to Fuzhou and with my second sister to mourn for him according to the old custom.

My mother Chen Ruyu

My mother was born on June 27, 1880, the lunar calendar, and died in 1961, at the age of 82. She was the eldest daughter of my grandfather, and had three brothers and a sister. At the Chen's Family, she was Ranked 5 among her peers, so the relatives of the Chen's Family called her 5th-mei, 5th-jie, 5th-gu and 5th-gupo. Because her third brother reads foreign books, he was called Fanzai. So when she was a child, she was called Fanzaimei by adult. In the past, calling a woman by her name was not allowed. My mother married the Zheng's Family, because my father was ranked 28th, so she was called the 28th young mistress, 28th-aunt, 28th-mother, even 28th-old mothers. I didn't know her name until I was old. She was married to my father as a continuation wife. At that time, the Zheng's Family belonged to official family, the Chen's family belonged to private family, and the marriage of the women of private family married into the official family was considered outmarry. In fact, the Zheng's Family was a broken feudal official family and the Chen's Family was an emerging merchant family.

Thrift and Keep a Family

When my mother married to my family, both my grandfather and my uncle had passed away. There were grandmother, aunt and my eldest sister born by my father's first wife. My father had no work, and his gambling addiction was still strong. The family was entirely dependent on my grandmother to work hard. At that time, there was still some ancestry left, and each Fang could still receive a certain amount of ancestral income each year. With that small pool of money, grandmother supported the family, and you could imagine how difficult it was. When I grew up, I often heard my mother talk about the grandmother pinch and scrape, the food was coarse mussels, occasionally meat, a bowl of meat to eat for several days, wear were modified and mended old clothes, use of course more economical. My mother and grandmother had lived together for many years, and she had learned the experience of hardworking and frugal housekeeping from my grandmother. She first gave birth to my second sister, and later gave birth to a boy and a girl, all unfortunately died early, and then gave birth to me and my younger brother. The second sister and younger brother were adopt to my aunt when they were born. So my second sister called my aunt as mother, and called my mother as aunt, and my father as uncle. When I was a kid, I called them as same as my second sister, and called my parents as my aunt and uncle, but I did not call my aunt as mother. Because I was born to be a rare son, so the adults let me call them in that way, and did not want me to change.

When I was only three years old, my grandmother passed away and the entire burden of housework was laid on my mother alone. At this time, there were seven persons in our family including parents, aunt, two sisters, my brother and me, the family had a lot of living expenses. My father had to go out to work, and often could not return for a long time. All the housework was left to my mother, and her hardship was conceivable. The young widowed aunt and step-sister also increased her troubles. Fortunately, she inherited the grandmother's thrifty tradition and had admirable patience. At the same time, she also received the necessary support from her siblings to manage many difficulties. A few years later, after the widowed aunt died and the eldest sister got married, she had relax a little.

The Le-3rd Fang of Zheng's Family, especially the 18th aunt "Big neck", unreasonably bullied us, often causing trouble to my mother, and also caused her a lot of mental suffering. After my uncle and aunt bought a big house in Meiwu, my mother with us moved to live with them for six or seventh years, until my uncle died, then we move back to Zheng's mansion. At that time, Le-3rd Fang had broken, and there was no longer a tendency to bully others.

While we lived with my aunt and uncle, my father spent most of his time in the Northeast. I only remember him coming back once, around

1922, when we were living in the Meiwu. My father stayed at home for only a few months, then went to the Northeast and didn't come back for five years. My mother lived in the back room of the half-building where my aunt lived and when my father came home, he temporarily lived in the front room downstairs. My 6th aunt and uncle were away from Fuzhou half the time, so we were actually helping them look after the house. When we lived together with my 4th uncle and 6th aunt, we got their care and financial help, but my mother's pride was so strong that she would not turn to them for help unless she had to. Both families, mother and child usually eat their own meals. During the New Year (Spring Festival), if my 6th aunts was in Fuzhou, the two family would eat a few meals together. Two sisters rejoiced that they had discussed what to prepare for the Chinese New Year long before the Spring Festival. They all talked about this matter before getting out of bed early in the morning. They talked many times, as if they had nothing to talk about otherwise.

In Meiwu, one summer my mother had a high fever for several days. My 4th uncle almost had no choice but to take a lot of heavy drugs (aspirin, quinine, etc.) to reduce the high fever. After a lot of sweat, the disease was relieved. As a result, my mother became very weak after her illness. At that time, a person who had a high fever was called a fever, not sure what kind of inflammation, typhus or scarlet fever? Doctors were still confused, they just use a lot of drugs to sweat. After this illness, my mother never suffered any serious illness, her health gradually got improved. Later, she took ginseng beard (my father sent from the northeast) and American ginseng for a while, That's probably why she lived to 82.

When my 4th uncle from Meiwu moved to Tian'an Temple for temporary stay, my mother followed him. After Meiwu's house was built, we moved back to live. Shortly after we lived the new house, my second sister got married. So when our family moved back to ZhengZai, it was only my younger brother and me with my mother. Soon my father returned from the Northeast, then stayed in the south. When we didn't live in ZhengZai, the back room was rented to Xihou (DuDu) of Le-7th Fang, and we only charged him two yuan per month. For these two dollars, I had to run several times a month to collect the debt. But the two yuan was a part of the money that my mother depends on to support our family, how difficult she was.

Parenting

My mother had never read any books and of course the level of education was very low, only knew a few words. But she pays close attention to my study. When I studied in a private school, I had to read the Four Classics, the Five Classics and Ancient Chinese, my mother urges me to recite it all every night. Under a kerosene lamp or a dim electric lamp, she held a book in her hand and listened to me recite it word by word. When I could not recite it back, or if I missed some words, she would know and asked to read again, I would not dare to neglected until learn my lessons by heart every night. After I went to school, she could not check my homework except to urge me to study.

Many men and women of the Zheng's Family often gamble, and there were always some people come to gamble at my 4th uncle's home. My mother not only did not participate, but basically did not to watch. She seemed to have so much clothes need to mend every day. During the day, except for cooking and washing, under the lamp at night, her hands kept doing needlework. When my younger brother and I were young, our clothes were basically made from the old clothes of the adults. Most of the underpants worn on the inside were had made up or been replenished, the gowns or trousers worn outside were rarely patched because she did not want her sons to look too shabby, and let other people laugh. Our socks were replenished and replenished. They were thick and uneven, making them uncomfortable to wear on the feet.

Three Treasures in Heart

My mother was very frightened of leprosy, thinking it was caused by dampness. She exposed the washed clothes under the sun again and again until it was very dry, then we were allowed to wear it, and all the clothes she washed had to starched with rice soup, they were almost able to stand up after drying. My younger brother and I often cried uncomfortably or refuse to wear them, especially color pants made of coarse clothe was very uncomfortably to wear on the body.

My mother liked the sun very much because it needed strong sunlight to dry clothes. As soon as the sun came up, she was busy. Not only should the clothes you change every day be exposed to the sun, but clothes you wear all year round should also be exposed to the sun in summer. Some clothes that were not often worn or not worn at all, were also exposed to the sun, causing sweaters to become fragile or fall off and leather become fragile and broken.

My mother was very happy to hear the magpie's scream, thought that the magpie's scream was to tell someone good news. It was a superstition, of course, but she always thought that was very effective. There were probably many times in her life when she heard magpie's scream, for example, my father in the remote place sent a letter, or a bank-letter (a letter of remittance), or a relative getting better and so on. Like the sound of a magpie's scream would inevitably hate the crow's cry, because many people believe that the crow cry was extremely bad news. Whenever heard the crow cry, the superstitious people scolded, or spit, Thinking that doing so would eliminate bad things, and so did my mother.

My mother was also quite superstitious about ghosts and gods. In addition to offering sacrifices to ancestors according to the old customs. She was always busy folding or pasting a lot of paper ingots before the Spring Festival every year, and hanging them in a string to prepare for the worship to the Kitchen God, New Year's Eve and the first lunar month. All the copper and tin incense burners, candlesticks, and the copper pieces on the cages and utensils at home should be polished and cleaned, because she believes that "would be dead if you don't wipe copper in the new year". When sweeping the tomb in spring and autumn, she would prepare tin foil to burn, before the arrival of the Mid-Autumn Festival in July on the lunar calendar, she would make paper ingots and origami clothes to burn during the ancestor sacrifice. Every date of our ancestors died, she had to prepare a few bowls of food and burn some paper ingots. For the Buddha, for the exception of Guanyin, which was worshiped at home, she did not seem to worship very much. She neither went to the temple for burning incense, nor did she read Buddhist scriptures and knock on wooden fish at home. She believed the Taoist, this may be because the grandfather often set up a dais and invited Taoist chanting had a profound influence on her mind. Every father's birthday, she always invite a Taoist priest to come to "Rid taisui". When I was young, she used to ask a Taoist priest to pray "get through barrier" for me several times, and when other family's children to do "get through barrier", she always asked me follow them to do the same. When I was a child, on the first and fifteenth day of every month, she would ask me to offer incense to the sky in the front and rear courtyards, as well as to the Wenchang Emperor, Kuixing and Kitchen God placed in the hall. When I was a child, there was a witch who worshiped the Three Generals as my foster mother, which was also a manifestation of her belief in Taoist. My mother worshiped the kitchen god very much and the annual sacrifice was very ceremonious. She especially believed in the Land God, whenever something unclear happened to her family, someone was sick, something important was missing, or she wished for something, she would turn to the Land God for help. When the matter was settled, she also wished to give rewards after the incident, and she never went back on her word. If the catastrophe was eliminated she would make her own rice dumplings and place them on the ground at the gate to be served to the Land God, and also burnt paper ingots made of tin foil. If it was just a small misfortune, she would only use the small noodles she bought as offerings and burn the money she bought. Every time my mother thought that the Land God was the top spirit.

Because my mother rejoices to the sun, the magpie and the Land God, my father often jokingly her said that these three treasures were always hidden in her heart.

Gratitude to Mother

My mother attached great importance to my studies. No matter how difficult it was at home, she must tried to let me go to school and wouldn't let me be a tradesman's apprentice. She did not expect much of me, just thought that after reading a few years of foreign books, I should had an "iron rice bowl" for life, just like some uncles and cousins of my maternal grandfather. But her wish did not come true, when I was in middle school, the Northern expedition took place, and none of those units recruit new staff. Therefore, my mother waited year after year and I had to continue my study until I entered the University. I could graduate from University mainly because of my mother's insistence on her wishes and my excellent academic performance, and in the last two years with the financial support of my two sisters enabled me to complete my University study. But I had never forgotten my mother's kindness, she put up with all kinds of hardships to cultivate me.

Another thing I was also grateful for my mother kindness, she found a good wife for me as a lifelong partner. I was influenced by the feudal idea of "men and women should not be too intimate" since childhood. When I was very young, I didn't had much contact with the girls from my relatives and neighbors. The schools I went to, including high school and college were only accept boys, so I did not have any opportunity to socialize with young girl. In addition, I was diligent in studying. and didn't spend my time or my mood to meet any girlfriend. If only depended on myself, I really did not know when I would get married. When I was in high school, someone took a fancy to me, a bookworm, and offered me a girl from their family, and asked my mother for advice. Their family were better than our family, but my mother did not want any of this, she wants a good, thrifty girl for my wife. When asked, she would politely say that I was not yet established and would not talk about it. I wonder if she ever had a girl in her mind, for she never talks to me about finding a mate for me, perhaps for fear of interfering with my studies. In 1925, my 4th uncle was dying, he told to my mother he hope his third daughter Pinying, the poor girl to marry me.

At that time my mother promised that, if I could become a talent, she would accept Pinying as daughter-in-law. My mother concealed this from me, and did not tell me about that, so I did not know whether she had taken a fancy to her long ago. But one thing was certain, she would rather want a virtuous and thrifty girl whose parents were dead than a spoiled girl from a rich family. The girl married to my younger brother was also a lonely cousin, a virtuous and thrifty wife.

I never left my mother until I was twenty-one, except for living in a middle school for one and a half years, boarding in a University for two and a half years, and going to Shanghai for more than a month in the summer of 1928. Even during in school, weekends and summer and winter vacations were mostly spent with my mother. It was not until the summer of 1930, when I went to University in Shanghai, that I left my mother's house. In early 1932, just before six months I would graduate from university, my parents suddenly asked me to get married. They brought Pin Ying to Shanghai to marry me, I guess they did it for a purpose. They want me after graduation return to Fuzhou work, and could live with them, thinking that if I had a wife in Fuzhou, I would definitely go back. But before graduate in summer, I was offered a teacher position in University and did not want to go back. This of course disappointed them, especially my mother, they had already found a job in Fuzhou for me in advance, as a teacher in Trinity High School, where I had studied. This job was not suitable for my major, so I did not want to settle for it. At the same time, I didn't like the backward situation in my hometown.

I went home in the summer, discussed with Pinying and decided to bring her to Shanghai. This decision disappointed my parents even more, because my mother had a strong feudal thought that daughter-in-law should stay with the old elderly and serve them. At first, she objected strongly, because I was very determined, then she put forward the condition that I should send 50 yuan every month to support the elderly, and I should repay my two sisters more than 200 yuan of tuition that they supported me in the last two years. My monthly salary was only 75 yuan, if there was no extra income, it could not even afford to live for two in Shanghai. But I was sure I could make ends meet with a tutorship student, and would be able to maintain the difficult days. So I promised the old elderly the conditions, sending them 60 yuan a month, using 50 yuan as alimony, and 10 yuan as the amortization of the two sisters. Only in this way, I could move my wife and me out of my hometown Fuzhou to settle down in Shanghai, up to now. Our life was really difficult at the beginning. When we left home, we had only bring an old bed cabinet and a wooden box with us to Shanghai to form a new family. It could be said that we had nothing but hands, we could meet in difficult situations. But we were freed from difficulties very quickly, the better the future, the richer the family. If it were not for a hardworking wife, I did not know how have overcome such difficulties.

Because I had always kept my mother's kindness in raising me through my University education and finding a good wife in my heart, I had little resentment for the temporary difficulties that my mother had caused me during this period. In those days a man could live well with a dozen yuan a month. The 50 yuan alimony I remitted each month was more than enough. Later I learned that my parents had used the extra money to build ancestral tombs. Some of them superstition thoughts, I understand them. They thought would do this, and our ancestors would bless their children, make them prosperous, that make me considerate of them.

Parents Come to Shanghai

After I with Pinying settled in Shanghai, I wanted to find a suitable place to pick up our parents to Shanghai for living together. From 1933 to 1934, Pinying aborted twice in succession, which required our mother's care. In 1934, the Kuomintang 19th Route army General Uprising and the establishment of the People's Government took place in Fuzhou. For avoid chaos the two elderly rushed to Shanghai. At that time, I lived in Anrenli, Beijing West Road, with only one front room, so I had to immediately move to Wanhangdu Road on the second floor of a building in Xinyi Village a house in the new style. My parents lived downstairs and I lived in the pavilion with Pinying, and the former building was sublet with a colleague from the same town. A few months later, I shared a house with two of my sisters in a newly built three-story building opposite Xinyi Village. This place was named Yongle Village. We lived on the number 11th and had a total of eight rooms, which was quite comfortable. My eldest sister and second sister lived separately in the front room on the third floor and the second floor, and our parents lived in the back room on the second floor. I and Pinying lived in the back room on the third floor. The small pavilion room on the second floor was used by as my study room, the large pavilion room on the third floor was used by my eldest sister, the front and back halls downstairs were used as guest rooms and dining rooms, and the toilets on the second floor were also shared by everyone. With the care of my mother, Pinying had to keep her third pregnancy and gave birth to her first son in January 1935. The birth of the son made my parents extremely happy, especially my father. He loved the first grandson very much, and besides taking a walk in the park, he also had fun at home. During this period, my parents lived with us and it was the happiest time of their lives.

At this time there was a conflict between my mother and me. Under the influence of the old ideas, she was determined to have a maid to serve her, while I was opposed to keeping slaves and maid servants in my home. I thought it was inhumane. But the 6th aunts in Nanjing sent my mother a little girl, called Chunrong. At that time, the 6th uncle was the secretary of the Kuomintang Party History Compilation Committee, and he had the way to buy cheap girls plundered by the Kuomintang troops from Jiangxi. His family had bought two or three girls, Chunrong. being one of them, small and very thin. At the end of 1935, Chunrong was sent to my mother in Shanghai, both of her hands of chilblains chapped erosion, not only would not do any thing, but also need Pinying for medicine dressing and take care of her. She drowned almost every night, and I joked about letting her sleep in the bathtub. Once she was found stealing food in the kitchen of the next house, which made me feel extremely angry. About this girl, conflict with my mother was inevitable, and then my mother returned to Fuzhou with Chunrong. Later, my mother probably felt it was not a good idea to keep such a girl, so she sold Chunrong to the second daughter of my eldest uncle. I was deeply sorry to hear that Chunrong soon became ill and died, This incident made me think that I was lack of virtue in my life. I deeply regret it.

In 1936, my younger brother graduated from Tsinghua University, and my parents wanted him to get married first. They returned to Fuzhou in the first half of the year. I moved to University for temporary stay, and my two sisters moved to Jianguo West Road and Fuxing Middle Road respectively. During the summer, I returned to Fuzhou to pick up Pinying and my son return back to Shanghai, and lived in an old house allocated by the University. At the beginning of the next year, I obtained a teaching position at the Lester Engineering College and moved to Yongle Village. At this time we lived on the fourth floor, except the third floor which we sublet to other people, and we used most of the house. It was very comfortable. After marriage, my younger brother with his wife went to Beijing, and our parents had no one to tack care in Fujian, so they came to Shanghai again. At this time, we were not only had grandson, but also had a new born granddaughter, that were enough to entertain our parents and make them happy. My father also named his granddaughter, our parents do not dote on their granddaughter as they do on their grandson. In the summer of that year, the tenant on the third floor moved away, so our family lived in the whole house alone, which was more spacious. Therefore, my parents lived in the front room on the second floor, my wife and I with two children lived in the front room on the third floor, the guest hall on the ground floor served as the study, the pavilion and the back room on the second and third floors were all empty. The building faces south, and there was a large private garden in front of it, so it gentle breeze in summer and quite cool inside. At this time, enough furniture had been added to the home, and a maid was employed, the life could be said very good, our parents were of course extremely satisfied.

Good Time did not Last Long

Unfortunately, the good times were not long, the summer was not over, War of Resistance Against Japan exploded on August 13. My younger brother with his wife in Beijing soon took refuge in Shanghai, and then returned to Fuzhou with our parents. By the end of the year, Shanghai had fallen, and Huxi had become a dead ground. I had to move to live at No. 3 Yucun Village, Huier Road in the French Concession. This house was similar to Yongle Village, except that each floor was not divided into front and back rooms, so the depth of the room was quite longer. We rented some rooms from the fellow countryman where we lived. They lived on the third floor. We first lived on the first and second floor. After then, they took back the ground floor guest house for their own use. We only lived in the front room on the second floor and the pavilion room. In 1939, I introduced my younger brother to work as a teacher in Lester Engineering College. At this time, Fuzhou also fell, and our parents had come to Shanghai again and lived in my home or my second sister's home. Since then, several unfortunate incidents had occurred. First, my son was scalded by boiling water. Later, my second brother-in-law was killed by car accident in Berlin Germany. Soon my father began to get ill and my family entered a bumpy period. If my father's illness was today, it was possible to be cured, but at that time, my mother refused to send my father to hospital for treatment, thinking that he was suffering from an incurable disease, and eventually died. My mother thought my father should die at home, and advocated use Chinese medicine for treatment, but there were no any improvement until my father died in early 1941. At this time, my second sister and her children returned to Fuzhou one year ago and lived in our old house in Zheng's mansion. After my father died, my mother rushed back to Fuzhou, with two of her daughters together to prepare my father's funeral in Fuzhou. In fact, my father's funeral was carried out in full accordance with the old tradition familiar pattern of mourning. It was more than a year before my mother came to Shanghai again.

When Pinying and I had one son and a daughter, we did not want to have any more children again, so we tried birth control. My mother was extremely dissatisfied, had taught us countless times to ask us had to raise more children, because she thought that there was only one son was too weak and also uninsured. As a result, It took more than five years after the birth of our daughter, we added two more boys one after another.

Not long after my father died, my daughter did not be well because of measles and gradually developed into tracheitis, pneumonia and pleuritis. As a result, the hydrops in the chest became suppurative. After three hospitalizations and three major operations, she recovered, costing a lot of money. I had stomach problems myself and had several episodes of stomach bleeding. At the same time, due to the economy collapsed with the fake currency flooded, the real purchasing power of my salary became lower and lower, so that it was difficult to maintain a family life. At the beginning of 1943, I took a job in a biochemical pharmaceutical factory, with an increase of income, but only a slight respite. During this time two sons were added to my family, with the population increased, my wife Piying got extremely hate hemorrhoid disease, had two times operations, was really poor and ill, even more difficult. My old mother, who was almost in sparse age, also suffered for several years, and I still feel uneasy now. Our family had no choice but to return home on a sailing boat in April 1945. Soon after arriving in Fuzhou, I was fortunate to work in a Unit of the American army with a very high monthly salary and abundant life in my family. At this time, my mother had been living in her favorite old house, My younger brother and his children also came back to Fuzhou meet together. Pinying and I took our children to live in the unit dormitory. Less than half a year, the victory coming, the War of Resistance against Japanese aggression ended, the Unit revocation. I returned to Shanghai, Pinying and the children moved back to our old house, Zheng's mansion. My younger brother's family went to Yongan. So during this time, my mother was accompanied by many adult and children in our family. At that time she was less than 70 years old, quite healthy. In addition to my children in the home, there were two elder sister's orphans one son and one daughter, and a son and a daughter of Pinying brother were also in our home. Because of all of them were no mother, and needed Pinying to care. There were so many children, she felt very happy, without any complaints. There was a maid to help my mother do housework, so my mother was not too hard.

In early 1946, I returned to Fuzhou to work in the Fujian office of the Disaster Relief Department, I spent a year and a half in Fuzhou living with my mother and my family in our old house Zheng's mansion. until the Fujian office closed in October 1947. I went to Shanghai again, shortly after my arrival at the end of 1947, I joined the Asian Oil Company at the beginning of 1948. The monthly salary was very high, and my family economic situation had greatly improved. Pinying had traveled between Fujian and Shanghai several times. Except that our eldest son had already come to Shanghai and studied in middle school, the other three children remained in Fuzhou. Later, because my younger brother got a scholarship for studying in the UK, and his wife brought their children back to Fuzhou to stay with our mother.

Memorable Happy Hour

In 1949, just before the liberation of Shanghai, my mother was 70 years old. She was impressed by the tradition of celebrating birthday from her grandfather, So that the 70th birthday must be celebrated, although Fuzhou was facing liberation, the people life were very unstable, but she still want to Pinying to arrange a big banquet for celebrating her 70 birthday, so she had a large feast and lively day. Just over a month later, Fuzhou was be liberated. Soon Pinying took the first postal bus to Shanghai with three children. At this time I had moved to the current site at Jiangsu Road. The spacious house with a front garden was more comfortable than any house I had ever lived before. My mother was accompanied by my younger brother's family stayed in Fuzhou, and I remitted a considerable sum of money every month for the their using. More than a year later, my mother came to Shanghai with my nephew. Since prices were stable after liberation and my salary was high, our life was better than ever before. Of course my mother was extremely satisfied. For several years, 4th aunt, cousin and my eldest sister in Shanghai often came to live in my home and accompany my mother to go to the theater every day. Sometimes they play Mahjong at home. Pinying and I also participated. Every year on my mother's birthday, Spring Festival, National Day and Labor Day, I had a banquet in the restaurant. At that time, we were almost eaten in all famous restaurants in Shanghai. This period could be said to be the happiest time in my mother life.

But my mother was also unhappy because she ate too well, especially in 1952, our family ate chicken, duck, fish with other good food almost every day. My mother ate too much meat and to be fat. Sometimes she felt chest discomfort and thought was sick and depressed. Later, I invited my classmate, who was also a doctor, to examine my mother and told her that her heart was not sick, she felt sad because her body fat was too much, which made her heart very depressed. My mother felt relieved after hearing this, and at the same time she pays attention to eating less fatty dishes, and the feeling of illness also disappears.

Since 1951, Pinying had participated in the District Women's Federation, created a nursery in the district, and was responsible for the work of nurseries and kindergartens. Pinying go out to work during the day. When there were no guests to be companions, my mother felt that she could only play the game of "passing five levels" with Pai Gow poker at home, which was too lonely and dreary. This year, she went back to Fuzhou by land, then lived with her nephew's granddaughter who lived in Zheng's mansion she also the eldest uncle's granddaughter. This house was my mother asked me to bought from the Le-6th Fang when we returned to Fujian in 1945. Later, she felt that not satisfied with the life in Fuzhou, so she came to Shanghai with her neighbor who opened a tea shop in Shanghai. In the second half of 1952, I went to Xiamen on a business trip for the Asia Oil Company. At that time, my younger Brother had returned back China and as a teacher worked at Xiamen University, with whole of his family lived in University campus. Before the end of the year, my younger brother went to Beijing on business, when he went back to Xiamen pass by Shanghai, my mother went to Xiamen with him. My mother lived in Xiamen for only a short period of time, then she got bored, she went back to Fuzhou and lived with 9th aunt for a while, because of uncomfortable then my mother came back to Shanghai, after that she never left Shanghai again.

My aunt, cousin, sister (they and my mother used to call themselves "the four Evils") came to our house more often to keep my mother from feeling lonely. In 1957, unfortunately my younger brother was labeled as the rightist. My mother was deeply touched and very unhappy. In 1958 my family moved from downstairs to upstairs. my mother lived more comfortably, but because she was nearly eighty years old, she couldn't go out to the theatre as often as before. At the same time, she was often depressed about my younger brother situation. In the following years, China entered a so-called "difficult" period, and the supply of non-staple food was extremely short. Although she was suffering from nothing to eat, I brought back a portion of the meat dishes that from outside for her every day, but the amount was limited, unable to meet her requirements.

She was more upset that cakes and biscuits and fruit were hard to find on the market, which makes her unhappy. 1959 was her eighty years old, and was also the most difficult period. But I still held a feast for her outside, of course, very different from her hopes. In November of 1959 the daughter gave birth to a son for the first time after her marriage, and My mother was delighted to see her fourth generation.

Before and After Mother Death

In 1961, my family bought a black-and-white TV set, which was transported from Beijing to Shanghai by air. I originally wanted to have this machine, my mother could watch some plays at home every night to entertain her old age. A few days later, she opened a drawer in her room, broke her hip and was bedridden. We used an ambulance sent her to the hospital for filming. The diagnosis was a cracked hip bone. The doctor thought he needed hospitalization. At the age of 82, she refused to be hospitalized, let alone undergo surgery, she had to go home and bedridden. Due to the severe pain, she could not move, and soon she developed bedsores on her back. Although she had been treated by doctor, but she could no to return my mother's life. She finally died at home nineteen days after falling. My brother came from Xiamen before my mother was close to death, but she was already unconscious. In accordance with the customs of our hometown, we had a big funeral for her in the hall of the World Funeral Home on the same day, and dozens of relatives, friends and colleagues came. She had already bought very good coffin materials in Fuzhou many years ago, but when shipped to Shanghai, she passed away prematurely and was inconvenient to use. It was a pity for that, late resold to others for a price of 1,000 yuan. During the funeral, we set up a worship for her at Jing'an Temple to inform relatives and friends in Shanghai to come to express condolences. There was a cemetery in Zhabei District, Shanghai, named Lianyi Mountain Villa, and there was Kang youwei's name on the archway at the gate.

There were a lot of elegant tombs built by Shanghai's large merchants and some celebrities were buried there, which was already very crowded. I spent hundreds of dollars, only bought a cemetery on the edge, moved my mother's coffin from the World Funeral Home to the earth, and covered it with concrete and erected stone tablets. I originally planned to wait a few years for my mother's remains to be moved back in Fuzhou, then buried in our ancestral tomb.

Unexpectedly, the "Cultural Revolution" broke out in 1966, the entire Lianyi Mountain Villa was completely destroyed, the land was taken by nearby factories, and the mother's remains were buried deeply. At that time, I was in a very difficult situation. I couldn't even go to see it. So far I still don't know where my mother's remains were. The ancestral graves in Fuzhou were also excavated shortly. The remains of grandparents, uncles and fathers were all buried on the top of Gaogai Mountain, and could not be visit them at all. It was normal for people to go to graves and sweep tombs in spring and autumn every year. Descendants who had left their hometowns regard sweep tombs as their top priority whenever they return to their hometowns. Not only I could not sacrifice my ancestral tomb when I return home, but my mother buried in Shanghai had no tomb, what inconceivable was?

CHAPTER 9

First Education

My Private School

Adults said I began to read at the age of three, but also said vividly that I recognize the word "call" situation. That I was holding a tablet of the word "call" in my hand and read aloud "call, which means to call a girl in the countryside". In fact, I did not recognize many words before school, because adults did not teach me in a planned way, but sometimes taught me as play. I was in a private school when I was 6 years old, when my cousin Meng Ge set up a private school in the back hall of Zheng's mansion. to enlighten students, many children of the Zheng's Family were entrusted to him for study. But my parents did not hand me over to him, because he did not get anything, he was a "White Ding". My parent intention was to find a teacher who had been a talented person (Xiucai or Juren) or a celebrity to enlighten me and ask me to follow virtuous teacher study well.

Just in Xiaolingding near my house, there was a school teacher named Chen chengfu in the hall of my eldest sister residence. He was the same ancestor as my eldest brother-in-law, he was a scholar (Xiucai), and had a talent in writing, he wrote very well. My mother decided send me to him. On the first day I was sent to him, and I brought incense. When I got there, I was asked to bow down to the sacred candlestick of the

Most Holy Master Confucius, and then asked me to bow to the teacher. There were already several schoolchildren in the school, some of them read “The Beginning of Man”, some read “Thousand Characters”, and some read “Childhood Qionglin”. Somehow, my parents did not want me to read these enlightenment textbooks first, but asked me to read The Analects and Mencius. The teacher taught me a paragraph every day and asked me to recite it to him the next day. I read it aloud in the school like a Buddhist monk. Since I had a strong memory, did not read it a few times and memorize it, but Teacher Chen still want me to read it. But I did not understand much about what was described in the book, or seem to understand. Later, I also added the Book of Songs and the Book of Classics, which made me even more ignorant.

Every day, I had to practice writing with brush strokes. At the beginning, I used red strokes, but I still had not mastered good writing skills. In the Zhong Hall, there were the gods of Wenchang emperor and Kuixing. The teacher asked students to bows every day of the first and fifteenth day per mouth. In the summer of Fuzhou, there was plague pandemic and a lot of people died. The teacher asked the students to line up every morning when they were enrolled in the school. There was also a god called Tengshan White Horse King in the hall. Teacher Chen was quite superstitious about this god. He said that there was a fire nearby, and the house where the private school was located in danger of being burned. Fortunately, the white horse king rode around on the top of the fence to protect the house. When he talked, he made a roaring sound as if hearing it with his own ears. He spoke arrogantly, and the students believed that.

In August, Confucius was born, on his day, teachers stopped teaching for one day. let the students play in the school, and eat that they brought. I still remember that everyone was very happy that day. But I was no idea what Mr. Chen had done in past. I had only seen him write couplets on several occasions. was the couplet written by him? Did he got pay for couplets? I do not know. When he taught me, he was probably over 50 years old. He had severe lung disease and was very thin. He fell ill the next year, and I dropped out of school, so, I had get his taught less than two years.

Recall that for more than a year, in addition to memorizing part of the Analects, Mencius, Book of Songs and Book of Classics, I also read Zuo Zhuan and a few ancient essays, and I would also memorize them well. I had also imitated several papers written, most of them were empty talks like travel notes. In addition, because of my familiarity, I could recite the enlightenment books that my classmates read. If I say that I had not learned anything in private school for more than a year, that was not necessarily the case. I always recognize a lot of words and recite some useful words and phrases. If said I had learned a lot in this year, that may be not necessarily true.

In short, the ratio of my knowledge to the time spent could be said the loss outweights the gain. With my understanding and memory, if I could get the right teaching from a good teacher and read the appropriate book, I believe I could benefit more. During this period, I went to school during the day, and at night my mother still supervised me under the lamp. Although she did not know how many words, but she could hear the missing or added words in the book I recite. At that time there was no electric light at home, so I studied under the oil lamp. Only then did I discover that I had night blindness. Under the dim light of the oil lamp, the big characters could not be seen clearly, let alone the small ones. It was often necessary to wipe my eyes with hands and squint to read the characters before you could barely see them. Night blindness was caused by a lack of vitamin A. Later, someone taught my mother to cook lamb liver with stew chaff for me to eat, and I did get better after eating it, probably because that was rich in vitamin A. I've had this prescription for years, but I only take it when I need. Later, the doctor's uncle recommended me to take cod liver oil for several years. In fact, in addition to my night blindness, my eyes also had problems with astigmatism and presbyopia. It was a pity that no one wore glasses for children at that time. I suffered for many years because I did not wear glasses. After I entered school, the words used in textbooks were all very small, especially in English-Chinese dictionaries, which made more difficult for me to read.

Yiwenshe Primary School

After Mr. Chen died, my mother couldn't find a good teacher nearby to teach me, so I dropped out of school at home. At this time, my father came back from the Northeast and was at home. He taught me to continue reading Mencius, Zuo Zhuan and some ancient writings. After I finished reading Zhongmeng (Mengzi's second volume was Le Lou), one day he asked me to carry this volume from head to toe, and I stood in front of him and carried it out. I got appreciated. I like Zuozhuan very much, because there were a lot of stories in it. My father had a copy of Zuo Zhuan Hua Hua, edited by Lin Shu, which he used as supplementary textbook. Unfortunately, my father was so eager to find a job at this time. he was in a very bad mood and failed to teach me well. At the same time, he was worried about whether I would be able to earn a living when I grew up. He always thought "chicken up jin, child up ten". If my mother allows me to be an apprentice, I may stop studying in the future and change my life. But my mother insisted that I read more, then I could have an "iron rice bowl", not afraid of unemployment, and regarded as a noble profession.

Fortunately, my father found a job and left home. My mother sent me to a nearby Yiwenshe Primary School. The primary school was located in the Ancestral Hall of Zhu Zi in Xiaoling Lane, very close to my home. I didn't know if it's official or not? When I go in? which class? What books to read? I did not have any impressions now, but I was first introduced to arithmetic there, and I soon rejoiced in this subject. I had studied in this primary school for less than one year, I stopped attending classes because I was moving.

Teacher We Family School

In 1920, My 4th uncle and 6th aunts bought a house in Meiwu. This house was originally built by Sheng Yuan Qianzhuang, so everyone called it Sheng Yuan. The house was three two-story old-fashioned houses, with a hall in the middle downstairs, a back hall in the back, and two front and back rooms next to each other. A thick iron door leads to the front room. This room was dark and wet. It only used for hold things, no one could live in it. There was a small patio in front of the hall. On one side of the patio was the compartment rooms and on the other side was the entrance hall. There was a gate leading to the road outside. Upstairs, there was only the back hall and the two front and back rooms and the compartment room. There was a large kitchen outside the right wall, and the ladder upstairs was located in that wall. The house had been equipped with electric lights, so no oil lamps were used for lighting at night.

The 4th uncle and 6th aunts used the right and left sides of the house, and the front and back halls and kitchen in the middle were shared. The 4th uncle used the anterior room downstairs as a practice clinic, and the wing room downstairs as a medicine room. All of 4th uncle's family lived in the anterior and posterior wing room upstairs and the posterior room downstairs. The 6th aunt's family lived in the anterior room and wing rooms upstairs, while the posterior room upstairs, and the anterior room downstairs were basically empty and unoccupied. The 4th uncle had four daughters and two sons. Except for the youngest daughter who was adopted by the 5th uncle, the rest were at home and had not yet married. Because the 4th aunts had passed away, later the 4th uncle remarried and gave birth to a boy and a daughter.

Apart from the couple, the 6th aunts had one stepdaughter and one son, only a few people. The 6th uncle often work in other places, the whole family followed, their home were empty. Therefore, the 6th aunts invited my mother to move in and help take care of their house when they left Fuzhou. My mother spend most time in the back room upstairs and only moved to the front room downstairs when my father returned shortly. The three daughters around the 4th uncle were all older than me, so they were all my elder cousins, and Pinying was one of them. One of the two sons was also elder than me, was my elder cousin, and the other was born the same year as me, but younger than me, so became my younger male cousin. Except the oldest female cousin who took care of the housework, also took care of her siblings at home, the other four all go to school. When my family moved in, the 6th aunts were all in Fuzhou. My second sister and my younger brother lived with our mother. So there were five girls and five boys in the same house. The five girls were elder than me, except for one boy, I was the eldest, and the 6th aunt's son was the youngest, but it was only three or four years younger than me. Four boys of similar age often play together in the hall, and the 6th uncle treats us as the four characters in "Journey to the West ". He shielded his son and called him a Tang monk. My 4th uncle's son of the same age of mine, born in Malaya, was naughty and called Sun Wukong. my younger brother was often bullied and liked to complain to adults. he was called Zhu Bajie, and I was called Sha Wujing. However, although the young Tang monk was 6 or 7 years old, he still Standing up to move bowels. He was savage because he was coddled by his parents. He liked to beat people. He often bullied my younger brother. He was honest only when he was standing up to move bowels. Therefore, he really was not worthy of being a Tang monk. The four boys eat together at the time of reconciliation, and each of them takes out their pastries and eats together, just like a few big girls get together to spend money on food. At that time, adults could take things not used at home, such as old clothes and daily necessities exchange pastries with hawkers. The little Tang monk especially liked to eat orange-red cakes and plantain sugar, and once brought a large bowl to change, which made the adults laugh. He had not yet reached school age, and my younger brother went to nearby elementary school with his cousin Sun Wukong after moving to Shengyuan. My mother did not let me go to elementary school, but wanted to find a good school teacher to teach me. Before I found the teacher, the 6th uncle taught me. Although this period was short, I had read a lot of ancient texts and poems, and some of them I could still recite it today.

There was a customs broker named JinJi near Meiwu sheng yuan, the boss was very wealthy, but also some knowledge. He had several daughters. The eldest daughter was married and had two grandchildren, one older than me and one younger than me. The businessman attached great importance to the study of his grandson and specially invited a teacher named Wei to set up a school at his home to teach them to study. There was a garden in his house, and the family school was located in the flower hall beside the garden. My mother heard about this and asked the boss to let me go to the school. Teacher Wei was a Juran and was over half a hundred years old. He was very thin and I did not know whose idea, asked me to study the dry and useless Zhou Li. But Teacher Wei also taught me how to write ancient poems and how to make pairs. I really like to make a pair. After the teacher asked a question, I always get the fastest and most complete. Once, a teacher came to the family school and asked the three of us to make a pair. The sentence I praised was appreciated by him. This fact showed that I had learned a lot from Teacher Wei. Unfortunately, after several months, Teacher Wei passed away due to illness, so I once again lost the opportunity to study well. He was another school teacher who died in the middle of teaching me. The death of the two school teachers became a precedent for many events in pairs in my life, because such things had happened many times in my later life.

While studying at the JinJi Customs Brokerage Office, I was quite happy, because the garden was just outside the family school, sometimes I could play inside the garden. Probably because I was very handsome when I was a kid, and the clothes were neatly dressed, the two or three girls of JinJi's boss liked me a lot, and sometimes took me to play in the garden under the flower shed. But the good times were not long.

The 4th Uncle's Medicine Clinic

The 4th uncle was a Western medicine. He retired from Malaya and returned to Fuzhou. He wanted to open a clinic in Shengyuan to practice medicine with attached a pharmacy to sell medicine. During this period, every time I fell ill, of course to asked my 4th uncle. In the summer of 1919, cholera was prevalent in Fuzhou, and there were many deaths. One day, I suffered from vomiting and diarrhea due to inadvertent eating. I was so afraid that was cholera, which was in critical condition. Fortunately, after my 4th uncle gave me Brandy and Tincture of Goro, I recovered. Since then, I had never suffered from a similar disease, It was possible that I had a real cholera and was cured and immune. I no longer suffer from the same kind disease. I was afraid to meet the 4th uncle, but I was very interested in the room where he opened the clinic. The furnishings were very simple. Several pieces of furniture were brought from Nanyang, which was quite chic. The writing desk placed in the middle of the room, it could be completely covered. The cover was composed of flexible plates. When pulled down, it become a quarter circle on the entire desktop, that was the little frame that showed the back. When pushed, it revealed the small frame behind it, the four treasures and so on, placed on each floor of the shelf. His chair could be rotated and could be adjusted in height. There were some rattan seats and a bed with backrest, that could be used for both sitting and lying. There was also a rocking chair that could swing back and forth, when lying down which was very comfortable. There were two extra large pictures hanging on the interior wall, one was the grandfather and the other one himself. They were basically just head-shots, at least 18 inches high and 14 inches wide. Both were wearing suits, which were extremely fashionable at the time. A coat and hat stand made of antlers was suspended from a post. The antlers were real, and the heads of the deer were made of wood, which looked more like the heads of horses than deer head. When my uncle was not at home, I sneaked in his room a few times to lie in a rocking chair.

The 4th uncle seemed very friendly when he didn't lose his temper or scolded others. In the summer, my 4th uncle had made soda (Dutchwater) to drink. I saw him take a glass of cold water add citric acid, stir well, then add a white medicine powder (baking soda powder), the water just like boiling with boiling many bubbles, he would drink. Once he made one cup for me, and I suddenly felt it was cool to drink. At that time, I thought that the 4th uncle could make a lot of money by selling this kind of water in the summer. He didn't seem to care about any child at all. He never talked to me, but once I heard his talking about me in the clinic with some adults (the oldest uncles, 6th uncles, etc.) in the clinic. The thing about reading. At that time, I was taught by Teacher Wei, and I heard he said, "TaunTaun could to learn geology when grow up." I heard this sentence even if I did not to ask why he had this idea, and what was the purpose of study geology? Later, when I recalled this matter, I realized that people around world were looking for oil mines at the time, and those who found oil mines made a fortune. Perhaps my uncle thought that I should do such a fortune. I only heard he said this time, never heard he talk about me again.

My primary school

After Teacher Wei died, I temporarily suspended school. It was in the fall of 1922 I entered a primary school to continue my studying. This was the second elementary school I entered, But the new primary school attached to the Trinity Middle School run by the Anglican Church. In this elementary school, I learned a lot of new things, such as Arithmetic, History, Geography, English, Music, Drawing and Crafts. I had a very good brain for studying Mathematics, and soon caught up with the rest of the class in arithmetic. I also like drawing and handwork, but because the eye was bad, drawing was bad, also could not make good craftsmanship. I did not like music because I had a poor voice and could not sing well. I also took physical education for the first time, but because of my weak body, I could not learn any sports well, but other homework was pretty good. In this elementary school, I only read for one year. At the end of the first semester, my grades were excellent and ranked first in the class. The school made me jump from the second semester of the first grade to the second semester of the second grade. By the end, I got the first place again. I still had kept this year primary school report card.

At the beginning of 1922, the 4th uncle and the 6th aunt sold the Shengyuan to a bank at high price, and then bought a piece of land on the roof of Meiwu, preparing to build a private residence. During the new house was building, they temporarily moved to the two new residences built by Mr. Chen Yikai at Tianan Temple in Cangqian Mountain, and our home also moved. From there to the Trinity Primary School, I had to cross a ridge. For convenience, my 4th uncle arranged for me through the British Consulate (Fuzhou called Hongmao Mansion) go to school every day. The consulate was built on the top of the ridge. Through it, I could walk a little less. There were many peculiar plants in the consulate garden. One of them was called mimosa. Its leaves were compound and there were a row of small leaves on each side, as soon as your finger touches it, the leaves on both sides would close together and then spread out slowly. When I pass by, I often went to play.

On top of Maywood Tianan Temple was destroyed. The main hall no longer exists, only the Maitreya Hall was near the bottom of the mountain, and the Maitreya Buddha image was still there. There was a temple near the mountain, and many houses had been built next to the temple. Our house was building on a hillside beside the temple. The back of the house face northwest and overlooks the Minjiang River. When the weather was fine, we could also overlook the white pagodas and black pagodas in the city. The scenery was quite good. However, but in summer, because of the sun, it was very hot. The Minjiang River seemed to be right under your feet, the two bridges and various boats on the Minjiang river could be clearly seen. There was still a temple house nearby, called Shuang jiang tai. Looking down from the front of the platform, you could see the Minjiang river with two tributaries across the Zhongzhou Island. Every time I walked by, I would stop and watch, I felt the scenery was really beautiful. It was a pity that I don't know how to draw pictures. Second, I don't had conditional photography. I could not record that good scene, so I could only remember it from memory. During the Dragon Boat Festival that year, I enjoyed the dragon boat race from our house. That year, I did not know what kind of disease I had, every afternoon I had a bit of fever. My 4th uncle given me Quinine pills for a few months, the fever had completely disappeared. Quinine pills were very blood-enriching and long term use may be beneficial to my body. my longevity may be related to this, But my tinnitus, which was caused by it, had not gone away.

English Tutoring School

In the summer of 1922, after I finished one year of elementary school, my mother wanted me to go to middle school as soon as possible, and hoped I would go to the post, telegram or customs after a few years of middle school. At this time, Mr. Qi Weixin, the English teacher of Trinity Middle School, opened an English tutoring school in the lobby of Lingshang's temple. Teacher Qi's home lived in a house next to the temple. This house used to be the former residence of the famous Song Dynasty official Li Gang. It was called Song Feng Tang. A large pine tree planted in the patio inside the house covered the whole house like an umbrella. Mr. Qi's father's name was Qi Burch, a staff member of the British Consulate. After graduating from Trinity High School, Mr. Qi went to St. John's University in Shanghai, then returned to Fuzhou Trinity High School to teach English. He taught very well in the cram school, I had benefited a lot, and made rapid progress. When I applied for the Trinity Middle School in autumn, I was admitted. Therefore I was promoted straight from the first year of high school to middle school, I jumped two grade, so in the autumn of 1922, I entered the middle school.

Recall that when I was in the private school and primary school from the age of 6 to 13 years, I attended two private schools in seven years, died two school teachers, and entered two primary schools. I studied for less than two years, not only did I not accept systematic education, and a lot of good time wasted, was really a pity. If I had a systematic education in those days, with my intelligence and memory, I was afraid that I was not such a sparsely educated person with so little knowledge, so my childhood could be said to be semi-desolate. My mother used to say I was unlucky at school, so I could not read more old books from my school teachers, so my knowledge was very shallow. During those seven years, my knowledge basically came from the books I read, and I did not learn more at all. My father was often away from home. My mother and other adults rarely talk to me. There were no books except the four books and five classics at home. I had no chance to get in touch with new books and newspapers. And since I was a child, I was not good at asking questions, so my source of knowledge was very narrow.

During this period, except for a few days to escape the war to shanggan township, I had never been away from home, so I had little social experience. At that time, during the era of warlord separatism in China, I only knew that the governor who ruled Fujian Province was Li Houji. Who was only a small warlord, and his dominion could not be extended to the whole province. At that time, there was a bandit army in northern Fujian, whose head was Tang Xingbang, who occupied Longxi, GuTian and other counties. There was another in southern Fujian. the leader was Chen Guohui, occupying counties like Longyan and Liancheng. In the world during the First World War (people call it the European War), I did not understand the situation of the war, nor could I understand it. But I know that during that period, the price of gold was very low. Ever the low price was only about twenty silver dollars. Many rich people rushed to buy gold jewelry. Even Guanyin opened a gold shop. At the same time, due to the depreciation of the British pound, the 4th uncle monthly pension from the British consulate was getting less and less, which make him often be furious. My understanding of the society at that time was so ignorant, and I entered the middle school age so ignorantly.

CHAPTER 10
Chinese-English School

Christian Trinity Middle School

In September 1922, I passed the entrance examination for the Trinity middle school. The full name of this school was Trinity Chinese-English Middle School, which was a part of Trinity School. Trinity School was a church school founded by the Church of England in Fuzhou, and only open to boys. The Trinity took its name from the Christian Trinity (the Trinity, meaning the Trinity of the Father, Jesus the Son and the Holy Spirit). The whole school was divided into three parts: Trinity Chinese-English Middle School, Trinity Normal School and Trinity Primary School, with primary and middle schools as the main body. The normal school was small and was only used to train teachers for primary schools run by Anglican Churches in Fujian Province. The primary school was attached to the middle school and provided part of the students for the middle school. "Chinese-English" ("Han-ying" in Chinese) meant that Chinese and English were equally important in teaching. In fact, schools payed more attention to English teaching. There were eight classes every day, four in the morning were English classes, all in English, and four in the afternoon were Chinese classes, all in Chinese. The school system was eight years, students could graduate after eight years of study. Therefore, all Trinity middle school graduates could begin their third year when they enter St. John University in Shanghai.

At that time, Fuzhou had several Christian churches, all of which had their own schools, where they preached doctrine and persuaded people to believe in religion. In Cangqianshan, there was a Trinity School run by the Church of England (known in Fuzhou as the Anglian) only for boys. It also runs two girls' schools, Taoshu School and Xunzhen School. In addition, there were monasteries. American Union University and Heling Yinghua College (Middle school) only admit male students, and also founded South China Girls' University, South China Girls' Middle School and Yuying Girls' School. Fuzhou had a Gezhi Middle School run by the American Presbyterian Church; Nantai wenshan had a Catholic Middle School for boys and girls. In addition to these missionary schools, the YMCA run a middle school. Some churches were more conservative, others were more open. This was reflected in the clothes worn by the students in the school they run, especially the ordinary girls. Fuzhou people used to have a song about the girls of a missionary school:

Beauty to beauty, gold ring with gold rim glasses; Meibei Association, Lao Beibei (meaning old-fashioned), Anrijian, red and red pants white "Shirt".

Meibei Association (the Presbyterian Association)

That was fairly vividly described, the more conservative, the more religious and the more disciplined the student was.

I did not know when Trinity School was founded. All I know was the founder was an English priest and his Chinese surname was "wan" (mean ten thousand). In order to commemorate him, a small bell tower, three-story high, was built in the school, named Siwan Building. The entire campus was located at the southern foot of Cangqian Mountain, covering a considerable area. The entrance to the school gate was a straight uphill slope, with the Siwan Building on the top of the slope, on the right was a small church and on the left was the middle school building. Behind the Siwan Building, on the left was a bungalow. that was the teaching building of the normal school, on the right was the teaching building of the primary school. The middle school building was a U-shaped two-story brick-wood structure with clear red brick walls, eight classrooms, an auditorium and a canteen on the ground floor, and student dormitories on the upper floors. In the U-shaped wing, the dormitory was ten small rooms with the names A, B, C J, each room could only accommodate one senior student. The other side was also divided into small rooms for single teachers. In the middle were seven large rooms named K, L, M Q. Suitable for lower grade students. Room K had a large space above the auditorium, which could accommodate more than a dozen people. Room Q had a large area over the dining room. The remaining rooms each could accommodate eight people. The kitchen was a bungalow, built behind the canteen. The primary school building was a single-storey red brick house, only used as a classroom. There were six classrooms for the six classes of students. Facing the primary school building, there was a big banyan tree, next to the tree was a small physics and chemistry laboratory. At the bottom of the slope behind the primary school building was a large flat area with a large football field and track field. There were two large playground in front of teaching buildings of the middle and primary schools, which could also be used as sports venues. In addition, there was a small gymnasium next to the church near the school gate, so there were many sports venues on the campus. There were also small foreign buildings on campus for principals, supervisors, English teachers and some Chinese teachers to live in. There were about 100 students in each primary and middle school, so the campus looks very spacious.

Because it was a church school and the Anglican Church was very conservative, the religious atmosphere in the school was extremely strong. Before the class, we must do a short time of worship. The annual course includes reading the Bible, the New Testament and the Old Testament, must read. All the students were required to attend Sunday Morning Service. There was also a prayer meeting on Friday night, which students living in dormitories must attend. Every time I pray, sing hymns, read the Bible and pray. On Sundays, I also listen to pastors or preaching sermons and sometimes invited people from outside to preach for us. Students who eat at school must also pray before eating. Principal, all English teachers, and most Chinese teachers were Christians and most of them also serve as pastors or preachers. There were also many students from religious families who, of course, had been Baptists after baptism. For other students, the school always tried to convince them to believe. Some students were baptized and taught in church, but some remain non-religious. I was one of those who remain secular and non-religious.

I didn't believe in ghosts and gods when I was a child, and of course there was no heaven or hell. I don't believe in the saying "put down the butcher's knife and stand on the ground to become a Buddha", and "as long as bad people believe in repentance, God forgives them". What I believe was what Confucius said, "Sin in heaven, don't pray". Therefore, I think people should do good deeds, as long as they did not do bad things, they had nothing to fear. But at the same time, I recognize that religion had a role to play, it could persuade people to be good, it could also encourage people to be good from evil, it had a great role in the purification of society. No matter what kind of religion, its doctrine contained the principle of doing good, which had a positive impact on education.

I think it was a waste of time and energy to pray, repeat the same song, read the same text, and listen to the same sermon every day. Even more interesting was praying and thanking God before each meal. Later, I was disgusted with adoration. When I pray, I often secretly read the Bible by myself, from Genesis to Revelation as a novel, I was interested in the Jewish history of the Old Testament. I could say that I was very familiar with the Bible, and that so far most of its contents could be told. Some students dozed off during the sermon, others whispered, some of the worst even masturbated, and few actually listened to the sermon and prayer. In retrospect, I fond it absurd to force students to worship in a church school. After the establishment of the Kuomintang Nanjing Government, all church schools were required to cancel the compulsory participation of students in religious activities. It was not until about 1927 that Trinity School gave students the freedom to not participate, but religious students continued to perform their services at the school.

I was born in a very feudal family and my mother was very superstitious about ghosts and gods. Why should I go to a church to study? Originally, my mother's purpose was just to let me read foreign books for a few years, until I entered the third or fourth grade. When new employees were recruited by so-called units controlled by foreigners, such as the post office, telegraph or customs office, could apply for a job and then hold the so-called iron rice bowl for life. The mother's 7 th uncle's second son Zhao Zhang uncle, the 3rd uncle's eldest son Qi Fu cousin and 4th uncle's eldest son Bingfu cousin and so on, relatives and a few young people I knew were all like this. So in the years after I entered middle school, my mother always encouraged me to study hard and be ready to take the iron rice bowl when I had a chance. She never barred me from being a religious person. Instead, she told me to obey all the school rules, whatever the school was asked to do, including praying and reading the Bible. My disbelief could be said to be entirely my own choice. Individual teachers and classmates also advised me to believe in religion, and I insisted on my own belief. I did not want to be a pious or nominal religious immigrant, and I did not want to be easily favored by forcigners in order to work in a foreign institution.

When I entered the school, the principal was British Williams. He used "Lai Bi Han" as his Chinese name. Everyone called him "Lai Lai" or "Mr. Lai". In addition to being a headmaster and teacher, he was a clergyman. Later he got married, and his wife was also a teacher at the school, which was dubbed "Laim" by the students. Other British teachers include Collins and his wife "Com", teacher Gao, and teacher Kong. Mr. Kong also served as the principal of the Primary School, and Mr. Gao also manages the Normal School. They were both priests. Then came two English teachers who taught Mathematics, Physics and Chemistry, teacher Miller taught Mathematics, and teacher Carpente taught Physics and Chemistry. Chinese teachers include Zhang Guangxu, Zhang Boshi (Zhirou), Chen Shizhong and Qi Weixin. There were also two teachers who specialize in teaching Chinese, teacher Chen and teacher Guo, both of them were passed the imperial examinations. Later, teacher Zhao was invited to replace teacher Chen, who was also passed the imperial examination. Except my Chinese teacher, all the Chinese teachers were Christians and some also serve as pastors or preachers. There was a supervisor under the principal to manage the students. When I entered the school, the supervisor was Mr. Song. Later, he died and was replaced by Mr. Tong.

Bilingual education

Unlike other middle schools, the trinity of Chinese-English middle schools could learn Chinese and English respectively. Some students only had Chinese classes, others only had English classes. The students took part time Chinese and English classes may not be in the same class, but most of the students took part time Chinese and English classes were in the same class. The school attached great importance to English class. The class time was arranged in the morning, six days a week, four classes a day and twenty-four classes full. According to the school report form, students must study a total of 30 subjects after eight years of study. But I suspect that there were individual classes that could not be opened. For example, 11 of the 30 lessons were related to English, including reading, practicing reading (i.e. reciting), speaking (i.e. dialogue, conversation) and intercepting characters (i.e. pinyin), memorization, practice writing, composition, letters, translation, grammar and literature. There were other 11 courses in mathematics and physics, including arithmetic, algebra, geometry, trigonometry and science (scientific common sense), physics, chemistry, astronomy, botany physiology and sexology. The remaining 8 subjects were Bible, history, geography, economics, theory, French, pictures and physical education. The content of these courses could be extremely rich, but some courses took very little time, and some were not even opened. Only eight subjects were taught in the first year, and the number was increasing year by year. In the sixth grade, you had 15 subjects to study. In eighth grade (that is, the senior year), you might add a little more. All morning classes were taught in English, and all used textbooks were in English except French.

Chinese language classes were scheduled in the afternoon, five days a week, four classes a day, and twenty classes were full. The content of the course was mainly 20 Chinese language courses, including vernacular Chinese, ancient Chinese, the Analects of Confucius, idioms, composition, discussion, scripture reading, Sanmeng, Zishu, Zhuangzi, Zuozhuan, Shiji Qinghua, history, rulers, celebrity books, Tang poetry, poetry selection, literary history, grammar and writing origin. In addition, there were 8 classes for History, Geography, Arithmetic, Legal system, Ethics, Sociology, Citizenship, and the Three People Principles, of which the last 3 classes were added after the establishment of the Kuomintang Government. Many of these Chinese courses were studied in eight years, and there were 8 or 9 courses per academic year, but some of them had not been opened during my study period.

The History and Geography taught in English classes were all foreign. Geography began to be studied in the 3rd grade until I left the school, and History began to be learned in the 5th grade. Therefore, I learned a lot of these two courses very carefully. Geography was a continent geography. History starts from the ancient history of the world, and then reads medieval history and modern history. Among them, the most learned was the history of European countries and the United States. I still had an impression of many major events in history and the deeds of big figures at all stages. I had read the Geography of Asia, Europe, America, Africa and Oceania, and I could still remember the names of many countries, capitals and important cities. I could almost tell all of the names of the states in the United States, and I could remember the names of famous mountains, rivers, bays, straits and islands on all continents of the world. I also know the important products and industrial and agricultural conditions of the major countries. I could tell the nationalities, customs, folk sentiments, religious beliefs and strange customs of many countries.

The History and Geography taught in Chinese were all from our country. Geography had been learned since the 1 st grade, and it had been studied for two years. History had also been studied since the 1st grade until I left school. Therefore, I had read in detail the history of the land in Fuzhou and the geography of all provinces in China. The history of China since the creation of the world by Pangu (Pangu Separates Sky from Earth, Pangu created the world) had been read in detail and I still remember quite a few of them.

Mathematics, Physics and Chemistry had less learning. Only the 1st, 2nd, and 3rd grades only learn Arithmetic. Only the 4th grade begins to learn Elementary Algebra, and the 5th grade began to learn Plane Geometry. When I left, I learned Triangle, Advanced Algebra, Solid Geometry and Analysis Geometry had never been learned. Because I learned very slowly, I did a lot of exercises, and often repeated them, I felt very fine, which made me more proficient in Elementary Mathematics. In the first four years, the school only taught general knowledge of science, and began to learn Botany in the 5th year, and Physics and Chemistry in the 6th year. Therefore, in this school, I took too few science courses, far less than the average middle school.

I jumped into the middle school from the 2nd grade of primary school. The English textbooks of the middle school were published by the British Macmillan Press. The content was very deep, the vocabulary was quite a lot, and the Chinese courses were relatively deep. At first, I felt quite difficult. For the first monthly test, I ranked 15th among 42, English classmates and 24th among 30 Chinese classmates. Seeing this situation, I had to dig in and study more. In the second monthly exam, English scores were still poor, ranking 18th, while Chinese had made some progress, ranking 9th. By the end of the first semester, my quarterly examination results had skyrocketed, ranking 3rd in Both English and Chinese, ranking 2nd on average and achieving the best results. From then on my examination results were basically the best and the rankings were very high. For the results of the first semester of the 2nd grade, I ranked 3rd among 31 English class students, and ranked 5th among 34 Chinese class students, ranking 2nd overall. The school let me jump into the second semester of the 3rd grade in the English class. This jump made me feel that I could not keep up with the English class. The results in the first month ranked the 13th among the 27 people in the English class, and the 1st place in the 2nd grade of the Chinese class. So I had to catch up and try to catch up with English class. By the end of that semester, my grades were 6th in the English class and 4th in the Chinese class. Therefore, in the third year after enrollment, I read the 4th grade in the English class and the 3rd grade in the Chinese class. In the second semester of this year, I also jumped up one level in the Chinese class, making me study English and Chinese in the 4th grade. Since then, I had achieved the best results every time, and the rankings were listed 1st.

When I entered Trinity Middle School, my family still lived in Tianan Temple. In the first semester I lived in the school and in Room K. There were more than a dozen students sharing a room. The supervisor of that year was Teacher Ning. He was older and he was strict with students. Especially in the evening, he often visits the dorms to see if the students go to bed on time. Some classmates resented him and tried to trick him, but they did not dare to do it. I was timid, relatively detached, and seldom interact with my classmates. I spend most of my time studying hard to catch up quickly. This year, I often had low temperature, and my uncle gave me Kuiyu pills daily, and it took a long time to cure. The next year, in 1923, the house jointly built by the 4th uncles and 6th aunts at MeiwuDing was completed, and then moved from Tianan Temple to MeiwuDing, and my family also moved with them. The road from our new lodgings to Trinity Middle School was closer, so I no longer lived in the school, instead went to school every day.

Life at Maywood

The house on the top of Meiwu was located opposite to the Temple of Plague (known as the Five Emperors Temple in Fuzhou) called "Mingzhen Temple". The house was two side-by-side, two-story buildings with a narrow terrace. In front of the gate there was a row of single-room shop house along the street, also was two floor. The back was the rear patio, there were two kitchens on the left, there was a room and aisle on the second floor above the kitchen, there were two rooms on the third floor, there was also a balcony on the top. On right there was a kitchen with two rooms on the second floor. There was a very deep well in the rear patio. The water quality was quite good. The water for drinking and washing was taken from this well. It was very difficult to hang the water up. The 4th uncle gave the 6th aunts one house on the right and the front shop house, and he had the one house on the left and the three-storey side house behind. As the 6th aunt was not often in Fuzhou, she rented out her house and the shop house separately. When she in Fuzhou, lived in the front building of the 4th uncle. My mother lived in the back room, and my 4th uncle and his family lived on the second and third floors of the side house. The front of the house faces west and behind was relatively high, so it was very hot in summer. On hot summer nights, everyone liked to chill out on the balcony after dinner. Girls tend to wash their hair first, and then went to balcony to blow-dry their hair. Everyone talked together on the balcony, sometimes eaten snacks and laughs while eating. At this time, I was 14 years old. I thought I was different from the girls. I seldom went to their snack parties, except to listen. After moving to the new residence, cousin Chen Lanying, the eldest daughter of the 4th uncle, and my second sister got married one after another, and they married into the city. When the school was in class, the second and third daughters of the 4th uncle, Guiying, and Pinying and cousin Yuhua lived in their respective girl's middle schools, the three-story room was often unoccupied and I slept in the small one. This room had a window facing south, which was brighter and cooler, It was my cousin Yuhua who lived at home. When she wasn't in Fuzhou or at school, it was mostly empty. My mother told me to sleep in it, but still wanted me to do my homework in her back room. Although she no longer supervises me as she used to, she still worries about me living alone. One night, after I finished my homework, I went upstairs to bed and went to the bottom of the stairs. When I looked up and saw that the door to the balcony was open. Against the background of the gray sky, the dark figure of a woman in a cloak passed by. By then it was so cold that no girl wanted to blow-dry her wet hair on the balcony. I thought for a moment and then called out who was on the balcony. Of course there was no answer, so I thought I saw a ghost, and I was so scared that I didn't dare go upstairs to sleep. From then on, When I went to the third floor alone, I felt a little scared. Later, when I chose to study psychology in college, I realized that I didn't see a ghost that night, but a hallucination caused by a trance.

The shop house on the top floor was rented out to a tenant named Gao, who owns a photo studio. The shop was called "Body outside body", which was very unique, the photo hall was located on the upper floor. The ground floor was rented out to a fruit stand for a while. Gao's name was "Kindness", but its face was very ugly, appearance not only not good, and very fierce, the 6th aunts in the back gave him a nickname called "ghost face" Gao was a businessman, he opened a water vegetable shop at the top of Daling, specializing in the supply of beef and other food for foreigners and had a little money. In addition to his wife and children, he also married a concubine and lived upstairs. It said the concubine was a prostitute before, so she could not have children. Later, thc youngcr 4th aunt had a son and a daughter and then had two daughters again. When they was born, they was given to be adopted, and the youngest one was given to her.

About two years after my family moved to Mei-wu, my second sister was getting married. In order to prepare the dowry, one day my mother asked me going to cross the bridge with my seventh uncle to the West Building of Fuzhou to buy some suitcases, mirror box and so on. This was the first time in my life that I had done so much big things for our family. My second brother-in-law lives on Nanhou Street in the city, after the second sister got married, as a young uncle, I visited my sister in the city several times. At that time, I began to wear the cloth shoes I had bought, there was a cloth shoe shop on Nanhou Street. When I went there to buy the cloth shoes, I went to my sister's home. There were more than ten miles of road from Meiwuding to Nanhou Street. It took me more than tow hours walk to go forth and back, I feel very tired. Probably due to lack of vitamins in my body, I came back with a pain in my leg. It was the same to visit the ancestral tomb twice a year. The tomb of my grandparents was behind Duoling on Cangqian Mountain. When I was a kid, I always went to sacrifice with some adults. When I was in middle school, my mother asked me to go alone, but I had to ask someone to help me to carry the sacrifice. So at first I had to go to the tomb owner's house near the cemetery, the cemetery was bought from him, we still call him the tomb owner, he would be responsible for us to take care of the cemetery, notify them to send someone to take a hoe with us, and weeded our graves for us. After the sacrifice was over, we went back to his house, cooked the food and asked them to eat together. We also paid him a little money. I still remember the tomb owner's name was "Fajian", but the last name was forgotten. His family lived in a fir-covered farmhouse, and the furniture was also made of fir. It was extremely rudimentary, but it still had an excellent impression in my mind to date, that was all fir doors, walls, pillars, floors, and table and chair, pot covers.

They were washed clean, so they were very hygienic. The climate in Fuzhou was relatively warm, the summer was hot, and plagues often occur. People all know to pay attention to hygiene. Although there was no call from that aspect, every family hold did cleanup from time to time. Although there was no public health evaluation, every family was evaluating and supervising each other. The door walls and pot covers of that family were not washed clean, and people in this family, especially housewives, would be criticized or ridiculed by the women and neighbors. This was true not only in the towns, but also in the backcountry. This was indeed a fairly good practice and deserves praise.

When I was a child, my mother did not let me do anything at home, only asked me to study hard. After I entered middle school, I grew up, and she asked me to buy this and that from time to time, from buying small items to buying rice. Sometimes she went out and asked me to cook. The most unhappy thing was that she asked me to go back to Xiadu hometown Zheng's mansion. to ask Du Du (Xihou) for rent. Since our family moved out, we rented the back room of our old house to Du Du for only two yuan a month, But Du Du was a bad guy, he never payed the rent and always runs away from home. I had to go early, had to asked him for the rent when he just got up. He was always pushing and pulling, and I had to beg for several times a month. When I was in middle school, my father was basically in the Northeast, and the task of writing to my father fell on me. In the past, mother asked her second uncle second son, Yufu, to write a letter for her. My father seldom sends money back. I only go to withdraw money one or two times at the post office. Doing more things and gain more social experience, but sometimes it would inevitably affect my study.

Academic Performance

At the end of each semester, when I received my academic performance, I would attach a copy to my father, but there was nothing to reward me. Only once, when a friend of my father came back from the Northeast to Fuzhou, he sent me a letter from my father, together with a set of two volumes entitled Etymology. He just told my mother that I needed a reference book for learning. That day I was at school, not at home, my mother received him, but did not ask the details about the two books whether he gave or my father entrusted him to buy for me. But I believe my father was satisfied with my academic performance and asked him to buy these two books as a gift when he passed through Shanghai.

One year after I entered the Trinity Middle School, my brother-in-law ordered an English Book published by Zhonghua Book Company as a gift to me. The English of this book was very light, so it was for middle school students to read. At that time, my English class had jumped to the 3rd grade, and I was able to write some decent articles in English. It happened that the magazine needed articles, so I wrote an article about my study and posted it. To my surprise, it was accepted for publication, for which I received a dozen exercise books as a reward. It was the first time in my life I had ever handed in an article, and the first time I received the remuneration. Unfortunately, no one had encouraged me to write more articles for submission.

I had learned a lot of English in the English class. From the 2nd grade, the school had used famous English novels as textbooks. Therefore, I had read Dicken novels "Wudu Orphans", "Further Life of the Flesh", "Tale of Two Cities", and several novels written by Scott about the British invasion of India. In the Chinese class, I read a lot of languages, such as the Analects, Mencius, Zuo Zhuan, ShiJi, ancient essays, ancient poetry, and Qiu Shui Xuan Chi Zhi. Therefore, it could be said that when I was in middle school, I mainly study languages. English and Chinese took most of my time. Secondly, I learned a lot about History and Geography. But all I liked Mathematics and Physics were too little to learn, was really pitiful. Although Mathematics had been continually studied since the 1st grade, the progress was too slow. In the first three years, I only learned Arithmetic, only in the 4th grade, I learned Algebra, and in the 5th grade, I learned Geometry. By the time I left school, I had not finished Algebra and Geometry. I had not touched Advanced Algebra and Solid Geometry. I had learned Triangles by myself, and I had only learned Plane Triangles, but not Spherical Triangles.

There were many Chinese teachers in Trinity Middle School, but there were very few Mathematics, Physics and Chemistry teachers. In the first few years of Mathematics, the principal was still taught very slowly, then came teacher Miller, who taught Algebra and Geometry, but also very slowly, he did not teach the rudiments of Analytic Geometry until the year I left. We learned even less about Physics and Chemistry. We did not begin to study Botany until the 5th grade when "Rum" taught us. Instead of textbooks, "Rum" used her own lecture notes and did some demonstration experiments. I was very interested in her course, but unfortunately it was not comprehensive. It was only in the 6th grade that teacher Carpenter came to teach Physics and Chemistry. I remember in his first class, the classroom was in a small laboratory. He was talking about the three states of matter solid, liquid and gas. He told us that some materials were very hard, such as diamonds and agate. He took out the mortar and pestle made of agate in the laboratory to show us, and used the pestle to mortar to explain that the agate was very hard, and also let our students take turns to watch. When it was my turn, I hit the mortar heavily with a pestle, and I could not think of both being crushed. Teacher Carpenter flushed immediately and did not say anything and did not want me to pay, but I was embarrassed and I did not know what to do. Although the Physics and Chemistry class had few class hours and not much learning, but I was very interested. In that year, the school required students to wear colored sweat vests when playing basketball in physical education classes. The yellow vest I wore was dyed by Mr. Carpenter with chemical dyes. The vests of other students were also dyed by him. In addition to yellow there were also red and blue colors. Since I learned less Mathematics, Physics and Chemistry in the Trinity Middle School than in other general middle schools. Later, I found it difficult to study science and technology in university. I had to learn many aspects by myself.

Father and Daughter

The 6th uncle was a member of the Kuomintang and was said to be follower of Mr. Sunyatsen. At his home there was a horizontal plaque "the world is for all" by Premier Sun. Before joining the Kuomintang government, he had taught Mathematics at Shanghai Public School and had translated Geometry textbooks edited by Wendell Wasson of the United States. In his bookcase, there were a full set of Mathematics books written by Wen Shi in English, with Arithmetic, Algebra, Geometry, and detailed solutions to the exercises in each book. A full set of "New Youth" magazines and books on politics and brochures. I was very interested in Mathematics books, I had read a lot, and had done many practice questions. I had only browsed some of its political books, but I was not interested. I only remember those books talking about this or that doctrine, including the anarchism of Bakunin and Klubbutt. In addition, I had read some yellow brochures. His daughter, cousin Youhua, was studying in South China Girls' High School. At that time, there was a Langhua bookstore specializing in new books near the campus of South China School. In addition to selling many translated novels in the twenties, it also publicly sold several "sex history" edited by Zhang Jingsheng, a doctor of sex. She had bought every "sex history" and read it and put it in the drawer of her small room on the third floor. Because I went to sleep on the third floor, I secretly read a few books, but I just browsed. I was not interested in the yellow books hidden by the father and daughter. I could say at that time that I was not in love with any girl. I was deeply influenced by the idea of "Reading bring us everything", and I thought that when I was in school, I should concentrate on learning. As long as I could learn, I would not fail to get my wife later. During this period, I was like a bookworm, and I ate books all the time.

Life After School

Trinity School payed great attention to sports. In addition to morning exercises, students also had to participate in team games. British people like football, so there were several venues in the school for practicing football. The school divided all the students into three teams: lion, eagle, and whale. The lion team members wore red vests, the eagle team wore blue vests, and the whale team wore yellow vests. I was put on the whale team and played football on the playground two days a week after class. Because of my lack of interest, also because of my physical weakness, I could not play football well, and also other sports could not do well. Therefore, my semester's physical education class score was always lower than other homework, and I could not keep up with most students.

When I was in Middle School, I mainly studied hard to get good grades, but it was not that I had not played. When I was in the 5th grade, the school once used the Easter holiday to organize a tour, which I participated in with my classmates. That time, we visited Fang Guangyan in Yong Tai County, near Fuzhou, led by Mr. Chen shizhong. Unfortunately, it was very rainy when we went. We went up to the temple in the heavy rain. This temple was very special, embedded in the mouth of a large mountain cave, with the top of the cave as the temple roof, so it was called "a tile". In front of the temple, there was rainwater pouring down from the top of the mountain like a pearl. There was a waterfall next to the temple. There was a smaller hole along the plank road behind the waterfall. There were many bats in the cave, called "bat cave". Because it was raining during the day, and I had a little diarrhea at night, several students also did this. At that time, I was staying in the temple and felt very cold. The rain was still very heavy the next day, and some classmates and I had no intention of continuing to play, and wanted return to Fuzhou early. Teacher Chen also did not want to play, so some of us went down the mountain with him and went back, while the rest continued to play there for another day. When they returned, they said they had climbed to the top of "a tile," that day, but no one dared to walk along the boardwalk, because heavy rain, none of the students had entered the bat cave. However, there was a monk in the temple who walked along the boardwalk enter the cave, and many bats flew out in alarm. This was my first time traveling, but unfortunately Heavenly Father did not create beauty, which made us not interested in the scenery there. In the future, the school would no longer organize tourism, and I would no longer leave Fuzhou.

There were already movies in Fuzhou in the 1920s, but I only remember watching it once. The movie theater was located in a shed in Cangqianshan, named Da Luotian Moving Theater. The name of the film was called "Ancient well heavy wave" and it was a story about a widow's remarriage, I was not interested at all. At that time, Fuzhou people watched a lot of Fujian operas, and there were several troupes performing traditional dramas in theater. I also was not interested, so I had not seen it once. At that time, there was a performance by Cao Taiban in the Shuimingzhen Temple of the Five Emperors, which was free for people to watch. Spectators crowd in front of the stage or on balconies to look up or down. I had been there two or three times, but I was not interested, so I didn't leave any impression in my mind. The only impression was that I looked downstairs and saw many people squeezing their heads in front of the stage. The olive tray above floats like a boat on the black waves of the head. On the eve of the Revolution, some middle school students organized dramas. Trinity students also publicly performed a show to persuade people to quit opium smoking. The plot was completely self-edited and the performance was not bad. A classmate played the opium ghost, acting very similarly, and later got the nickname of the opium ghost. I did not take part in the show, only doing the preparation work. We were also performing one or two dramas for our classmates on campus. I only had participated as a work-on.

Because I lived just opposite Mingzhen for several years, every time sent the plague to sea, I waited until the middle of the night at my door. There were several customs brokers in Meiwu where Mingzhenan temple was located. They all had wooden barges that were used to transport goods between Fuzhou and Mawei. They were superstitious in ghosts and spirits, and they all worship Wenshen or Wugui (the impermanence of the day and the impermanence of the night) who travel the streets. They also donate large sums of money every year to Mingzhen Temple to make boats for the god of plague. Therefore, Mingzhenan's boats were made of wood, which was much more sophisticated than the paper boats made by other temples of Pestilence. As early as a few months before sending the god of plague, Mingzhenan began to hire workers to build ships in the temple. On the night of sending the god of plague, this boat was carried by many people to the riverside and burned. All the gods of war and martial arts had came out to take part in the parade and it was quite a spectacle.

Trinity school holidays were rare. Except for Spring Easter and Fall Christmas, the other holidays were the National Day on October 10, or Double Ten. But on such a day, the school refused to take the initiative to leave, and students still had to apply. One year, the principal came to the student representative who said: "What National Day do you have? In successive years of war between warlords, you only have China chaos!" The students felt indignant at this.

I rarely ask for leave, even when my body gets low fever every afternoon, I also go to class as usual, not taking sick leave. In five and a half years, I only asked for leave a few times when my eldest uncle had a happy event. Once his grandson got married, and I was sent to the bride's house to meet, it was my task.

Family Financial Constraints

Because my father did not return from the Northeast for a few years, and rarely sent money home, the our family economy had always been very tight. I did not have any pocket money. I only ask my mother when I need. She manages housework very frugally and sometimes extremely difficult. Every time a semester starts to pay tuition and miscellaneous fees, she had worked hard to raise funds. At the time, in addition to the use of silver dollars, Taiwanese-style tickets was sued by Xiaozhuang were also in circulation, each with a face value of one yuan. but the school refuses to accept this kind of ticket, so it must be changed to the silver dollar. So, every time we payed our tuition, we had to change it into silver dollar first. We could only change money through the bank, we had to pay more for the change. At that time, there was a mixture of counterfeit silver dollars on the market. The school stipulated that all silver dollars handed in must be accompanied by a small piece of paper with the name of the paying student on it, so that if a counterfeit was found, it could be returned and replaced. All of these also increased more troubles.

The clothes I wear at school were extremely frugal, most of them had been modified or amends by my mother, and the underwear was rough and ragged. I remember one time my father sent back some colored cloths of local origin from the Northeast. The color was cyan, so it was called cyan cloth. My mother used this cloth to make a long gown for me and my younger brother to wear for my uncle's birthday and New Year's Day. On the Lantern Festival night that year, there was a fireworks exploding nearby, and we all went to watch. Unfortunately, a rotating firework flew across my younger brother, burning his new gown into several holes, my mother was really anxious and angry. Probably when I was in the 3rd or 4th grade, there was a rule in our school that students should wear a black twill uniform with a black silk bar and a leaf-shaped loop on the sleeves. In order to make this uniform for me, although the cost was not too much, it inevitably puts an extra burden on my mother.

The shoes I wore were all made of homemade cyan cloth shoes, but later I changed to the shoes bought from shop, because I knew they were available in the Nanhou streets of town and they were cheap. On rainy days, I wore cloth-covered wooden soles and clatter on the flagstones. It was not until a long time later that I wore a pair of rubber shoes that were made by Mr. Tan Kah Kee's factory, but my feet were itchy and smelly from the heat. Later, I changed into a kind of very rough leather shoes with a cross strap on the sole, a heel horseshoe, and a pair of nails on the front, which sounds like the horseshoe was on the road. One year, in order to attend my uncle's wedding, my mother found a piece of gray satin in the family suitcase, was barely made into two pairs of vamp, then hand to the shoemaker for fitting with cowhide bottom ready for my brother and me to wear. My mother thought gray was unlucky, so she gave it to her cousin Lin Peiying, to dye black in his sock factory. Unexpectedly, the factory put these two pairs of shoes into the black dyeing tank to cook. As a result, the color was dyed black, but the soles of the cowhide were twisted and crumpled by cooking, and both pairs of shoes were so strangely shaped that could not be worn at all. After seeing them, my mother was very angry and funny. When I was a kid, I wore cloth socks, later I changed to wearing cotton yarn socks, which were also home made. The bottom of the socks was high and low, and it was very uncomfortable to wear on the feet. In order to make up the socks, I did not know how much my mother's hard work.

I did not wear well, and my diet also was poor, I did not have much to eat except for three meals a day, three meals were coarse grain and vegetables, as a result I was chronically undernourished and skinny. Fortunately, I didn't have any serious illnesses. Otherwise, I would not be able to study, nor would be able to live to this day. I lived in the school twice, my luggage was an old bamboo box with wheels underneath it that I could drag to the floor, and some bedding. I didn't know if these were my grandparents who rushed to the exam with these luggage. One of the mattresses in my bed had been rotten for a long time, the cotton tread on the blue and white cotton quilt has not re bounced for a long time. A straw mat was half broken, and the mosquito nets were pieced together. I was so shabby in the school, but none of my classmates looked down upon me, because there were plenty of classmates liked me. Looking back, I feel that the social atmosphere of that time was much better than now!

When I was in the 4th grade, my younger brother also entered middle school. He attended Ying hua College, a church middle school run by the United States-Israel Association. My mother really went to great lengths to put her two sons through middle school. I didn't know how she manages to maintain our family finances. I missed it very much and I was very grateful to my mother for her kindness to us. My mother hoped that our two brothers would be accepted by the post office or customs a few years after we graduated from middle school. Unexpectedly, due to the country's political turmoil and economic recession, these institutions were not recruit new personnel, so we could postpone year after year of study, and my mother had to pay our study and living expenses year after year, which was really difficult.

My Cousin Pinying

Trinity School did not accept girls, and I did not have any female classmates. My parents basically had no friends, and my father was away from home for a long time, so I had no chance to contact any girl other than relatives. Although my grandfather had many cousins, these cousins were much younger than me. Only two of them were slightly older than me, and the rest were much older than me. A cousin who was slightly older than me was the girl who was my host mother gave to 9th aunt as her daughter. I seldom see the girl except for the happy event of my uncle. Later, she married to Xiamen early. The other one was Chen Pinying, the third daughter of my 4th uncle. During the period when our family with the 4th uncle family lived together, she lived in the same house with me, could be said to be childhood sweetheart. However, she lived on campus as soon as she entered middle school. She only back home in winter and summer holidays. I also lived in the Trinity middle school, so it was rare to get together. Because of the difference between men and women, and by the influence of feudal thought, we gradually alienated. So when I was in middle school, I could say that I did not had any contact with girl of my age.

My mother determined not to choose a spouse for me until I graduated to work. Someone once wanted to marry their daughter to me. My mother always said to her: "TuanTuan was still studying. I did not know what would happen in the future? I did not want to trouble myself about his marriage, so as not to make a mistake". I remember that my 4th sister's husband, who were much older than me, had intended to match his orphan granddaughter with me and several times asked my mother for permission, but my mother declined. In 1920, my 4th uncle got a critically lung disease and asked my mother to promise match Pinying with me before he died. my mother unable to refuse at that time and said to him: "I would not let him marry your daughter until he was successful." That's how I got married to Pinying. Instead of telling me about it, my mother also managed to keep it as secret. So at first I was kept in the dark for months, but when I Just to hear a little bit about that. Soon, my mother moved our family back to Zhengr's mansion which meant she wanted to isolate me from Pinying. However, when the uncle's family had a happy event, I could not help meeting her, and we felt a little embarrassed to each other. I remember one day, she and I had to have breakfast before going to class. Wu Ma, who prepared our meals, arranged us to eat together on a small coffee table. Some people were laughing and joking, making us feel embarrassed.

Pinying took mathematics classes and needed a protractor and asked my elder sister to borrow it from me. I immediately lent her the only one I had. Later, she accidentally shattered it and couldn't return it. I knew it and told her indirectly that she didn't mind. This matter was still hidden from the mother!

One day I was wearing a faded blue cloth gown, an oiled paper umbrella under my armpit, walking on a wooden bottom with rain boots, and walking in a narrow Xiaoling lane. Unexpectedly, Pinying with a classmate came across from each other. No one even nodded to each other, so I bowed my head and walked past, feeling embarrassed. My ragged image was therefore passed on as a joke by Pinying's classmates, and also spread to my classmates.

When Pinying graduated from junior middle school, she entrusted her sister Guiying to give me an invitation card and wanted to invite me to attend her graduation ceremony, I did not go because of my shame and fear of being known by my mother that inevitably let her disappointed. After graduation, because of the death of her father, she unable to go to school again, Pinying worked as a teacher in Yuying Kindergarten and lived upstairs in the kindergarten. The house was originally an orphanage set up by the American-Israeli Association, so she had been with orphans for several years. Although the place was near Trinity Middle School, I had never been there to meet her. I could say that throughout my middle school years, I did not want a girlfriend at all, not even a known fiancée.

Science Saving the Country

On the eve of the Revolution of 1925, many school students secretly engaged in the revolution. Most of them participate in some kind of organization and secretly activities. At that time, the warlords who ruled Fujian Province tried to suppress it. A special agent named Zhang was sent to several middle schools for reconnaissance under the cover of teaching "Mandarin", people call him "Mandarin Zhang". Missionary schools were relatively backward, especially the Trinity Middle School set up by Anlijian Association. Only a handful of classmates secretly participated in revolutionary organizations. I did not know who it was and what organization they participated in. It was not until 1926 that there was a student union at Trinity Middle School, but this student union was just an autonomous organization. Apart from managing student meals, the only activity seemed to be organizing a drama. I worked as an accountant in collecting membership fees and managing food accounts, and announced accounts on a monthly basis. A few students who later learned that it was the extreme left opposed the student union and refused to pay the membership fee. At a conference, I ordered their names, and they were going to hit me. Fortunately, they were blocked by the students.

After the National Revolutionary Army led by Heyingqin entered Fuzhou, the Kuomintang Department was immediately established, and several demonstrations and conferences were held. At that time, "Mandarin Zhang" was still lurking in Fuzhou, and was soon caught. After being shot, his body was hanged upside down at the top of Maiyuan near Trinity Middle School. Afterwards, he was dragged down to show the public on the upper street. Since then, students in Fuzhou had mobilized students to march every few days. Every time, a mass meeting was held at the large campus outside the South Gate. Some people were beaten down and even executed after the meeting. I was not interested in politics at the time, and I did not want to understand it. Every time I followed the procession blindly, I felt very tired and bored. At that time, Trinity Middle School had stopped forcing students to worship and instead held a commemorative week every Monday morning to chant Premier Sun's will.

In order to seek to understand some of Sunyat sen's doctrines, I started to study "Three People's Principles" "Guidelines for the Founding of the People's Republic of China" and Jianguo Fangji, of which I was most interested in Jianguo Fangji Because I had long believed that the main reason for China's weakness was that it had not been well built for the country. Since then I had the idea of saving the country with science and technology, but I think that this doctrine and that doctrine were just empty talk, and could not help our poor country. There was a short period of time when I studied and discussed "Three People's Principles" with several classmates, but soon they were disbanded due to lack of interest.

In the second half of 1927, I was in 7th grade and could live in a small single dormitory on campus. In the middle of the night at the end of the semester, the school building caught fire, I woke up and escaped out. I did not take anything with me in my hurry, so I lost all my clothes. It was only afterwards that the fire was released by a very left student who opposed the Christian church. He went from outside the school to the wall, then broke the window and climbed into a toilet on the second floor of the middle school building. From there, he slipped into a mezzanine floor under the roof, where was a lot of old paper, which, once lit, quickly spread throughout the building, causing it to burst into flames in an instant. Fortunately, the students who lived in school all escaped in time, and none of them was injured, but almost all their clothing was lost. The building was burned down, and the school had to suspend and allow the students to go home, it was nearly the end of the year.

Soon afterwards, Fujian Union University recruited students. I and several classmates tried to take the exam, unexpectedly I was admitted. In this way, just like when I entered middle school before graduating from my primary school, I transferred to university without graduating from the middle school.

I had been studying in middle school for five and a half years. Since I skipped the first level, I finished the middle school in six and a half years. The level of English and Chinese meet or exceed university standards, The liberal arts courses in History, Geography, etc. could also keep up with the university level, but the Physical Chemistry and Biology of science were slightly worse. I was admitted to the university on an exceptional basis, and was required to practice some science courses as a preparatory student. So, I entered the university in early 1928.

CHAPTER 11

My University Years

Fujian Union University

At the end of 1927, the school building of Trinity Middle School was set on fire, I could not finish the middle school, did not graduate to apply for admission for Fujian Union University, I was admitted. I had no intention of going to University, nor was my family prepared to pay for it. Because of the continuous war in Fuzhou, the economy was very depressed, there was no employment opportunities in society, I could not drop out of school to find a job to do. Also my academic performance had been very good, if the family did not let me continue to study, it would a pity. My mother had to clench her teeth and squeeze money to cultivate me. At the same time, I was the first person in the Zheng's Family to go to University. In the Chen's Family at that time, only the eldest uncle son-in-law was a college graduate. Besides, no one had ever gone to University. Therefore, I could go to University was very enviable, My mother also thinks that having a son go to University was an honor and that a little hardship in life was well worth. Were it not for the destruction of the Trinity Middle School buildings, I would had been able to graduate and obtain a diploma, and I would had never been to University. So it could be said that fire to help me go to college, this was really fate arrangements.

At that time, Fujian Union University was a new established University. The original site was located in the northern foot of Cangqian Mountain, facing the hillside of Minjiang River, There was only one small building. From the river, we had to walk a lot of stone steps, which looks very imposing. In the beginning, there were few students and few teachers. However, due to the expansion of the school scale, the school site was not enough, then a new school site was found at the foot of Gushan along the Minjiang River. The site was located near Kuiqi Township between Fuzhou and Mawei, so it was often called Kuiqi Union University, or simply Called Kuiqi University. Most of the new buildings were built on the hillside with a number of bungalows below. The new buildings consists of two three-storey buildings with palatial roofs. One science building donated by the Roche Foundation (Rockmole, the boss of Mobil Oil), The physics, chemistry and biology departments of the Faculty of Science occupy one floor each. Another dormitory building donated by Alcoa king Hall (the aluminum magnate). There were two or three small buildings for professors to stay in, also with palatial roofs. The bungalows below were used by all departments of the Faculty of Arts. as teach buildings, and a number of bungalows were used as student dormitories and canteens. On the clear sunny day, from one side of the hillside you could see the twin towers and downtown urban areas of Fuzhou City, and on the other side you could see the ship's check point at the Mawei Luoxing Tower. The Minjiang River bends around Kui Qi liked a belt around the front of the campus. Across the river was Nantai Island, the island green trees, farmhouses scattered between them, looked like a beautiful picture. The river was dotted with sails, small fire wheel liked many stars, showing the heavy traffic scene. The campus scenery was very beautiful, choose such environment to set University could be good ideal.

Fujian Union University was run by American-Israel-American Society, so its English name was translated into Chinese as Fujian Christian University. The founder was an American pastor named Gao Zhi, as principal. Because of the Kuomintang government regulation that the principal should be Chinese, so instead by Lin Jingrun successor, and the provost was also Chinese, instead by professor Lintianlang. The number of professors was small. Scott who taught Philosophy, Kellogg who taught Zoology, and Mc Alfe who taught Botany, were all Americans, and Martin, an Australian, taught Physics. Lin Jingrun and Lintianlang, who teaches Social Science and Psychology. In addition, there was an American professor who teaches English. The Chinese professor used to be Mr. Wangzhixi There was also a Biology assistant named Chenzetuan. When I entered the school, there were less than a hundred students and the school was still very small.

At that time, there was no road between Fuzhou and Mawei, and there was only a small path along the Minjiang River from Fuzhou to Kuiqi, so land transportation was extremely inconvenient, so people mainly relied on water transportation. Union University had a small shuttle boat between Fuzhou Nantai Island wharf and University wharf for teachers and students. But the boat did not drive very often, it usually only runs on weekends. Most of the traffic relies on a few small steamboat running between Fuzhou and the towns downstream of the Minjiang River, each township had a daily voyage. The time was to start from Fuzhou in the morning, and drive back from the township in the afternoon or evening. In order to take such a small steamboat, we must go to the edge of the river to board the steamboat by a small rower boat, when we arrive School pier there were school-owned boats drawn up to fetch us, the boatman named Eli. From school back to Fuzhou, I used to take the small steamboat, through Eli's small rower boat to boarded the small steamboat. Eli's small rower boat without pay, and took the small steamboat was also cheap, but I forgot how much it costed. The school pier was just a ramp into the river. The first time I went to school, as soon as I stepped on the dock, I was attracted by the beautiful campus. To see the mighty new school building standing on the hillside, my heart was filled with joy and excitement, I swore to myself that I would study hard here. In the first semester, I lived on the first floor of the new dormitory building, and my Trinity middle School classmate Yang Sunlao, who was admitted by the University at the same time, we lived in the same room.

In the University, there was a chemistry student named Huang who was in a class higher than me and engaged with my 2nd maternal uncle's daughter, also Pinying's cousin. As it was arranged by his parents, he opposed the marriage and refused to get married. My 2nd maternal uncle died early, and my 2nd aunt, anxious to have her daughter married as soon as possible, entrusted me to ask Huang. Huang insisted on breaking off the engagement. At the same time, I learned that his mother was mentally ill, and that his own nerves seemed abnormal. Therefore I suggested my 2nd aunt that to call off the engagement. So this cousin's betrothed gift by my hand back to Huang. Before that, the eldest daughter of my great uncle, also the cousin of Pinying after marrying a graduate of Peking Union Medical College, the couple had a bad relationship and separated at an early age. With these two things, I worried that Pinying might worry that I was also a student of Union University, or would abandon her. So I decided to write a letter to tell her I was a sincere lover. After the letter was sent, I waited for weeks in vain for her reply. After marriage, I learned that she was very conflicted after receiving the letter. She wanted to write back but dared not, for fear that her correspondence with me would be criticized, and for fear that it would affect my study, so she finally decided not to writ. After my disappointment, I felt no anger; I did not think it necessary to write a letter to express my feelings. Therefore, I only passed this letter with Pinying before marriage. The University opened to the public. a lot of people came, including many of my classmates' girlfriends or fiancées. I had not invited Pinying, but I had looked forward to her arrival on campus that day. Then one person walks back and forth along the river shore, hoped to see her on the dock. As a result, she did not come, I was a little disappointed, but later forgot. Recall that I had refused to attend her graduation ceremony, and forgive her for not coming. When I studied at Union University, which was still an all-boys school, so In two and a half years I had no contact with anyone of the opposite sex close to my age.

Because I did not graduate from high school, and I learned only too few science courses in middle school, I had to take a biology preparatory course in the first semester of Union University, not a college credit. In addition, my English, Chinese, Mathematics, Philosophy and Physics were all University courses, which could be counted as credits, Philosophy was a compulsory course, and Physics was a major course I had chosen. In middle school I thought I was very knowledgeable, as if I knew everything. After arriving at the University, saw so many courses, visited the laboratory and the library, only then opened the eye, realized that the study sea profound, oneself knew was only a drop in the ocean. While studying Biology prep, hand-made some experiments, from the microscope to see the microbial world, immediately interested. This lesson was taught by Assistant Chen, he taught very well, he spoke very organized, the textbooks used were very informative added to my interest. But I thought reading Biology was of little use at the time, so I wanted to learn Physics and thought that Physics could be used directly in industrial production. At the same time, because Physics was closer to Mathematics, in fact, the Mechanical part of Physics was called Applied Mathematics, I like Mathematics, so I want to learn Physics. In studying Physics, I personally did a lot of interesting experiments, but also increased interest in physics. While doing the experiment, I had learned some craft from the copper smith at school, tried metalworking with hacksaws, hammers, chisels, files and tongs, and tried to assemble an ore radio, but it did not work. Mathematics was still my favorite course, English and Chinese classes I could keep up quickly. Professor Scott taught a wide variety of Philosophy courses with everything. The lecture notes were made up by himself. They were brief and to the point and he spoke so vividly, I gained a lot of new knowledge from him. I still remember that the book classification, originally belong to the knowledge of Library science content. The Bible is no longer a compulsory subject, so I did not choose to read it. I was curious and wanted to acquire almost any new knowledge, so I was interested in all the courses and wanted to take all the courses.

Union University was located in the Gushan scenic area, above the Yongquan Temple, drinking water rock and other scenic spots. I had been attracted to fame scenic spots for a long time, but I had never had a chance to play. After entering University, this scenic spot was very close.

The day of April 8, 1928 lunar calendar bath Buddha festival, with several classmates, we first went up a few miles along the river to the lower house of the temple, and then picked up a mountain climb from there. Before arriving at the temple, five pavilions were passed along the way, each with a plaque. The plaque in the fourth pavilion had four big characters "Can't get enough", which I still remember to this day, because these four words do write the mentality of mountain climbers. People who were not used to climbing mountains would feel tired from climbing up the mountain to the fourth pavilion. But there was not far away from the temple, and would feel that the courage to reach the destination, really want to give up or not give up, not give up had to fight. A few of us had this kind of contradictory mood, whether study or work, as a career adult must had "Can't get enough" fighting spirit.

St. John's University, Shanghai

In the summer of 1930, I transferred to St. John's University in Shanghai. My life after arrival in Shanghai will be described detail in the chapters of "my parents", "my eldest sister and second sister" and "my younger brother".

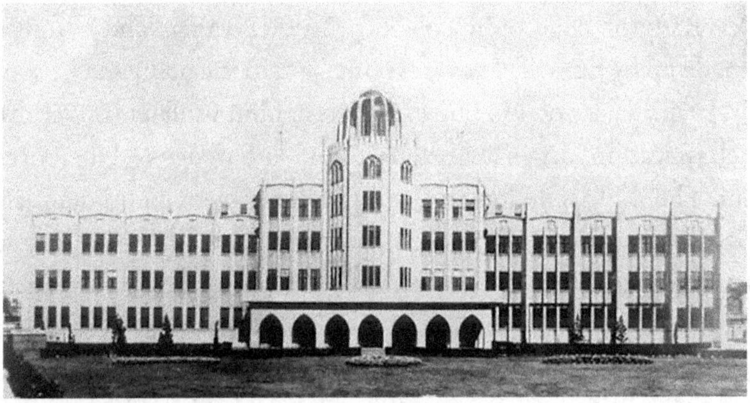

CHAPTER 12

Eldest and Second Sisters

My Eldest Sister

My eldest sister, Ruirun, also known as Changrun, Ruirun. She was born to my father's first wife Feng, so she and I were half siblings. She was born in 1893, 17 years earlier than me. When I was a child, I called her Sister Run. When I grew up, I changed her name and called her Ten Sister (because she was the tenth female of Zheng's Family). Despite the age difference and the different birth mothers, our sister and brother had always been very affectionate and could be said to be much better than the same mother. So now I didn't remember if she took care of me when I was child, so I didn't have any memories of her before she got married. She got married in 1912, when I did the math.

My Eldest Sister's Family

My eldest sister's Father-in-law's surname was Chen, and her residence was at Xiaolingding, very close to Zheng's mansion. At that time, although the Chen family was not as good as the Zhou, Wang, Zheng, CAI four big families, but it was not a small family, there was a Chen Ancestral

Hall next to the Shijing Temple. Although they all lived in Xiadu, it had nothing to do with my maternal grandfather Chen's family.

The eldest brother-in-law's ancestors had six brothers, most of them were serving in the Navy. When they were on board or admiralty officials, their descendants were mostly Navy officials, so this family could be called the Navy's Family. And yet, strangely enough, almost all of them had no offspring today. My eldest brother-in-law's father was an only son, and he and his son (my nephew) were also only son. Now my nephew had no son and only one single daughter, he was nearly seventy, and seemed afraid that he would be no offspring, the 2nd and 3rd granduncles had long lost descendants, the 4th granduncle was an only son and no offspring, the 5th granduncle had a few children, but I had not heard of any offspring that existed, and it may had been a heir; The 6th granduncle had only one son and an illegitimate daughter, and the third generation had only one daughter seems to have no offspring. A formerly vigorous family died off so quickly. Some their ancestral graves were not good for Feng Shui, which was of course an untrustworthy superstition. So what were the consequences? I could not say.

My eldest brother-in-law had lost his mother long ago. His father remarried and had only two daughters. Later, he adopted a Uncle Borer. Although he grew up, he did not had a son. When my eldest sister married Chen's Family, the father-in-law was dead. There were a stepmother, two cousins and cousin-borer, all of whom were supported by my eldest brother-in-law. My eldest brother-in-law, Changqing, was of the same age as my eldest sister. He had been studying driving at the Mawei Naval Academy since he was young. After graduation, he studied and practiced in Shanghai and Qingdao. They were married during an internship in Shanghai. After being married my eldest sister returned to Fuzhou and lived in the Chen's house. As soon as she entered the Chen's house, she became the master. After leaving home, she was very attentive and took care of her family nearby and often came back and brought some food with her. She could said that she loved her two younger brothers, especially me. The food brought back was mainly pastries and fruits for me. The fresh longan produced in Fuzhou was called Longan by Fuzhou people. It was used as a tonic for children. Whenever the autumn season was on the market, the family bought longan more or less for children to eat. Every year as soon as this season arrives my eldest sister kept buying longan for my younger brother and me to eat. She also often gave me things to play. She sends me lamps before the Lantern Festival every year, and before the Mid-Autumn Festival, she gave me clay figurine to set up towers. Therefore, in my young heart, there had long been my eldest sister a deep love for me.

Like her biological mother, my eldest sister was also very gambling, play Mahjong and Paigow, which she learned from Zheng's mansion, an old gambling nest. After she got married, she often returned to Zheng's mansion. to participate in gambling, most of them in the second entrance where there were more gambling descendants of Zheng's Family and neighbors. But her gambling skill was very big, very shrewd, also may be gambling luck was better, so she mostly win money, rarely lose money, but the wins or losses were small. But neither wins nor loses. she was very generous to people, and any family member of her relatives was in difficulties, she was willing to help out, so the Zheng's Family respected her very much.

When met her always greet 10th aunt long, 10th sister short to hello her. When I was young, I went to her home and slept with her at night. My bed was made of very thin rattan sheds, while her bed was made of wooden planks. I remember when I first slept in her house, I thought her bed was very hard, I asked her why? There were the 4th grandaunts and 6th grandaunts who lived with her. The latter had a son who was about the same age as me, so I had a child of the same age in her family to play. The first private school I read was located in the hall of her home. The teacher surname was Chen, probably her relative. Later, there was a wealthy businessman named Huang lived in back hall. During the Spring Festival every year, they all set off fireworks and invited Dragon Lantern to dance in the patio. My eldest sister took me to her house for two or three years to watch, and slept at her house at night.

Baby Lamp and Orange Lamp

After my eldest sister got married, she had no children for nine years. According to the customs of Fuzhou, after a girl was married, her family would send a lantern before the Lantern Festival every year. Before she gave birth to a son, her family would send a lantern of the children's bidet. If two or three years had passed and the fruit had not been born, her family would change to send a orange (urgent) lamp. Until the boy were born, changed sent the lamp to children. So, after my eldest sister got married, my mother would usually send a "baby" lamp every year, for about three years, she had not yet had child, so my mother sent an orange lamp for another two or three years. In the ninth year, 1921, my mother was a little anxious, so she sent two kinds of lamp at the same time and that worked. This year, my eldest sister raised her first child, and the time was really long enough. After the fist nephew, she had two more daughters. The first one died when was swaddled, and the second died when she was eight years old, so she had only one son left. my nephew was a rare son, and he was born in a very thin family, so he was especially precious. When he was born, I was only 11 years old and I liked him as much as adults. What's wrong with him. my eldest sister always asking for my 4th uncle to heal him. He had boils in summer and my 4th uncle also squeezed pus for him. When he was big enough to go to kindergarten, Dongmei, his maid, carried him to the Cangqianshan Yuying Kindergarten every day for education. The scene of Dongmei carrying him on her back while walking on Cangqian Mountain road was filmed. which was quite interesting. When my nephew was in kindergarten, Pinying was a teacher there. After graduating from Yuying Girls' High School, because of the death of parents, Pinying unable to go to school for further study. My eldest sister offered finance her for continue education. Later Pinying decided to go to kindergarten work, not accept my eldest sister's funding. Pinying was engaged to me by that time, and my eldest sister's kindness showed her affection for her brother, and on the other way to show her generosity.

Naval Officer

After completing his studies at the Naval academy, my eldest brother-in-law was assigned to be the third mate of a ship. After a few years, he was promoted to be the second mate, he served as the third officer of the Hairong, the largest warship in China Naval at that time. When his ships were not at sea, they were stationed mostly at Shanghai, Qingdao, or Guangzhou, and seldom at Fuzhou. Sun yatsen was shipwrecked in Guangzhou. At that time, due to Chen's rebellion, a war broke out in Guangzhou. Sun yatsen took refuge in Zhongshan warships. When the news reached Fuzhou, my eldest sister was very frightened and worried when she heard that someone had been killed on board of the warships. Fortunately, she quickly learned that my eldest brother-in-law was fine and she relieved. A few years later, my eldest brother-in-law was transferred to the Marine Survey Bureau under the jurisdiction of the Navy. where he first worked as a second officer on a survey ship, and then was promoted to captain. The Bureau was located in Shanghai and the Survey Scope was mostly near Shanghai. In 1928, he was transferred to the Bureau and stopped going on board. His third uncle, Caijunbao, was an early Naval officer. While working in Shanghai, and lived in an apartment at No. 3, Lane 286, Lafayette Road (now Fuxing Middle Road). In 1929, Cai was transferred to the Admiralty of the Navy as the director of personnel, and his family moved to Nanjing. and his Shanghai residence was given to my eldest brother-in-law. In that year, my eldest sister from Fuzhou moved to Shanghai with her children and my second sister-in-law and maid Dongmei. Soon after, my second sister moved to Shanghai to live with them. My second brother-in-law was also an officer in the Navy. He married my second sister, and the matchmaker was my eldest brother-in-law. In Shanghai their house was a two-story Shikumen house, but it was a little larger than a single house. and relatively wide in front. There was a wing beside the patio, in which my second sister lived. The downstairs hall also served as a dining room, and on three walls hung foreign oil paintings said to have been brought back from abroad by Caijunbao's ambassadorial brother. The upstairs room was used by my eldest sister family.

In the summer of 1930, I transferred to St. John's University in Shanghai for further study, which would cost a lot and my parents could not afford it. My eldest sister voluntarily subsidized all the expenses except tuition fees, and my second sister also funded part of the expenses for two years until I graduated from University. During this period, I never went back to Fuzhou. During summer and winter vacations and most weekends, I lived in the eldest sister's house and got her a lot of care. Caijunbao's eldest daughter, named HeHe, who also lived at my eldest sister home for weekends and holidays, I politely called her Lotus Cousin, and she was a high school student in Shanghai. She died of a sudden illness in the first half of 1931. I was told that she died of poisoning by swallowing red pencil leads because of world-weariness. In 1931, an unemployed bachelor named Wu yongjian about 40 years old, came to live in my eldest sister's home. I don't know what kind of relation with my eldest sister? But we called him as 6th uncle. It seems the 6th uncle with our alkaloid expert Hou Debang to have a relative relationship, so he had worked in Nanjing alkali factory, Perhaps because he was too lazy, he only did it for a very short time. He came back to Shanghai and lived in my eldest sister's home for a long time. When I was at the eldest sister's house, I set up a camp bed in the guest hall to sleep at night, and the same was for the 6th uncle.

One middle night, a thief tried using a blowtorch to burn a hole on my eldest sister's back door, so could unlock the key, for reach in. The thief presumably mistook my eldest sister's rich family because he saw a valuable painting hanging in the parlor and wanted to steal or rob it. Just 5th uncle get up to urinate, see the blowtorch come in the flames, startled, so that big shout "Ho, Ho". And pulled my foot to wake me up. We quickly turned on the lights and woke up the rest of the room loudly. The thief heard the noise inside the door and ran away immediately, thus saving my eldest sister's family a loss.

Generous and Helpful

My eldest sister was very generous, as was my eldest brother-in-law. In addition to their relatives who often lived in the family for a long time, some relatives and friends in Shanghai come to visit and often stay for dinner. My eldest brother-in-law had an uncle (the son of the 4th granduncle) as a technician in the Navy factory, Caijunbao had a younger brother studying in Shanghai, and a cousin named Liguisen who was introduced into the Naval hospital as an assistant. They come from time to time walk around, Li was very interesting. My eldest sister liked ply Mahjong very much, but sometimes there were only three people available, and need one more to joint the play. As it happened, Li was drawn into the seat, because of Missing One Player. But Lie didn't understand anything, and even the eight cylinders and nine cylinders could not be distinguished, causing people to laugh. Sometimes he was sitting on the table, and the person who really played the card was the person behind him who looks at the card. He often tells Li to play a certain card in the back. There was also a young man who was the son of my aunt's maid named Cheng Fu, came from Shanli Township, Fangzhou, Fuzhou. Because of poor family and poor life, my eldest brother-in-law introduced him to work n a unit of the Navy. He was very honest, and sometimes he came to help my eldest sister. There were so many people coming and going, so my eldest sister's family was lively and busy most of the time. I had been in Shanghai for two years and could say that I was not homesick.

In 1931, my eldest sister moved to a new built Ruihua Square just across the road. The house was a single three-storey Shikumen house. It was rented from one household and two landlords. What reason she moved, I could not remember clearly, probably because of fear of thief. My second sister moved to the second floor front building on the other side of the same block. I forgot how to deal with the old apartment. After the summer, my eldest sister moved again and moved to the second floor of a house nearby Lu priest Road (now Hefei Road). At this time, the

6 th uncle had returned to Fuzhou, and no one else lived in my eldest sister's house.

In January 1932, my parents wanted me to get married and sent Pinying to Shanghai. They also brought the 6th aunt's unwed daughter-in-law to live in my sisters homes. Dongmei had leprosy when she was in Fuzhou, but they didn't pay attention to that. At this time, because my mother, who was very afraid of leprosy, would coming soon, I was asked to take Dongmei to the Red Cross Hospital (now Huashan Hospital) for examination by a doctor who was my classmate. Then arranged Dongmei to enter the Leprosy Hospital in Hangzhou for treatment. On the morning of the January 28th, I sent Dongmei to Hangzhou. On the same day, I returned to Shanghai. When I arrived at Xinlonghua Station, I realized that the Songhu Anti-Japanese War had broken out. Because of the war, I got married on February 4th and used my eldest sister's room as a cave. A few days later, the 6th aunts and 6th uncles and their sons come from Nanjing to Shanghai, and the 6th aunts temporarily stayed in my eldest sister's house, causing her house to be overwhelmed. After the 6th aunt's son got married, they turned back to Nanjing. Songhu War was dragged on for a long time, and the battle was getting worse. My parents and I with Pinying fled back to Fuzhou by boat. After about a month, I came back to Shanghai alone to continue study in school. When I graduated in the summer, I invited my eldest brother-in-law to attend my graduation ceremony. He was very happy to see that I received the best student award.

After graduation, I stayed in University as a teacher and returned to Fuzhou to picked up Pinying and settled down in Shanghai. we were frugal and saved money, then I could remit an extra ten yuan every month to my parents, they would accumulate on behalf of us. After about one year, we returned the more than one hundred yuan to my eldest sister's financing aid during the two years of my study. Although the money was paid back, but my eldest sister subsidized me to graduate from University with all the kindness to me, I would never forget it.

In 1934, after my parents came to Shanghai, I moved twice. When I moved to No. 11, Yongle Village, Wanhangdu Road, my two sisters families also moved in. My eldest sister and her stepmother lived in the front building and the pavilion on the third floor, and Pinying and I lived in the back building. At this time, Pinying was pregnant and were taken care by my eldest sister in many aspects. On the evening of January 18, 1935, Pinying was about to give birth with abdominal pain. My eldest sister and I were accompanied by a taxi to Xieqiao Red House Hospital. My eldest sister and I had been waiting outside the delivery room. After the birth of my son, I first went home to report and take a rest, and she stayed in the hospital to take care of Pinying and busy all night. During the confinement period, Pinying also was helped a lot. In the spring of this year, my eldest sister daughter unfortunately suffered from measles, poisoned her brain, and suddenly became unconscious. Her sister-in-law and I carried the sick child together, and was sent to two hospitals for treatment, but neither could save her. The death of young girl make my eldest sister very sad, I was also very sad. This eight-year-old girl was very lively and cute, and she was very good at singing and dancing. Everyone loves her, Her early death made many people feel sorry for my eldest sister.

In the first half of 1936, my parents and Pinying returned to Fuzhou to have my younger brother married. The three families were torn apart. My eldest sister moved to Fululi Road, 36 East Lane, Jianyeli. I moved alone to the school, and quit often visited my eldest sister. During this period, my eldest sister bought a lot of furniture for me from her next door neighbor, which was piled up in her house first. Until I picked up Pinying, returned to Shanghai and lived in St. John's dormitory, then I moved these furniture out. In November of that year Pinying was pregnant for the second time and was about to give birth. Pinying and I moved to my elder sister's house which was very close to the Red House hospital in advance for fear of going to the hospital too late. During the delivery, Pinying was taken care of by my elder sister.

During the Anti-Japanese War

At the end of 1937, because the west of Shanghai had turned into evil soil, my family moved to No. 3 Fishing Village, Baier Road in the French Concession. I rented a room on the first and second floors, which was relatively spacious. My parents were not in Shanghai, so I invited my eldest sister to come and lived with us. At that time, only my eldest sister with her husband and son were in Shanghai. Soon, the 3rd aunts (Cai junbao wife) and their second daughter LingLing from Nanjing moved to Shanghai and they stayed in my house for a few days then transferred to Fuzhou. By this time the Survey Bureau had ceased completely, and my brother-in-law had nothing to do, so Just did the research that he loved. Early on, he strongly supported the reform of Chinese characters and advocated the popularization and application of phonetic symbols. When he named his son with two letters "ㄌㄦ" as nickname. But this name was very bad, because in Chinese writer "ㄌ" like the inferior part of "劣" (meaning of "bad") "ㄦ" like "兒" (now was simplified to ㄦ) homophones, "ㄌ ㄦ" would be read as a bad boy by many people, was it a joke? When the eldest daughter was born, he used letters "ㄈㄙ" as her nickname and call it like an English fox (fox), it's even more bizarre and the girl was born and died. The second daughter used "ㄠ西" two letters as her name, even called with the Chinese sound as "yao xi", (meaning of "will die") and later she died at the age of eight. So many people, including my eldest sister, said he was a bit dumb. He also spent a lot of time creating a shorthand method, which was said to be based on the mouth shape with tongue shape of the pronunciation. Printing and distributing this creation with his own money had not been appreciated and accepted. He also wanted to plot the spherical triangle according to its projected on the plane, and to find another function value, which took several years. When he lived in Fishing Village, he once laid a big curtain on guest hall, and asked a cartographer of the Survey Bureau to draw a picture for him and he asked very precise to the four digits that were impossible at the time. Before this picture was completed, he was sent to Chongqing, while my eldest sister stayed in Shanghai. Later, since my apartment was restricted to a room on the second floor, my parents came to Shanghai again, my eldest sister moved back to the house she still kept in Jianyeli, soon my eldest sister son was admitted to Jiaotong University. Some of his close friends were arrested for resisting Japan, afraid of being involved, he sneaked into the interior and continue studied at Southwest Associated University until graduation, he majored mechanical engineering. When my eldest sister's son left Shanghai, he was live alone at home, and I was disappointed that neither my place nor my financial situation would allow me to invite my eldest sister again. During this time, she often visited our parents, and when our father died, my eldest sister sat and served by his side.

In April 1945, my family returned to Fuzhou by a risky sailing ship, while my eldest sister remained in Shanghai alone. A lot of our furniture in my family were stored in her back room and attic. Soon after the victory of the War, my eldest sister's son returned to Shanghai as an Air Force ground crew. He was assigned a Japanese house in Jiangwan and soon got married, my eldest sister moved in and lived with them together. During the Spring Festival in 1946, I came to Shanghai from Fuzhou. I went to Jiangwan for New Year's Eve dinner. At this time, my eldest brother-in-law had also returned to Shanghai, I was overjoyed to see my eldest sister's family together. Soon after, my elder sister son resigned from the Air Force and went to work for Mobil company, responsible for the sales and technical business of lubricating grease. My eldest brother-in-law still returned to work at the Survey Bureau and was assigned to the residence at Fenglin Bridge near the Survey Bureau, where all of the family lived, and I visited them every time I came to Shanghai. The eldest sister still keeps the house she rented in Jianyeli. However, all the rooms except the back room and attic were sublet. From 1946 to 1949, I lived intermittently in the back room and attic, also lived the front room for several months. In April 1949, after the People's Liberation Army attacked Nanjing, the Kuomintang government's offices in Shanghai successively withdrew to Taiwan, and the Survey Bureau was also among the retreats. My eldest brother-in-law went alone, and my eldest sister did not go, but her family needed to move out of the Survey Bureau's house in Fenglin Bridge, so I moved out of Jianyeli.

Sister life after liberation

In September 1949, after the liberation of Shanghai, I rented a big house at 134 Jiangsu Road. Soon, Pinying with the children came to Shanghai, and so did my mother in 1951. My eldest sister had a maid at home, and her housework was greatly lightened, usually came to live in my house and accompany my mother and to go to the theatre with my cousin and my 4th aunt. At that time my economic and living conditions were quite good. I often invited them to come and hosted banquets in many restaurants outside. From 1958 to 1960, I also invited my eldest sister to travel with me. We had been to Suzhou, Wuxi, Beijing and Fuzhou, Xiamen and other places, eating and sleeping were abundant and comfortable. My mother could not go out with us, because she was nearly 80 years old, but my eldest sister was younger, not yet in her 70s. She was in good physical condition and still very healthy, so we invited her to travel a lot. I treated her like my mother during the trip. I did this by doing my best, repaying her kindness to me, and a little peace of mind.

When our mother died in 1961, my eldest sister was served by her side. During the funeral, she came to participate in every mourning event. Later, she would come to my house from time to time, and sometimes stay for a few days. But as her daughter-in-law was sickly, and in order to give her more careful attention, and more or less incapacitated by her own age, she came less and less. One day at the end of 1965, my eldest sister's daughter-in-law called us that my eldest sister had a stroke the night before, and was rescued in the hospital. After hearing the news, Pinying and I rushed to hospital. Although my eldest sister was rescued, but was paralysis of half of her body. She was hospitalized for more than a month, Unable to relieve paralysis of the right upper and lower limbs, she went home to recuperate. After she became ill, I visited almost every day. At the beginning of 1966, when the Asian Company was ended, I was sent to "study" in North Cao Xi Road, where was close to my eldest sister's home, and I visit her every day before I go home. But unfortunately, "Cultural Revolution" began in mid-May, making it was impossible for me to continue visit my eldest sister every day. At the beginning of September, I was overwhelmed and by property. The mood was very bad, the economy was also greatly hit, My stomach disease recurred, I was hospitalized because of stomach bleeding. In May 1967, I was admitted to Zhongshan Hospital for Gastrectomy due to massive stomach bleeding. My live up and down made my eldest sister worry about me. At the same time, she also fretted about the shock to her son's short period of isolation and censorship. In July 1968, I was also quarantined and censorship for a year and nine months before I was freed in April 1970. These unfortunate events all increased the anxiety and resentment of my eldest sister. During almost four years from 1966 to 1970, Pinying went to visit my eldest sister from time to time. My eldest sister understood my family's economic situation. Whenever Pinying refused, she was very anxious and even insisted to Pinying accept it. Her love for her younger brother made me grateful when I knew that later. When I was in quarantine, I didn't know anything about my family, so I often missed my wife and children, and especially missed my eldest sister. She had been broken the candle before the wind, and with a bad mood, I always miss whether she was still in the world, and I had always been worried about whether I could see her again when I was free. So, as soon as I got out of quarantine and went back home, I asked about my eldest sister how she was. When I heard that she was still alive, I felt relieved and immediately wanted to see her. But at that time, I was worried about whether my visit would had suspicion of cascading and implicated my eldest sister's family. As a last resort, I had no choice but to invite my hemiplegic eldest sister to my house, lest in case of her sudden death, brother and sister would not see each other, would regret for the rest of their lives. With the help of my eldest sister's neighbors, my eldest sister was finally brought in. The joy of the both sister and brother meeting was really beyond description. When my youngest son got married, we managed to invite her to come my house for wedding party, and after stayed one night, then sent her back. This was her last visit, when she was seventy-nine years old. When I got back some of the copied money, I returned to my eldest sister the sum of money she had given to my family during my isolation, I paid wayan back in round Numbers the money she had given me during my isolation and deposited it in the bank on her behalf. After I retired in 1971, I often went to visit her with Pinying, at least once a week, I brought some food for her when I went there. Later, as my deposits were gradually recovered, I also gave the money to my eldest sister for the neighbor bought her nutrition. When she and my eldest brother-in-law's birthday, I would give them a good filial piety.

At the beginning of 1980, my eldest sister's illness became worse, and she was bedridden. Every time needed someone help to pick her up for urinate. Fortunately, my eldest sister's neighbors helped. I sent a chair specially made of light wood by carpenter When she was bedridden, she needed cushions. I prepared rubber bands and sent them with cotton pads and straw paper. While my eldest sister couldn't get up, Pinying and I went to see her almost every day. On the morning of her death, Pinying and I rushed to my eldest sister's home. After seeing the last time, the body was taken away in a car from Longhua Funeral Parlour. My eldest sister was eighty-eight years old and had lived a long life, but the unspeakable sufferings she went through in her later years were remembered with great pain today. On the third day after my eldest sister's death, at the Longhua Funeral Parlour, I and Pinying cried again. In addition to presenting a large wreath, I also wrote a couple of offerings.

Has passed the high age,
    has not enjoyed the high age,
        Has lingered on the bed for fifteen years;
Although not the same mother,
    It is better than same mother.
        Love will last a lifetime.

I also wrote a couplet on behalf of my eldest sister's son as follows:

Sixty-one years according to Their parents,
    Has not been filial,
        worthy of my mother
More than five thousand days of lingering bitter,
    Although the end of life,
        pain through my heart

My Eldest Brother-in-law

Later in the same year that my eldest sister died, my eldest brother-in-law also died in Taiwan, at the same age of 88. Since he went to Taiwan in early 1949, he had not communicated with his home, even indirect communication. He was a member of the Kuomintang with an officer. He was extremely loyal to the Kuomintang and loyal enough to ignore even all his relatives on the mainland. He had an aunt who also went to Taiwan in 1949, after marrying, she settled down in Brazil with her husband. One year she returned to the mainland and visited relatives in mainland and Taiwan. When she was in Taiwan, and told him about the situation of his family in the mainland. When I wrote to my second sister's daughter in Taiwan and asked her to tell my eldest brother-in-law about my family and his family, he did not listen. He was so stupid and loyal.

Thirty-one years in Taiwan, he never had a home. After retirement, he lived in a retreat for KMT veterans. He reached the highest rank of major, but his residence in the so-called Rongjun Institute was extremely rudimentary, and the poor living conditions could be seen in the photos that was sent back from Brazil. My eldest brother-in-law was alone in Taipei, and the only relative close to him was his cousin. It was not known whether there were other relatives or friends on the side when he died in the hospital. In order to praise my eldest brother-in-law, the Kuomintang buried him deeply after his death. I saw it in a funeral photo transferred from Brazil.

My Second Sister

My second sister and I were siblings of the same mother, my father named her Rebirth, why did he choose this name, I did not know. She ranks 13th among the women of our Zheng's Family. I called her Rebirth sister from an early age, and later sometimes called her 13th sister, but never called her the second sister. She was the first child raised by my mother, but she was stepdad to my aunt after birth, so she was my aunt's stepdaughter. I did not know why my aunt did not like her, so she was not affectionate to my aunt. Unlike my eldest sister, she did not love younger brother much. Although I had been with her for more than 10 years before she married, we did not seem siblings in each other. Her zodiac was tiger. I calculated from this zodiac that she was born in 1902, she was 8 years older than me. I did not remember if she played with me when I was a kid. Probably due to her being a tiger, she had a bad temper, a violent personality with a very ruthless heart. So my younger brother and I were afraid of her and had been beaten and scolded by her. But she was still a bit cautious about me, because I was the eldest son of my parents, and my mother especially loved me. She did not care about my younger brother, although he was nominally her younger brother, both were successors of our aunt.

Live at Meiwu

I remember that when our family lived in Meiwukou in 1923, one night, my second sister stayed downstairs, she came running up with vigour and fury, suddenly slap my younger brother on his face without asking. Did not know some one upstairs, who was dropping water on her, At that time she was 23 years old, and my youngest brother was 11, both not too young.

During lived in Meiwu, there were five big girls lived together. Apart from my second sister, among them there were the 3rd sisters (Lanying), the 4th sisters (Guiying) and Pinying, the daughters of the 4th uncle, and Zheng Youhua, the elder daughter of the 6th uncle. They sometimes piece together pocket money to buy or cook something to eat. My second sister always was one of the initiators, but most of the work was done by other girls. She reaped the benefits and said nothing but annoyance.

My second sister was vain and snobbish, and often sneered at the poor and envied the rich. When we lived in Meiwukou Port, there was a Wanfeng customs broker nearby, which owned several barges for the transportation of goods between Fuzhou and Marwe, and for handling customs formalities on behalf of them, business was very good. Therefore, the boss was very rich, and people called him Wanfengding. His wife died early, leaving behind a lustful prostitute son, already married long ago and, begging another prostitute to be his concubine. Wanfengding himself remarry a wife who was much younger than him. Wanfengding's wife was very young when she got married, that she soon had two sons but no daughters. Of course she wanted one daughter. Somehow, my second sisters would knew this family and actually worship her as mother-in-law, but the age difference of the mother-daughter was no more than 10 years. After paying a visit to the mother-in-law, she certainly got some cheap food, but as far as I know, all she got was food and a few plays, and there was nothing worth mentioning. On one occasion, it was probably the uncle's family who had a happy event. When she was going to eat the wedding wine, she borrowed a gold ornament from her mother-in-law and accidentally lost. For this reason, she cried a lot and paid compensation, but she still treasured this friendship. When she married, the mother-in-law did give her anything, I did not know. But I know that my second brother-in-law had nothing to do with them. The two sons of this mother-in-law were married at a very young age. When the eldest son raised her first child, she was only 36 years old and became a 36-year-old young grandmother. When his second son later studied at Shanghai Daxia University, he married another female classmate to be his wife. During the war of resistance against Japan, my second sister handed over many years of savings to him to do business, but the results were empty.

My Second Brother-in-law

My second sister had been in the boudoir for many years. Somehow, few people proposed to match her, and some of them were unsuccessful. She may also be eager to marry herself, and often lose her temper. I heard my mother talk about her marrying, and then my mother asked my eldest brother-in-law to mediate for her. My eldest brother-in-law was extremely honest, but not good at making friends, and few people know. Because of my mother's repeated entrust he introduced an officer who was a second vehicle (the chief engineer's deputy) on the warship to my second sister as husband. My second brother-in-law, Li Kongrong, lived in Nanhou Street in the city. The family of the Li was originally very prosperous, and built a three-entry house. My second sister lived in the third-entry. My second brother-in-law's mother died before my second sister married Li's family. There was only one father-in-law at the top of the family, and four sons below. Her father-in-law worked as a clerk in a scented candle shop, his salary was very low, his second son was a mental patient, his third son had no fixed occupation, he married a wife first, his fourth son was young, but he did not study or work, live a hard life. My second sister was married in 1924. At this time my father was not at home, my mother tried her best with bitter and hard for her. Try to beat the money to prepare the dowry. All I just remember that there was a set of furniture made of fake mulberry in the dowry, and of course there were suitcases and so on. Although the second sister was not satisfied, her dowry was decent enough because the Li family was poor at that time. When my second sister returned to home, she also took away all the small ornaments (small porcelain vases and small porcelain basins) that I liked. As soon as my second sister got married, she became the head of the house. and my second brother-in-law's monthly salary was entirely her charged. She was very dissatisfied with supporting the three young uncles. Soon the mentally ill brother-in-law died and the third brother was forced to join the army and never returned, probably died soon after hearing nothing from him. The second brother-in-law wife was forced to run away, leaving the young husband unemployed at home, the second brother-in-law also got mental illness, after a period of time also died. In this way, in just two or three years, the three younger brothers of my second brother-in-law all died. Perhaps due to genetic relationship, the spirit of my second brother-in-law was not normal, often silent, staring, thoughtful. He had been on board and had been home only a short time. I had little contact with him and could not remember what we had talked about. As I grew up, I wondered if he might be mentally ill too. When I was in middle school, I went to the city several times to visit my second sister. From home to walk to her home, the road was quite far. It took half a day to go back and forth, so I rarely went. Two or three times I went to buy cloth shoes in South backstreet, by the way, After marriage, my second sister did not often go back to home, also because of the distance.

In 1930, when I went to Shanghai to study at University, my second sister lived in Lane 286 Lafayette Road with my eldest sister. She lived in the downstairs room. I heard something about my second brother-in-law, which was quite ridiculous. When his ship sailed to Shanghai and returned to his house for the first time, he could not find his home and returned to the ship. It turned out that The Reinfeld Road, lane

286, near the mouth of Baylor Road, in order to find convenience, customary to address them as lane 286, Lafayette Road, Baylor Road, keep your position on the front road and the back road points to the nearest intersection. When my second brothers-in-law came home, he thought they were on Baylor Road and blindly looked for lane 286 along Baylor Road. Of course, he could not find it. He had to return to the ship. Everyone laughed that he didn't know how to find it on Lafayette Road, and he did not know how to ask passers-by. Later, he probably asked his colleagues on the ship to find his house when he returned for the second time.

Prefer Boys to Girls

My second sister had raised a daughter before she came to Shanghai, a little younger than the eldest sister's daughter. Later in 1931 raised a son in Shanghai. She had a strong preference for sons, and often had what not to please, then make the daughter as air hole, beat and scold, referring to daughter but scolds others, made her daughter feel uncomfortable. When her daughter was young, often cried with said, "Mom beats me with feathers' dusters." When she first arrived in Shanghai, her mother and daughter were together lived in my eldest sister's house. Afterwards, she thought the food were bad, so they ate separately. She wants to hire a maid to work for her. At that time, hiring a maid usually went to the recommendation line, they would bring the rural women who were to be hired to negotiate terms at home to do so or to leave. One time, the recommendation line introduced a maid, when she saw my second sister, she did not talk about anything, but turned around and left. It was said that she was "afraid of the madam's face." When she was unhappy, her face was fierce and terrible indeed.

I had to continue to finish college in Shanghai, mainly relying on my eldest sister's financial assistance, and my second sister also helped a part. During the winter and summer vacations and most weekends in the past two years, I lived in my eldest sister's house, and my second sister occasionally asked me to eat at her house. A lot of money was provided to me by my eldest sister, but I remember that my second sister once bought wool and knitted a thick cardigan to keep me warm. The two sets of short sleeves and ordinary shorts I needed in the summer were also bought by my second sister. I remember all the money she gave and the money she used to buy things for me. In the two years, there were a total of 50 or 60 yuan (the real number had been forgotten). After I graduated, I remit an extra 10 yuan to my parents every month, just for returning back to my second sister. I always remember my second sister's help in this respect, would never forget.

In 1931, Both sisters' houses moved to Ruihuafang, just across the road, where they lived on the second floor of two buildings. My second sister only lived in a front building. During holidays and weekends, I still eta and lived in my eldest sister's house, and I also from time to time, went to my second sister's house to visit her and her children.

Second Sister's Saving Plan

My second brother-in-law had been working on the ship and only had a few time back home. Both he and my second sister desperately wanted to end their separation life as soon as possible. For this reason, they jointly worked out a plan to accumulate a sum of money within a few years (at that time, five or six thousand yuan was enough), so that they could retire as soon as possible. Live on deposits. They all strive to save, especially my second sister. Thrift was a virtue, not only blame it, but also commendable. But she was frugal to the point of being stingy, and she liked to take advantage of others' cheapness, which was wrong. Their money was stored in the Universal Savings Association (founded by the French) at that time, with small savings by Installment deposit and lump sum withdrawal, monthly deposit. This was rewarded and interest-bearing savings, lottery on time, there were many opportunities to win.

In addition, my second brother-in-law listened to the advertisement at that time and invested in the New Zealand forest development enterprise. It is said that a few years later, he will receive a large amount of principal and interest and preferential dividends. This shows the urgency of their desire to get rich.

At the beginning of 1932, I married at my eldest sister house. My father lived temporarily at my second sister house. At that time, her family had moved to the second floor of Yongyu Lane, Fuxing Middle Road. Her father-in-law, about 70, the old man anility, had come to Shanghai and lived in the back rood, was also responsible for taking care of his grandson who was only one year old. The little grandson was very thin, and his grandfather sat on a chair in back room all day, holding him with his hands, and looked pitiful. The Songhu Anti-Japanese War took place this year. After I got married, I went back to Fuzhou with my parents, and my second sister's family followed us back to Fuzhou. In Fuzhou they all lived in their old house in the city. Soon after I returned to Shanghai to continue my study in University, my second sister often brought her son back to our home in Fuzhou. At our house, she handed her son to Pinying for taking care, and then she went out, shopping everywhere, or spending most time in gambling or watching gambling, but she did not like my eldest sister, she just want to make fun on it. But for to have lunch or dinner, always need Pingying to invite her again and again, that made Pingying very annoying. She also often feels unhappy and loses her temper, said that she was in her mother's home, "unlike the owner or the guest, the actions were restricted and not respected." Pinying felt very distressed about this, and my father was very sympathetic. When I returned to Fuzhou after graduation, I determined to take Pinying to Shanghai, that also was a reason.

My second sister took her children to Shanghai after her father-in-law's death. In 1934, three families (my eldest sister, my second sister and my family) lived together at No. 11, Yongle Village, Wanhangdu Road. My second sister's family lived in the front room on the second floor, and my parents lived in the back room. At this time, she had already saved a sum of money, my eldest brother-in-law had a high salary, and my eldest sister also had some savings. I was the poorest, had a lower salary, and had to support parents. My second sister was afraid to disclose her savings because she was afraid of us. During this period, she was win one of the large IWC Savings Awards, and she did not dare to speak out, afraid would pay her money out for a treat or to entertain.

After the Sudden Bad News

In 1936 Chiang Kai-shek government had close ties to the Nazi Germany, required naval officers to Germany to study for establish a submarine force, My second brother-in-law was one of the dispatched personnel, and soon he was dressed up abroad, and everyone was happy for him.

In 1937, when the War of Resistance Against Japan broke out, my family moved from Huxi to No. 3 Fishing Village, Shunchang Road, close to Yongyuli where my second sister lived. In 1939, my parents came to Shanghai again because my house was very small, so they had to live in my second sister's house. But soon, the two elders moved back to my house in a hurry. When they came back, my father shouted, "Escaped! Escaped!". Although my mother did not say anything, we did not ask the reason in detail, but they all knew that neither of them could bear my second sister's bad temper. One day this year, my second sister received a telegram from Berlin informing her that her husband was killed in a car accident. The sudden bad news shocked and saddened everyone in our family. Of course, my second sister was heartbroken. It was very strange to say that when she and her children were having breakfast that day, the 10 year old daughter suddenly exclaimed: "Dad, come back!" It was often said that the souls of relatives who died in a distant place would fly home like electricity inspiring loved ones could perceive. Given the illusion of a 10-year-old daughter, was this credible? Later my second sister received a letter from a colleague who went to Germany with my second brother-in-law. When my second brother-in-law hear that my second sister had written to him, and they hurriedly rushed to there (probably the Chinese embassy in Germany) to take the letter, He was hit by a motorbike while crossing the road and died from serious head injuries. could not be rescued and died. It was said that the fault of the accident lay in his careless walking, while the cyclist was not at fault and not liable for compensation. He died so tragically, probably because he was mentally ill and crossed the road too quickly. Colleagues took care of his funeral, and the relics were later brought back by them. There were two new suits in the relics were I paid for. As soon as the second brother-in-law died, the savings plans made by my second sister and my second brother-in-law were completely lost. Her deposits at the Universal Savings Association were becoming less valuable because of the depreciation of counterfeit currency. In order to maintain value, she gave the money to her brother to do business. Probably all the money invested in New Zealand forestry was also lost. She never let me know about these things, and of course never even discussed with me, because I was poor in her eyes.

Shortly after the death of my second brother-in-law, my second sister with their son and daughter returned to Fuzhou and lived and stayed In the east front room and front wing room of the second entrance in Zheng's mansion, as well as the kitchen outside the wall and a room upstairs. This room was bought by my parents for a long time ago at a very cheap price, and had been rented to others. In addition to the saving and my second brother-in-law pension was sued by the Admiralty, my second sister also relied on the rent received to subsidize her family. Of course, it was economically quite difficult. I did not know if his family members had ever given subsidies. In early 1941, my father died, and my eldest sister, me, and my young brother were beside him, my second sister was the only person in Fuzhou who could not come to Shanghai. When my father died, he whispered her name and said, "Road was too far to come!" For my father's funeral at Fuzhou, my mother hurried back to Fuzhou. After my second sister assisted my mother in the funeral, my mother stayed in Fuzhou with her for a period of time and did not come to Shanghai until the next year. Not more longer my second sister died in Fuzhou, at the age of 41, she died of bowel disease. After her death, she left a very poor pair of orphans. her daughter was only 15 years old and her son was 11 years old. They were all taken care of by their uncles first. I did not know whether they were also taken care of by their grandmother. In 1946, according to acquaintances, my second sister's daughter married Mr. Lin who graduated from Jinan University. After marriage, they went to Taiwan to teach at a primary school in Kaohsiung. Mr. Lin was a secondary school teacher in Kaohsiung and later promoted to principal. They had two sons and had difficult life at the beginning. With the development of Taiwan's economy, their lives had improved greatly. Both children graduated from university in Taiwan and had studied in the United States successively. They both obtained a master degree in engineering. They were both now settled in the United States, and they both had a family and had children. After graduating from Fuzhou Middle School, the second sister son was admitted to a school in Northeast China. After graduation, he settled down to work in Northeast China and gave birth to two sons and one daughter. In 1983, he brought two sons back to Fuzhou, and now both of them had graduated from college, and the descendants of my second sister had been extended, I was glad to hear that.

CHAPTER 13

Younger Brother

I had only one younger brother, he was two years younger than me and was born in 1912. He was named Chaozong, and his little name was Haiguan. Our father gave him these two names, which means "Chaozong Yuhai". Later, he named himself Haifu and used as pseudonym for writing articles. Most of his life lived and worked in Xiamen near by the sea, so he loved the sea and was proud of the pseudonym Haifu.

Hard Study

In the Zheng's Family, my younger brother, Ranking 38, was the youngest one in the Zhao generation. After birth he was stepdad to my widow aunt. Although he was my aunt stepson, but when he was only 3 years old, my widow aunt died. So our brothers had always been very affectionate in our family. But some adults treat us differently. I was the eldest son of my parents and the only son in name. The family and relatives had a different look at me and my younger brother thought he was the nephew of our parents, not like me. For this reason, he had an inferiority complex as a child. The more he was, the more he was bullied by children of the same age and relatives. At that time, there were five such children in the first entrance of Zheng's mansion, One was Chaozhi, one year older than me, quite naughty, and ran away when something happened. Fortunately, he lived outside the front wall, and had to pass the front hall, where the fierce woman "Big Neck" often sat. He was so scared and didn't dare to go over. There were two nephews Tianxiong and Tianzhao living in the back room in the east. Tianxiong was one year older than me and relatively honest. His younger brother Tianzhao was two years younger than me, as same age as Chaozong. Tianzhao was naughty and brutal, and his mother 19th sister-in-law, often indulges and shields him. Tianzhao was fearless, like practical jokes, bullying Chaozong, causing Chaozong to be tricked by him, and punished by our mother. Once Tianzhao secretly stuffed a shoe of Chaozong into the gutter hole of the back patio. Chaozong found nowhere and was scolded by our mother. Later, the eldest daughter of the 14th sister-in-law found the shoe, and the 19th sister-in-law was still insisted that it was not her son's fault. The 14th sister-in-law who lived behind the wall had two daughters who was about the same age as my younger brothers. One was the elder sister who found the shoe, and the other was XiXi sister. They often play with us in the back hall and back patio. My family had a dining table in the back hall, and a bamboo basket was hung on the roof beam above the table. Children could stand on the table for getting this bamboo basket. One day, Chaozong and them climbed up on the table to fight for the bamboo basket. Chaozong was small and unsteady standing, so was squeezed down, his heads touched the ground, and was bleeding. In order to stop bleeding, an adult quickly grabbed a handful of dust from the door and put on the wound. The bleeding was stopped, and tetanus and fever did not occur afterwards, but the wound did not grow hair later, leaving a crescent mark on his head that had left a deep impression in my memory.

Because of the family's financial difficulties, our parents could not give the same education to our two brothers. When I was a kid, the school teacher I studied at that time was considered to be relatively good in the local area, because they were talented, and Chaozong studied at the enlightenment private school set up by one of my cousin.

I only read primary school for one year, of which half a year was Trinity Primary School. He spent much longer in primary school. Our parents intended him to be an apprentice after a few years of reading, to learn a skill. But he refused and strove to study well, so that might go on to school. After I finished primary school in grade one (now the fourth grade of primary school), my mother paid for my tutor English lessons during summer vacation. So I could went to middle school study early, and later I was admitted to Trinity Chinese-English Middle School. After finishing primary school, my younger brother was admitted to Heling Yinghua School (later renamed Yinghua Middle School, then known as Yinghuazhai), and continued study until graduation. Both Trinity and Yinghua were church schools. Trinity was run by the Anglica Church and Yinghua was run by the America-Israeli-American Society. Liked me, although my younger brother had been studying in a middle school with a strong Christian environment for many years, he also was not religious. Two of our maternal grandfather's family had studied in Yinghua for three or four years before they were admitted by the post office and took the iron rice bowl of that time. Mother also hoped that this would be the case for Zhaozong, but it happened that the post office and other agencies did not recruit new staff in those years, so had to read year after year.

After graduating from the middle school, our parents were no longer able to make my younger brother go to College. So from 1930 to 1932, he worked as a clerk of the Provincial Department of Education for two years. At the same time he also taught Zheng zaiyu concubine to read, Zheng zaiyu was the director of the Provincial Department of Civil Affairs, his golden house was located in the Nanxia Mountain Pavilion, and our cousin Liu boyu's house was also there. During this period, I was studying at University in Shanghai. My parents were satisfied to have him in Fuzhou and to be able to support them, I also was quite satisfied. In 1932, my younger brother was admitted to Tsinghua University with excellent academic performance and was awarded a scholarship. Coincidentally this year, I graduated from University, I could replace my younger brother to support our parents, so he could go to University in Peiping at the end of the summer. He was different from me. I like Mathematics, Physics and Chemistry, so I majored in Physics first and then transferred to Civil Engineering in University. He liked literature, since entering Tsinghua, he had been specializing in Chinese and Foreign Literature, so both Chinese and English were very good. He was very knowledgeable and had read many literary and historical books, all could be remembered, so later benefited greatly from writing articles. He was better at writing prose and ancient poetry and wrote and published a lot of essays and works.

Encounter War

In 1936 my younger brother graduated from Tsinghua and returned to Fuzhou to get marriage in the summer. His wife Lin Mingqing was granddaughter of the 7th uncle of the Chen Family, so they were sparse aunts and cousins. She lost her mother at the age of 13 and had one elder brother with two younger brothers. After her mother died, she took on the responsibility of raising the two younger brothers. Later, her father remarriage and gave birth to another bunch of children. Her housework was even heavier. Late her father also died, and of course she was more bitter. Our mother wanted to choose such a girl as my younger brother wife. After marriage my younger brother left home to look for job. That time just was during the Japanese invasion of China, quite difficult to find a job. Until the end of the year that he got a post of secretary of the president office in Peking Normal University, until December that he found out a residence that he could took his wife to reunite in Peiping. The following year, the "July 7" incident occurred, and they fled to the south. After passing through Shanghai, they lived in my house at No. 4 Yongle Village for a few days before returning to Fuzhou with our parents. For finding a job in Fujian province, he was displaced for two years. In 1939, I introduced him to join the Lester Engineering College and taught Chinese in the Middle School, he and his wife came to Shanghai. For the next four years, he lived a slightly more stable life, and giving birth to a daughter and a son. However, during this period, their live were not very calm. At first, they lived in the back room of No. 36 Jianye Dongli where my eldest sister lived. He once had typhoid fever and was hospitalized. Two children had tracheitis and whooping cough. Later, they moved to the second floor in Chengqingli, was close to the Fishing Village where my family lived. When our father died in early 1941, my younger brother was at the bedside. By the end of 1942, the British principal and teachers of the Lester Engineering College were locked up in a concentration camps by the Japanese. At the beginning of the next year I resigned my teaching work there and my younger brother also resigned in July. Then he traveled back to Fujian alone, and soon his wife with their children sail back to Fuzhou on boat.

Determined Return

In Fujian, he found a teaching position at Xiamen University and moved his family to Changting, where Xiamen University was located, since then he had taken root in Xiamen University. In 1945, he once worked in Yongan for a short period. His wife brought three children back to live in Fuzhou, one of whom was raised in Changting. After the victory of the Anti-Japanese War, Xiamen University moved back to the original site in Xiamen. His wife with their children settled down in Xiamen, where he gave birth to the youngest daughter and became the father of one son with three daughters. In 1948, he received Sino-British heptyl scholarship to study in the UK, and went to Britain, and his wife with four children returned to live in Fuzhou. In the UK he entered Oxford University to study English literature. New China was founded in 1949, and the following year a group of scholars abroad, such as Li Siguang, tried to return to China. Taiwan Kuomintang exile government embassies and consulates in foreign countries also tried every means to attract scholars,

Graduate students and students who were still abroad, prompting them to betray the motherland. At the same time, his mentor asked him to specialize in Western classical literature, and disagreed with his study of progressive literature, so he gave up his degree and resolutely returned to his homeland. When he arrived in Guangzhou via Hong Kong, the Central People's Government and Xiamen University sent personnel there to welcome him back. He decided to return to Xiamen University to teach, teach Chinese and Western literature, and later served as the head of the Chinese Department. At this time, his family lived in the Professor Building of Danan Xincun on the campus, and was adjacent to Professor Lujiaxi. In the second half of 1952, I from Shanghai to Xiamen, for Asia oil company to close the Xiamen branch, I lived in Gulangyu for half a year. I often went to my younger brother's house to visit their couple and four children, we got along very well and happy. He joined the Democratic League as an ally and served as xiamen Municipal Party Committee and Fujian Provincial Party Committee of the Democratic League. He was also a member of the All-China Federation of Literature and Art, and a member of the Provincial Federation of Literature and Art. He also a member of the CPPCC National Committee at both provincial and municipal levels. For this reason, he often left Xiamen to attend various conferences, and teaching-related meetings. While I was in Xiamen, he went to Beijing for a business trip, and when he came back to Shanghai, he took our mother back to Xiamen and lived there for few weeks.

Care in Mired

Just when we were happy for him, suddenly a bolt from the blue came. In 1957, an anti-rightist struggle was launched in China, and the turbid current spread to him. Because he wrote several articles before and after the victory of the Anti-Japanese War, he was classified as a rightist and suffered a great unreasonable impact, so that his family suffered unjustly for twenty years. His position was reduced, his salary was cut, his house was compressed and ruined, and the mental blow was even harder to say. In those suffering years, when a person was pushed down to the ground and then put a foot trodden on again, would never be able to turn over, and he would be wronged forever if he was wronged. I squatted in a foreign business enterprise and got some asylum. These ultra-left characters did not dare to be arrogant. However, I dare not take the risk of being involved in protecting the "rightists" and being unable to make a difference. I really could not help, and felt extremely uneasy. Fortunately, both my eldest niece and eldest nephew had arrived at the year of entering higher education, so that was able to remit them monthly living expenses to their respective schools to reduce the burden of my younger brother. My eldest niece majored in physics, after graduated from college, she was assigned to a middle school as a teacher in Haikou, Fuqing. Insisted on her own to support her younger brother through college, do not want me to remit money to him, so I only support them for two years. In the second half of 1960, I went to Xiamen, Fuzhou with my wife and my eldest sister, and lived in my brother's house in Xiamen. At that time he lived in Dashengli and had two daughters by his side. Due to the narrow housing, he had to borrow the neighbor's room for a few days. When we went on a trip, invited him and his wife to accompany with us. On the trip, we found him were unhappy with a heavy mood and depressed, so we were very worried about them. My niece was about to get married in Haikou. At this difficult time, it was not easy to buy anything. We sent them some small household items as gifts from Shanghai. Although my youngest brother had removed his rightist hat, but his situation had not changed much. At the end of 1961, when my mother was in critical condition in Shanghai, I sent a telegram to him. He rushed to Shanghai immediately, on the next day our mother died. when our mother died, he was with us. After our mother was buried, he returned to Xiamen. Unexpectedly, he was a little loose for three or four years, and our country set off a 10-year catastrophe that was much worse than the anti-rightist movement. my younger brother was so persecuted that in 1970 he was exiled to Liancheng Mountains to work as a farmer. At this time, Asia Oil

Company was closed, and I was assigned to the Shanghai Housing and Land Bureau to "learn". During the robbery, My house had been raided. Later, I was quarantined for nearly two years. While he was in Liancheng, his wife also voluntarily accompanied him and spent two years with him. During this period, after graduating from Xiamen University, the second daughter was assigned to work in Chongqing Iron and Steel Factory, and the third daughter was forced to leave family and go to countryside. Although he was transferred back to Xiamen University from Liancheng in mid-1972, but his situation was still not good.

See Light

It was not until 1976 that the "gang of four" was crushed that his mood was comfortable, but his life has not been greatly improved. At the end of that year, Pinying and I returned to Fujian and lived in his home in Xiamen. At this time he was still living in Dashengli, but the house was slightly more comfortable than before, and his situation gradually improved over time. After a few year he was completely vindicated. He was resumed his position as full professor with the head of department, and his salary was restored. The residence was moved to the newly built lecturer building near Xiamen University, which had two rooms with one hall. By the end of 1980, when Pinying and I returned to Fujian, again, we lived there for a few days. At that time, his children were all away from home. The eldest daughter and son-in-law were teaching at the worker school set up by the Fuzhou Federation of Trade Unions. The son and daughter-in-law were teaching at the Fuzhou Normal University Affiliated Middle School and the Primary School. The second daughter and her husband were still working as engineers and doctors at Chonggang. The third daughter was admitted to Fujian Medical College and studying in Fuzhou, and her husband worked at the Xiamen Institute of Oceanography and lived in the dormitory of the institute. Only left their old couple and a little grandson needed their took care, so it seemed quite comfortable. At this time, he was in a good mood, writing and publishing a lot of essays, and compiled into a collection of essays, received a lot of manuscript fees, so the economic situation was good. After staying in Xiamen for a few days, we traveled to Quanzhou with my brother and purchased new clothing such as Nilon shirts imported at the time.

In the autumn of 1982, they came to Shanghai with high spirits. After my younger brother participated in a meeting of graduate student oral defense in Shanghai, we accompanied them to tour Hangzhou, Nanjing and Yangzhou, everyone was very happy. By this time the three were over seventy, and my sister-in-law was not yet seventy, while touring the Nanjing Yangtze River Bridge and Zhongshan Mausoleum, She was the only one who was able to climb to the top of Bridge and climb up to the Zhongshan Lingtang. After returning to Xiamen, my younger brother published a prose named "Tour record of Four Hao", which was quite interesting to read. Traveling with him this time, my younger brother felt his health was worse than before, and his spirit was also very poor. On the train from Shanghai to Hangzhou, we all sat on a hard seat. He sat on the edge of the aisle. Soon after the train start moved, he fell asleep and leaned over the passing conductor. We were all shocked when the conductor called us, thinking that he had suddenly fallen ill and had asked the announcer to call the doctor on board for medical attention. The result was not illness, but drowsiness, and then he and my sister-in-law moved to the soft seat. In Shanghai, we let him had a good rest for a few days, then we took soft seats to Nanjing, and took big bus from Nanjing to Yangzhou for a half-day tour. Finally, we crossed the River from Yangzhou to Zhenjiang, then transfer to a soft seat backed to Shanghai. When visiting Hangzhou, Nanjing and Yangzhou, we tried not to tire him out too much, but he paid great attention to the cultural relics and copied a lot of words for writing. After returning from Shanghai, he spent several months for recuperating in Gulangyu Island Sanatorium, accompanied by his wife. He suffered from coronary heart disease and hypertension, as well as frequent episodes of stomach ulcers. It could be said that these diseases were caused by his long-term unhealthy mood, which was exacerbated by repeated stimulation. Fortunately, his wife took good care of him, often measuring his blood pressure, and giving him medicines and foods such as mashed celery.

In 1984, when Pinying and I visited Xiamen again, we were traveling with them in the Huli Special Economic Zone and the Sea Paradise, and I was very pleased to see that my younger brother was well maintained. At this time, he has two daughters working in Xiamen, close to him. The second daughter and her husband had been transferred from Chongqing to Xiamen. The second daughter worked as an engineer at Xiamen University. The son-in-law worked as a physician in the First Hospital of Xiamen. The third daughter had graduated from the medical University, and worked in the city hospital as obstetrics and gynecology doctor, her husband was a researcher at the Institute of Oceanography. During this period, my younger brother still went out from time to time to attend meetings, such as he was accompanied by someone to go to Beijing to participate in a cultural federation meeting, and accompanied by his wife went Fuzhou to attend the Fujian Provincial committee of the Chinese People Political Consultative Conference.

Sunset Afterglow

In the second half of 1985, my sister-in-law accompanied my younger brother to attend a meeting in Fuzhou. After returning to Xiamen, my younger brother did not feel any discomfort, but his wife felt quite tired. Her digestive system had problems early, but she was still strong and did not seek medical attention in time. On the evening of November 1, she suffered from acute pancreatitis and was admitted to a hospital in the city. The doctor gave him medical treatment instead of surgery. As a result, she was hospitalized for more than a month, exhausted all the good medicines, and still no improvement. she died on the winter solstice, and was only 70 years old. Recalling that three years ago, when my younger brother and my sister-in-law travelled together in the three cities of Jiangsu and Zhejiang with Pinying and me, she was the youngest with the toughest body, but she died first, that was not what we expect. Both Pinying and I were greatly shocked when she fell ill. We sent a telegram of condolence until we heard of her death, and deeply regretted her untimely death. We were also worried that my younger brother would no longer be cared for by his wife. He felled ill and was hospitalized for a few days. He was admitted to the same hospital due to high blood pressure and heart problems. Fortunately, he had two daughters at home, a daughter and a son-in-law was also a doctor, could serve at any time. Four years had passed and he was as well as ever. We were all glad for him and wish him happy and healthy.

People's life, unless the life was short, could not be smooth sailing, there were always up and down. In the turbulent 20th century, China experienced a long war of warlords, Anti-Japanese War, War of liberation, and continuous class struggle after the founding of new China, It was rare that a man who was near or over the age of seventy could not go through without ups and downs. But some people had long periods of prosperity and short periods of adversity. Others, on the other hand, had short periods of prosperity and long and frequent periods of adversity. Those who believe in fate would say that the former was good and the latter was bad. Who wouldn't say so afterwards? If one could tell the story of a newborn child's life, he was either a fortune-teller or a physiognomist. To believe such people was called superstition, I was not superstitious, but there were things that I could not help believing. Take me and my younger brother for example. We were brothers, when I was a child, no one in my family counted my life and the same was probably true of my youngest brother. But my mother told me very early that my life was relatively smooth and better than my youngest brother, but he had a lot of lives with unlucky. On what grounds my mother neither knew the art of fortune-telling nor the art of physiognomist, I was still at a loss to understand.

In the old days, people often said that the upper body long people live comfortable life, the lower body long people live laborious life. My mother also said. I had a short body and short legs. Up to now 80 years of my life, the first 20 years of living in Fuzhou, the next nearly 60 years of living in Shanghai, it could be said that there was no much hardship in my life. On the other hand, my younger brother was tall with long legs, he had travelled to countless places in his life, had studied abroad and been exiled to the poor countryside to work as a farmer, It's hard enough, I had two bumpy periods, one was caused by national calamity during the war of resistance against Japan; other one was the "Cultural Revolution". It was caused by political catastrophe (political havoc). But my two calamity, compared with the average person, were only short time. But after graduating from university, my younger brother suffered from many setbacks, repeatedly bumped up and down, from "anti-rightist" injustice to the "Cultural Revolution" suffering wrongfully, which lasted as long as 20 years. It was only when he was fast forward to his seventies, he was at ease, but not for long, then he was bereaved of a wife who had long shared his joys and sorrows. I could not write about him without sighing for the doom of his life. Now I wish him a long and healthy life.

CHAPTER 14

Song of Golden Wedding

Time was gone,
Ran Fifty years,
This was blue silk hair,
Frost was on the temple side.

Knotted for half a century,
The scene changes several times,
Together, together
The love was growing stronger.

Old wife and me,
Cousin Marriage Alliance,
My mother and my father,
Siblings and brothers.

That year was longer than me,
I'm Xiao Fangqing[1]
No need for a pearl tower[2],
My spouse was born naturally.

Each title when he was young,
Reunion famous[3],
The team was born in the homeland,
The beads were from Nanyang.

I was only seven years old,
Return to your hometown with your mother,
My aunt saw me happy,
Jokes and tricks.

Unfortunately she died prematurely,
Died the next year,
Poor Pearl was still young,
Eight-year-old bereavement mother.

The stepmother is very serious,
Sent Peto sad,
Whenever wronged,
Siqin tears.

Our two young days,
From time to time,
Later lived in a house[4],
The two little ones had no guesses.

Go to private school,
But separated from each other,
Slightly longer into school,
Different seedlings were planted in two places.

I went to the monk temple[5],
Bijin Nun Temple[6],
I was twelve,
She was 13 years old.

Although we met on the weekend,
There were rare chats,
Study well,
Not willing to fall behind.

Pity the lot, nor was it good
Soon the Father will return to heaven,
Only fifteen years old,
Suffering alone.

His father's deathbed,
Call the mother to the bed,
Entrust him,
Get in touch with me.

My mother kept silent,
His father did not declare,
In the two little masks,
There was no care in my heart.

Get along as before,
Traveling together with you,
I had been aware of it for a long time,
Unnatural at first.

In order to avoid misconduct,
the mother Moved back to his old home,
Participating in business was not[7],
But it was more sparse to meet.

No distractions in my chest.
Study diligently,
Do not play Phoenix[8],
Never learned[9]

The adults do not know,
Half suspicious,
Unexpectedly, my classmates,
Someone actually learned.

As a joke,
Play with each other,
Blush and ears,
Happy in my heart.

Because of my light clothes,
Do not wear satin and tassels,
Hold a paper umbrella on a rainy day,
The clogs were half stained with mud.

Seen by classmate Zhu,
Humiliating,
Once on a narrow road,
Shyly head down[10]

Pinying graduation ceremony,
Invite me to love[11],
Chao Qiang did not dare to go,
Frightened to be teased.

After graduating from high school,
Go their own way,
Pin Ying lacked funding,
School dropout[12]

Chao Qiang studied further,
Study and study[14],
A cousin of Pinying,
Xu Pei Wang Mou Gong.

With me as a classmate,
I will rush the engagement,
Because of the sadness of beads,
Comfortable information.

Waiting for more than ten days,
There was no response,
Nianbi was shy,
Never complained.

Concorde Open Day,
Classmate Girlfriend Pro,
Hope that people have not arrived,
Riverside alone.

In the summer of 1930,
Transfer to Shanghai Binhai,
Study the engineering class hard,
No time to read Iraqi people.

I have never graduated,
I did not want to get married,
It is hard to violate parental orders,
End marriage early.

Follow each other[15],
Strange to meet,
I saw an umbrella in my hand[16],
Forget the old times.

No smile on his face,
Two pairs of eyes straight,
The dialogue was speechless,
Not speaking to each other.

Sanni Tatsuka[17],
Yu Feicheng Phoenix,
Wedding gift,
Borrow lecture hall[18]

Acacia candle night,
My sister made a cave,
The Japanese attacked the artillery,
The sound was long all night long[19]

Looking back on childhood events,
The memory was still fresh,
Learn to be an adult,
Several times Jintai[20]

Ask who plays, Zheng and Chen[21],
Unexpectedly this day,
Falsification actually came true.
Japanese invaders were in a hurry to invade,

Japanese invaders were in a hurry to invade,
Songhu Anti-Japanese warfare,
To avoid swordsmanship,
The family turned back to the south.

Go home by boat,
Watching the people on the fence,
Marry first and fall in love,
Promote the knee as a long tan.

Honeymoon was over,
Return to Shenjiang,
To finish the competition,
To the cold window again.

Add acacia debt,
From time to time,
Yuyu Lai Yuyan,
Paper short stories were hard to understand.

Read diligently day and night,
The cousin was very ambitious,
All grades[22],
Cousin's face was light.

Know me like Ji Zi[23],
For my private bag,
Receiving the school title day,
Have to wear new clothes[24]

After parting,
Flying south liked an arrow,
Seeking parental promises,
The two branches had been connected since then.

I stay in school to teach[25],
Return to the same boat,
Long night and night,
Traveling together.

Taohongliuluji,
Traveling together in Hangzhou,
Jiang Xing took pictures of Qianying,
West Lake rafting.

After dozens of years,
Revisit again,
Group photo to find the old land,
Three frames remain today.

We came to Shanghai,
Only bring a wooden box,
One piece of furniture,
Former Toko Todoroki.

Starting from scratch,
Duan Lai wife virtuous,
Be diligent,
Thrift with money was an outline.

Parents were generous[26],
Daily use was quite unacceptable,
Everything to be added,
Arrangements are troublesome.

Soon to grow a child,
Immediately adopted daughter,
The burden was heavier,
The more difficult it was to maintain.

Zhengxi changed jobs[27],
Salary had doubled,
The economy was turning abundant,
Life was rising.

Unfortunately, the War of Resistance,
Began to suffer,
Prices were soaring fast,
The disadvantages were like landslides.

The delicate girl suffered from chronic illness,
Also lost by his father,
Pinying had a fistula,
I had a stomach ulcer.

Years of ups and downs,
Panic all day long,
Fortunately, Xianli help,
Suffering was common.

We planned early,
Do not ask for more births,
A man and a woman,
The days were bad.

Mother reprimanded,
Helpless mercy,
After having two more sons,
Life increases torture.

Determined to sterilize[28],
Tired wives often suffer,
The day of war was approaching,
The whole family was trapped in poverty.

Take the risk[29],
Drifting back to Fujian,
Get rid of the desperation,
Withered wood and spring[30].

It's only been a few months
Looking forward end of the war,
Back to Hudu alone,
Reinstatement into a dream[31]

Three years of work[32],
Fluttering like a canopy,
Rong and Shanghai go,
Lao's wife came and went.

Jiang Dangcheng was violent,
Renewed the civil war,
The bandit army was vulnerable,
The defeat seems to melt ice.

The frauds fell sharply,
The people were suffering,
My family was in trouble,
Si Shi and Sun Rise.

Shanghai old nest lost,
Inability to camp a new nest[33],
Although the salaries were not small,
It's just depreciation.

It was a lot,
It's a bag of grass,
Had the chance to go abroad,
Can't bear to throw home[34]

Sincerely stay at home,
Waiting to see the light,
The speed of liberation of the mainland,
Forehead Qing Taiping.

Family reunion[35],
As dry as Ganlin,
Life honey,
Thank you very much.

Elder went to North Korea,
Join the volunteer army,
Saner was against Jiang,
Throw a pen to Congrong[36]

The wife was in a duty,
Work harder,
elected to the city generation,
Ten years busy[37]

Children grow up well,
All of them were members,
Had entered the university one after another,
Each had its own special.

Married one after another,
My son-in-law was lucky,
Five symbiotic males,
There was no female Chanjuan.

My wife and I,
Let's increase the parties,
Nine Three and People's Progress,
Separated from each other.

Often busy activities,
Actively praised,
Keeping the house work hard and frugal,
Life was simple.

Only happy to hike,
Become good friends with each other,
Range Rover scenes everywhere,
Ancient monuments were also requested.

Also love to watch drama,
Appreciate the famous people,
After all,
Still feeling long.

On the path of life,
It's hard to sail,
Cultural Revolution caused catastrophe,
Attacked for no reason.

Copy home for ten days,
Everything was evacuated,
Sunny day comes to Lili,
Suddenly become poor and poor.

Imprisoned for more than 20 months,
was isolated from the family[38],
Su Yewei was lonely,
Thinking of his wife was only Chi.

After 36 years of marriage,
I often sing along,
Even though there was a difference,
When the audio was uninterrupted.

Ten years of disaster,
Hardship had been rewarded,
Fortunately, old and young,
Have security and health.

Once got anyway,
The property was fully repaid,
Reunited with the prosperous world,
The joy was extraordinary.

All children were handsome,
The post was won[39],
The grandchildren were not evil,
Learn to contend with Yan Yan.

If the education was good,
The old wife had merit,
Serve Weng Guxiao,
Xiangfu was also comprehensive.

My zodiac was a dog,
The zodiac was a chicken,
Who said chicken and dog,
Couldn't be a couple?

Now both of us,
Are more than ancient,
Kindness grown thicker,
It is comparable to Zhaohui.

Looking back at the old years,
It can be called bittersweet,
Although it was easy,
You were pure in love.

It 's not easy to suffer,
Love was more precious,
Dozens of cold and summer calendars,
Rarely like a guest.

Fortunately for all ages,
Smiling golden wedding,
Give this hundreds of sentences,
Unfortunately, it was difficult to speak.

Talking about wife virtue,
Used to give birth to children and grandchildren,
Take care of each other,
Happy birthday to Kunlun.

(1) Fang Qing was a scholar in traditional drama Pearl Tower. He married his cousin.

(2) Fang Qing's cousin gave him a pagoda made of pearls to show his affection.

(3) When I was young, I was named Tuan, and Pinying was called Xiaozhu when I was young. My relatives used to call us by their small names, which was still true today.

(4) My father worked in the Northeast for a long time and once moved to live with his uncle and aunt for a few years.

(5) The No. 1 Boys School of Sany Chinese-English Middle School

(6) Yuying Middle School attended by Pinying was a female middle school.

(7) Two stars from the participating business lines that did not appear in the sky at the same time.

(8) Refers to an ancient tune of music "Phoenix".

(9) Refers to Sima Xiangru, who teases Zhuo Wenjun by playing the piano, courts her, and becomes a couple.

(10) I once walked in a narrow alley, wearing a plain cloth shirt, feet on wooden bottom rain boots, holding a paper umbrella in my hand, just came head-to-head to Pinying and her friends, which made me feel ashamed and embarrassed, Walked quickly with his head down.

(11) When graduating from Pinying Middle School, ZengYangren gave me an invitation to invite me to the ceremony.

(12) After graduating from Pinying Middle School, she entered Yuying Kindergarten as a teacher until she got married.

(13) Before graduating from high school, I was admitted to Fuzhou Union University to study science, and two and a half years later transferred to Shanghai Saint John University to study civil engineering.

(14) Concord University was open to the public every year for people to visit.

(15) At the end of January 1931, my parents wanted me to get married, and they brought Pinying to Shanghai to get on well with me.

(16) My parents and Pinying took the carriage from the boat dock to my sister's house to get the mouth. I went out to meet and saw her sitting in the car with three paper umbrellas in her hands.

(17) We were married on the 4th of February 1932 on the Spring Day.

(18) Since the Songhu Anti-Japanese War broke out on January 28th, we were unable to hold a wedding in a hotel, so we hurriedly borrowed the Jingwu Sports Club practice martial arts hall in the sister's home.

(19) It was only seven days before the outbreak of the Shanghai-Hangzhou War on the day of the wedding, the violent gunfire was heard all day and night.

(20) Marriage was also said to be good for Qin Jin.

(21) Whenever I participated in the marriage among relatives as a child, the children learned how to make a marriage. Once or twice, I was sent to play the groom and Pinying to play the bride.

(22) When I graduated from St. John's University, I was the best student in the whole class, and I had a bachelor's degree.

(23) Ji Zi was an alias of Su Qin. When Su Qin went out to lobby, he didn't return home, and his pockets were empty, so there was a saying that Ji Zi's pockets were empty.

(24) The suits that I wore on the graduation day ordered by the British grant.

(25) After I graduated, I stayed at St. John University as a teacher.

(26) When I started working, my monthly salary was 75 yuan, and I would send 50 yuan as support for my parents.

(27) At the beginning of 1937, I transferred to the Netherland Institute of Technology to teach.

(28) In 1944, Pin Ying raised the third child and ligated the fallopian tubes.

(29) In April 1945, the whole family returned to Fuzhou from Shanghai on a wooden sailboat with a load of only five hundred dans (i.e. 25 tons).

(30) Soon after arriving in Fuzhou, the Japanese invaders retreated, and I entered the US military rescue agency. The salary was high and the accommodation was comfortable.

(31) After the war, I wanted to go back to teaching at the Netherland Polytechnic Institute. The school was occupied by Jiang Jun and

failed. During the three years from 1945 to 1948, I worked in the Fujian Office of the US Military Agency, Shanghai Industrial Trust Letter, the Aftermath Relief Administration of the Puppet Executive Yuan, and the Shanghai Office of Fujian Paper Mill.

(32) When the whole family left Shanghai in April 1945, they lifted their houses to the top and came back to Shanghai after the victory of the Anti-Japanese War. Because there were few golden roofs that could not reach the house, they could not let their families return.

(33) At the end of 1948, I had already obtained a Chinese passport and could go to New Zealand as an engineer. Because the Liberation Army was about to go south, I couldn't bear to abandon my mother, wife and children.

(34) In September 1949, I rented my residence at No. 134 Jiangsu Road in Shanghai and reunited my wife and children from Fuzhou.

(35) The third child, when he tried to counterattack the mainland in 1962, just graduated from high school, gave up enrolling in the university and was recruited into the army.

(36) From 1956 to 1966, Pinying was elected as the second, third, fourth and fifth Shanghai Municipal People's Representative.

(37) From July 1968 to April 1970, I was isolated for 21 months without reason.

(38) After the Cultural Revolution, both young children were admitted to graduate school, and they went abroad for further study. Now they all learn to return home to work.

My four children

All my four children, All had a family,
All making money different,
All spending also different.

The first one conservative, earn
less spend not much;
The second had a salary,
got money soon ran out;
The third one had a lot skill,
easy earn easy spend;
The fourth made enough money,
alway reluctant to spend.

All economy were good,
All not spent to much;
All no worry,
All happy day by day.

APPENDIX I

The Life of Mr. Zheng Chaoqiang

On February 24, 1910, as the eldest son of family, Mr. Zheng Chaoqiang was born in Xiadu Zheng's mansion. Fuzhou City. At the age of 6, he entered an old-style private school and started his enlightenment education, However, the enlightenment teacher died after a year later. When father came back home from northeast China, he continued primary education by his father. At the age of 10, his father went out to seek a job again, and he was admitted to Yiwenshe Primary School near his home for further study, then transferred to Trinity Elementary School. In 1922, entered Fuzhou Trinity Middle School, Mr. Zheng studied extremely hard and achieved top results. Although he was went to church school one after another, even he was bound to participate in some church activities, but Mr. Zheng had never been a religious.

At the end of 1927, Fuzhou Trinity middle School buildings were set on fire and burned down, Mr. Zheng could not continue his studied, he directly applied for Fujian Union University, was admitted and entered the university to study, became the first University student of the Zheng's family. In 1930, Mr. Zheng was still eager to learn more and transferred to St. John's University in Shanghai for further study. In

1932, Mr. Zheng passed the graduation examination with honors and able to stay on St. John's University as a teacher.

On February 4, 1932, Mr. Zheng Chaoqiang and Mrs. Chen Pinying got married in Shanghai.

In March 1934, Shanghai Leicester Institute of Technology was established, Mr. Zheng promoted to be a lecturer in the college. Mr. Zheng had been able to play important role and cultivating a large number of students, so he had planned to work at Shanghai Leicester Institute of Technology for long time. Unfortunately, By the end of 1942, the Japanese had imprisoned the British President and teachers of The Leicester Institute of Technology into concentration camps, and intended to change the school into a Japanese school. The matter was immediately met with a unanimous revolt by all Chinese staff, therefore Mr. Zheng began a period of displaced life, In order to maintain the livelihood of a family of seven, he often moved between Shanghai and Fuzhou, frequently changing different jobs, and even often lost his job, making it difficult to sustain life.

At the end of 1948, on the recommendation of fellow township Mr. Chen Hongduo, Mr. Zheng Chaoqiang was employed by the British Asian Thermal Oil Company (namely The Asian branch of Shell Oil Company) as the chief of engineering section, with a good salary. In 1949, shortly after the liberation of Shanghai, the whole family moved to Shanghai, his wife Chen Pinying brought three children who had stayed in Fuzhou to Shanghai, so all of Mr. Zheng's family settled down in Shanghai.

Because of the American trade embargo against China at that time, Mr. Zheng's work in Asia company was almost zero. In spare time, Mr. Zheng studied the structure of building projects, and had published many papers in the National Professional Journal "China Civil Engineering Journal", reviewed a large number of professional papers for the journal, and was soon appointed as the editorial committee member of the journal. After the liberation, Mr. Zheng and his family lived a stable and happy life, he sincerely grateful to the Communist Party of China, and as a senior intellectual identity, joined the Jiusan Society, served as Huangpu District committee members in Shanghai. He gave full support to his wife Chan Pinying in her work of preschool education. All four of there children graduated from university. After the Cultural Revolution, two youngest boys passed the examination of graduate students, had gone abroad for further study. Now them of both had returned to China. Two of the three sons joined the army, while the eldest went to fight in Korea for volunteers.

In the early days of the "Cultural Revolution", Mr. Zheng was, suffered unfair treatment, even inexplicably isolated examination for nearly two years (all staff of Asia company, more than 40 people were isolated), but he had a clear conscience with spirit of optimism. After the end of the "Cultural Revolution", Mr. Zheng firmly supported the party's reform and opening policy and actively participated in various activities organized by the Jiusan Society as always. In order to support the first municipal engineering relocation project in Shanghai, Mr. Zheng signed the relocation agreement of Jiangsu Road housing with the relocation team, which was published in Shanghai Xinmin Evening News.

Mr. Zheng valued education all his life, and was deeply aware of the importance of education to the country and the nation. Therefore, he not only attached importance to the education of his own children, but also helped to support the education of the children of poor relatives and friends. He once sponsored many young people to go to university and complete their studies.

Mr. Zheng was filial to his parents and devoted to his wife. The couple celebrated their 60th anniversary in 1992 with the blessing of their four children.

On January 6, 1995, Mr. Zheng Chaoqiang died of illness at the age of 85

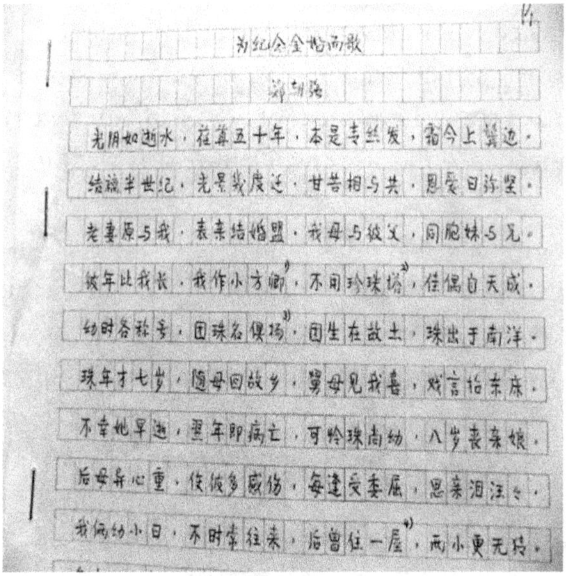

为纪念金婚而歌

郑胡骆

光阴如逝水，荏苒五十年，本是青丝发，霜今上鬓边。
结褵半世纪，光景几度迁，甘苦相与共，恩爱日弥坚。
老妻原与我，表亲结婚盟，我母与彼父，同胞妹与兄。
彼年比我长，我作小方卿[1]，不同珍珠塔[2]，佳偶自天成。
幼时各称号，团珠名俱扬[3]，团生在故土，珠出于南洋。
珠年才七岁，随母回故乡，舅母见我喜，戏言始东床。
不幸她早逝，翌年即病亡，可怜珠尚幼，八岁丧亲娘。
后母异心重，使彼多感伤，每逢受委屈，思亲泪汪汪。
我俩幼小日，不时常往来，后曾住一屋[4]，两小更无猜。

APPENDIX II

Historical Information About Fuzhou Tengshan (Cangqianshan)

Fuzhou Tengshan, also known as Tianning Mountain, was the ancient name of Cangqian Mountain, located at the northern end of Nantai Island, south bank of North Port of Minjiang river. At the end of the 14th century, during the Reign of Hongwu in the Ming Dynasty, merchants began to open salt warehouses and wharfs at the northern foot of Tianning Mountain and the southern bank of Minjiang River, forming the salt transport center of Fuzhou. Therefore, this area was called "Salt Warehouse Front", hence the name of Tengshan Mountain was changed to Cangqian Mountain. Cangqian Mountain was surrounded by rivers, with beautiful scenery and pleasant climate. Since the Ming and Qing Dynasties, Tengshan area had been a land of outstanding people and outstanding talents, with three generations of five scholars, seven subjects and eight jinshi. The literature and history materials were very rich. After the Opium War, Fuzhou was forced to become one commercial port of five ports in China. Seventeen countries, including Britain, France, the United States, the Netherlands, Russia, Japan, Denmark, Belgium, Hungary and Mexico, opened foreign companies and established consulates in Cangqian Mountain, engaged in importing opium, industrial products and exporting tea, wood and other local specialties. In the late Qing Dynasty, there were more than 30 foreign companies in Cangqian Mountain area, 55 foreign ships along the Minjiang River, and hundreds of Chinese merchant ships engaged in transit transportation. Cangqian Mountain area became the foreign trade base and shipping center of Fuzhou. In Cangqian Mountain, there was a Customs office set up by Britain, a Branch of Merchants Bureau set up by Westernization Group, the first State-owned bank in Fuzhou, the Daqing Bank (the predecessor of The Bank of China), and seven foreign Banks. Under the protection of unequal treaties, the original agricultural natural economy gradually changed, making Cangqian Mountain to be the birthplace of modern Fuzhou industry. At the same time, foreign religions and cultures were also penetrating into and expanding. Foreigners set up churches in Cangqian Mountain area for the purpose of preaching, and built missionary schools and missionary hospitals to spread Western culture. On this basis, many consulates, foreign firms, churches, hospitals, schools, private villas and mansions of various styles were built successively, including 11 churches and 8 missionary schools. In addition in Cangqian Mountain area also built foreigner's residence area and a foreigner's summer resort in Guling. Compared with Gulangyu Island in Xiamen, Cangqian Mountain had many more unique and numerous buildings. The modern architecture of both had the reputation of "International Architecture Exhibition", which was a common witness of the influence of world powers on the development of modern China.

By the 1920s and 1930s, there were more than 200 national industrial and commercial enterprises in Cangqianshan Port and Shangdu area, and the commercial districts with concentrated shops were mainly in the area from Meiwu to Guanjing The motley population of Chinese and Foreigners in Cangqianshan area had soared from more than 15, 000 to more than 56, 000 in 10 years. In Cangqianshan area there were several missionary schools, such as south China College of Liberal Arts for Women, founded by the Methodist Episcopal Church in the United States (the predecessor of Fujian Normal University) and He-Ling Yinghua Middle School, South China Women's University Affiliated High School, The Church of England's Tao Shu Girl's School (above three schools now affiliated high School of Fuzhou Normal University), Trinity High School (now No. 9 Fuzhou Middle School) Yu Ying female middle school, Xun Jane female middle school (above two schools now merged into sixteen middle school), etc. The modern economy, thought, culture, science and technology and education of Cangqian Mountain area in Fuzhou had great influence and contribution to Fuzhou and even the whole country. Until now, Cangqian Mountain area was still the educational center of Fuzhou with the more schools and the highest level centered by Fujian Normal University.

Today, there were some traces of the ancient deep lane in Fuzhou Tengshan area, churches, wooden houses, steps, stone walls and houses. Even a small part of the lush trees and the deep quiet of the old houses were preserved, scattered in the crowded city, waiting for us to find out and understand with their ancestors related to those bits of the past and smoke years.

Based on network information

第四屆大會會場

THANKS

In the editing of this book, first of all, I would like to thank my sister for keeping the hundreds of pages of the handwritten manuscript of our father's life, so as to achieve our father's 150,000-word legacy. I would also like to thank my sister for contacting friends of our family and giving me encouragement, so that I have the confidence to complete the revision and writing of my father's legacy.

Teacher Wu Guangan of Wuhu has a profound literary skills, in the layout of the overall structure of the book and the rhetoric of the text and sentences, propose more amendments that are worth adopting. About this book, Teacher Wang once proposed five or six title for choosing, but "Memory Marks" cobbled together by accident in my busy life, I did not expect to be approved by the editor-in-chief of the publishing house, Liu Xitao And selection; thank you very much.

After the preliminary writing of this book, I invited Ms. Chen Ling (granddaughter of my father's eldest sister) in Shanghai and Mr. Zheng Zaiqin (father's eldest grandson) in the United States to read this book in full to provide opinions and opinions, to make the content and vocabulary as perfect as possible.

My younger brother, Zheng Tianhui fully supported me in editing and publishing my father's legacy. After read the full text several times and write the preface. And agreed to present a batch of this book to Shanghai West Middle School as a literary and historical materials of scholarship named after our parents "Chao Qiang" and "Ping Ying"

To all of my friends who have helped in the process of editing and publishing this book, sincerely thank you!

This book is based on the memoirs written by my father when he was in his 80s, Due to its long history, it is inevitable that there are some omissions and inaccuracies. Please understand.

Zheng Tianzhong

September

CPSIA information can be obtained
at www.ICGtesting.com
Printed in the USA
BVHW070447120521
607047BV00009B/1895

9 781954 941144